Takai dance

John Miller Chernoff

African Rhythm and African Sensibility

Aesthetics and Social Action
in African Musical Idioms

The University of Chicago Press
Chicago and London

The University of Chicago Press, Chicago 60637
The University of Chicago Press, Ltd., London

Acknowledgment is made to the following for
permission to quote from the works named: Fela
Anikulapo Kuti, "Water No Get Enemy"; Fela
Anikulapo Kuti and Glenwood Music Corpora-
tion, "Carry Me, I Want to Die"; Harold Cour-
lander and Ethnic Folkways Library, "So Them
Bad Minded" (from the album *Caribbean Folk
Music*, recorded by Thomas J. Price, edited by
Harold Courlander); Warne Marsh Music, liner
notes from *Drums of Trinidad;* Bergman, Vocco &
Conn, Inc., "The King."

All photographs reproduced in this book were taken by
the author.

Library of Congress Cataloging in Publication Data

Chernoff, John Miller.
   African rhythm and African sensibility.

   Bibliography: p.
   Includes index.
   1. Music—Africa.   I. Title.
ML3760.C48   780'.96   79–189
ISBN 0–226–10345–5 (paper)

To my parents, Florence and Harold Chernoff

Contents

Plates

Acknowledgments

This book was written in 1973 and 1974. The basic field research was carried out in 1970 and 1971. In 1972, in the United States, I read the ethnomusicological writings and wrote an essay on which this book is based. Since the time I finished the rewriting in 1974, I have lived in Ghana, but I have had opportunities to review the manuscript in 1976 and 1978. I kept my revisions to a minimum, and aside from a few new illustrations and descriptive examples, the only major change was the addition of Ibrahim Abdulai's lectures. Nonetheless, there is a sense in which I have been living with this book for the past eight years, and looking back, I am astounded by the number of people who helped me in my work. While I have made extensive use of notes to provide scholarly references, I feel I owe more thanks to the great many people who, in their various ways, contributed to my understanding of African music and to the writing of this book, and I want to note their names because I consider this book to be a product of their efforts and ideas as much as mine.

My first thanks go to my drumming teachers, who gave me much more than mere technical instruction. In Ghana, I studied Dagomba drumming in Tamale under Alhaji Ibrahim Abdulai, assisted by Alhassan Ibrahim, Alhassan Abukari, Mohamadu Fuseini, and Adam Ibrahim, with further assistance from Abdulai Seidu, Yusefu Alhassan, and Fuseini Alhassan. I studied Ewe drumming with Freeman Donkor of Tsiame and Gideon Folie Alorwoyie of Afiadenyigba, with additional assistance from Edmund Ben Ahorlu of Keta, Seth Y. Nakey of Afiadenyigba, C. K. Ladzekpo of Anyako, and also from Jomo Vincent Danku. I studied Highlife and other contemporary forms of conga drumming mainly with Seth Ankrah of Accra and also with Daniel Banini of Accra. In Haiti, I studied "folklorique" drumming with Joseph Thèlus of Port-au-Prince. Special thanks are also due to my first African drumming teacher, Abraham Adzenyah of Winnebah, Ghana.

Many friends in Africa contributed insights, demonstrated important points, or helped me further my research in a number of ways. I would like to thank Steven W. Evans and Timmy W. Ogude especially, the late Alfred J. Prah, Farouk Mossolly, Samuel Nyanyo Nmai, J. S. K. Amewovie, F. K. Dogbatsey, Rev. I. K. A. Thompson, Davis Y. Glah, Lamidi Badaru, Amina Yaro Etibié, Felix K. Amenudah, Billy Onassis Atos, and also Bala Abdulai, Abena Aboatema, Isaac Abraham, Conrad Adusei, the late George Adzomani, Kwa-Anim Agyempaw, Victoria Aikins, Feyi Akinrujomu, Hawawu Alhassan, Big Kwame Amanu, Umaru U. Amateze, Gilbert Amegatcher, Alhaji I. A. Aminu, Josephine Adjoa Amoah, Martha Ankrah, Ernest A. Asare, Otchere Asare, Tony Asrilen, Husaine A. Attah, Willis Bell, Mohammed Malcolm Ben, Robert Biezui, Felicia Blankson, J. K. Brimah, Alan and Mary Brody, Ajax Bukana, Renato Chiarelli, Theophilus A. Codjoe, John Collins and Gifty, James Crocker, Dan Danies, Andrews Ofori Danso, Carmine DiMarco, Johnny Ebo, Victor Egli, the late Justice Eshun, K. Essandoh, Amy Eyeson, J. K. Fabi, Charlotte Folie, George Footit, Isaac Oti Frempong, C. K. Ganyo, Freddie Green, Mary Haizel, Joe Hammond, E. K. Hanson, Patrick Hayford, Sam Hero, Robert Heward-Mills, Jeff Holden, Garba Ibrahim, Peter Kassinikos, Mike Knock-the-Man-Down, Alhaji Amadu Labaran Cole Younger, Joseph A. Y. Lartey, Alex MacDonald, Samuel Maddy, Agnes Mensah, Nii Osah Mills, The Monkey, Ahmed and Kanaan Mossolly, Confort Nyako, Benjamin Obeng, Jimmy Okoye, Bernard Osei, Yaw Odei Osei, Osmanu Citizen of Metropole Hotel, Cynthia Prah Otoo, Dickson Owusu, William G. Page, Stephen Panford, Celia Pedersen, Nana Owusu Akyaw Prempeh, Rev. Dr. Samuel Prempeh, Gary Richards, Cyprian Rowe, Presley Sackeyfio, Charlotte and Eunice Sampson, Theodore Skoufis, Somewhere Something, E. P. Sowah, George Boye Tawiah, Yaazori Tengoli, Confort Tetteh, Mary Tettekor, Helen Thomas, Tongo Ra-Na, Sala Torbay, Fui Tsikata, Paul Uwakwe, Mohammed Yakubu, Issa Yatassaye, Guy Yoyo, Fati Wala, Zaga Walata, the Wango Wango guys, and all the members of The Club. In Tamale I would particularly like to thank Kissmal Ibrahim Hussein, Benjamin D. Sunkari, S. K.

Abbiw, Joseph Owusu, Rev. Daniel A. Wumbee, Alhaji Iddi Yakubu
and his wives, Askia Mohammed, Mustapha Mohammed Big Afro,
James Nuhu Salifu, Ishmael Ibrahim, Dr. E. Babah Sampanah, Alhaji
Adam Alhassan, Amadu Jaato, Fuseini Alhassan, Mumuni Abdulai,
Alhassan Kalangu, Natogma Naparo, Mohamadu Neena, Osmanu
Abdulai, Maalam Alhaji Shahadu Issah, Namo-Naa Issahaku Mahama,
Nanton Lun-Naa Iddrisu Mahama, Logambalbo Abukari Neena, Lun-
Zoo-Naa Abukari Seidi, the late Yo-Naa Abdulai II, Anane Gyan The
Old Man, Yakubu William, Sulemana Mahama, A. M. Bamford, L. A.
Iddi, Harruna Labaran, Fuseini Tia, Harruna Alhassan, Dr. Kwesi
Sackey, J. S. Kaleem, Alhaji Ibrahim Mahama, Rev. A. van der Broek,
E. T. Q. Pinto, Sulemana Alhassan, D. C. Eshun, Paul Yaw Ngisah,
Nana Kwame Attakora, Fulera Osmanu, Yaw Tufuor Joseph, Iddrisu
Harruna, Atia Duah, A. B. Sayibu, G. B. Kanton, Mahama Achiri,
John Atchulo, and the members of Gymkhana Club. Among the many
musicians I would like to thank are Tony Allen, Jerry Hansen, Fela
Anikulapo Kuti, P. S. K. Ampadu, Sunny Ade, Victor Uwaifo, Sonny
Okosun, Potato, Leslie Tex, Smart Nkansah, Elvis J. Brown, Tony Ben-
son, and also Berkeley Jones, B. B. Boogaloo, Pap Dingo, Frank and
Stanley Todd, P. S. Flyne, Geraldo Pino, Godwin Omabuwa, Ebenezer
Obey, and the members of Ramblers International, Africa '70, African
Brothers, and Sweet Talks. In Haiti I would like to thank Charlotte
Saint Jean especially, St. Fleur Charlot, Moravia Raymond, Bastien
Étienne, Armand Jean-Baptiste, Michel Jean-Louis, and Rolin Arbith-
nott. In obtaining recordings from various countries, I had help in
Accra from James K. Awuah and Francis Yaw Manu of Redeemer
Enterprises and from Francis K. Akuamoah of Keep Smiling Records;
in Ouagadougou from Kabré Paul Thierry of Poly-Disco; and in Lomé
from Koudoukou Akuesso of Kakadou Bar, from Pierre Akueson and
Koudakou Pierre of Aziza Disques, and from Gbassi Damien of La
Musette. During my stay at the University of Ghana, I learned a great
deal from my exposure to J. H. Kwabena Nketia, A. M. Opoku, Simon
D. Asiama, Alan Tamakloe, and K. A. Opoku. I would also like to
thank Trinity College, Legon, and the Evangelical Presbyterian Church
for sponsoring my residence in Ghana since 1974.
    During the preparation of this essay as a dissertation at the Hart-
ford Seminary Foundation, I was also fortunate to have had the help
of many remarkable scholars from diverse fields. Their interest in me
and in my work has undoubtedly influenced my presentation and en-
riched my life. I would first like to thank Kai T. Erikson, who was an
eminently sensible and sensitive editor for this book. Since the time he

was my undergraduate sociology advisor at Yale, his concern for my scholarly growth has been a major inspiration for me. My special thanks in this regard also go to Leighton McCutchen, who guided my graduate program. His extremely open and sensitive support for my work is deeply appreciated. Richard A. Underwood has been a wonderful man to have as an advisor, giving me both substantive and exemplary encouragement. Charles Keil, the third member of my doctoral committee, continually pressed me toward methodological clarity, always with an eye for the best result. The Hartford Seminary Foundation provided an ideal environment to pursue interdisciplinary inquiries. Its innovative curriculum, now unfortunately curtailed, was one of great academic freedom and sophistication. Those students and teachers who had a chance to listen to Willem A. Bijlefeld's lectures on phenomenology of religion or to profit from his thoughtful advice and his understanding of African religions will recognize the enduring impression he made on my scholarly sensibility. Kenneth Keniston's continuing concern extends from the time he helped organize and direct my undergraduate interdisciplinary work, and in our many conversations over the past twelve years, he prepared me to recognize more deeply and to use more thoroughly the relationship between my personality and my understanding.

In addition, a number of scholars took the trouble to read earlier drafts and offer responses and encouragement. In this regard, I would like to thank George Appianda-Arthur, C. E. Asante Darkwa, James W. Fernandez, William Graves, Wadi' Z. Haddad, Russell Hartenberger, James Hopewell, Raymond Kennedy, James Koetting, William Krohn, David McAllester, Daniel McCall, Marjorie A. Marks, Howard A. Mayer, David Neuman, Hewitt Pantaleoni, W. Hearne Pardee, Maurice Stein, Desmund Tay, Robert F. Thompson, Colin M. Turnbull, J. Michael Turner, and Ifekandu Ummuna. Of particularly valuable assistance were Dale Davis on musicological matters and my brother Michael Chernoff on sociological matters. As a scholar and an artist, Arthur Hall, director of the Ile-Ife Black Humanitarian Center, was especially helpful and kind, and I also learned a great deal from my friendships with Farel Johnson and Sam Smith, Jr., both of whom contributed generously to my understanding from their knowledge and experience as drummers. Eric Suliman Rucker is a devoted drummer; he has been a thoughtful and reliable friend.

I would also like to thank some of the people in the United States who helped me or with whom I discussed my ideas and clarified my perspective. Thanks go to Ralph Adams, Bob Barton, Lincoln Berkley, Stuart Bluestone, Jaymie and Nina Chernoff, Richard I. Closs, Robert

Cunningham, Mara Davakis, Jules Ehrman, Peter Fitzgerald, Ed For-stenzer, Robert Garfinkle, Arnold and Adrien Gefsky, Ted George, Sugar Glass, Sherman Goldman, Mark Hamilton, Marion Harper, Reginald Helfferich, Martin Hoffmeister, the late William Kiernan, Bernard and Selma Kraft, the late Rod Lack, John Levey, Harvey and Lenore Light, Martha McCutchen, Santo Mancarella, John Marks, Mary Anne Mason, Michael Mattil, Steven Mullen, Nicholas Paindiris, Chuck and Vicky Perilman, Dr. and Mrs. James S. Peters II, James S. Peters III, Rev. E. Neill Richards, Malaya Rucker, Tony and Maria Thomas, Rev. Sri Santo, Phil Schuyler, Anthony Sereslis, Debbie Solow, Chip Stewart, Robert Whitehill, Suzanne Glausser Widdoes, Sandra Williams and John and Martha Wolf. Several others were also invaluable during the preparation of the manuscript. Vasilios Haralambous provided more than can be accounted for; Nancy Taylor Roberts offered generous assistance in countless ways; Mary Wysocki helped me utilize to the fullest all the admirable facilities of the Case Memorial Library at the Hartford Seminary Foundation. Mrs. Ruth Emerson, an inspiration to all who know her, was exceptionally patient and considerate during the typing of more than one version of the manuscript; she is a true friend. From the first, Linnea McCaffrey has been an involved and insightful participant in my work, and I appreciate her sensitive concern for my efforts.

Finally, I would like to thank my parents, to whom this book is dedicated, Florence and Harold Chernoff. My awareness of their continuing support, confidence, and love throughout the years of my investigation made me happy and grateful to realize my luck.

Sitting at my desk, I have never been alone.

A ninety-minute audio cassette accompanying this book is now available separately. The cassette includes musical selections illustrating examples discussed in the book: multiple meter and cross-rhythms; call and response; supporting drum variations; drum language; and traditional music.

Asterisks on the following pages indicate corresponding selections on the cassette: 45, 46, 52, 53, 55, 56, 57, 58, 59, 75, 78, 82, 83, 85, 99, 101, 119, 120, 121, 123, 127, 128.

The cassette may be ordered by writing directly to:

Sales Department
University of Chicago Press
5801 S. Ellis
Chicago, Illinois 60637

Pronunciation and Transliteration

Most African languages are written phonetically, and therefore in pronouncing African words, one should try to pronounce all the vowels and consonants that are written. With regard to vowels particularly, pronounce *a* as in *bar*, *e* as in *weigh*, *i* as in *bee*, *o* as in *comb*, and *u* as in *boot*.

In order to avoid nonstandard phonetic typographical characters, I have modified the spelling of many words. In the case of Ewe words, I have maintained the common English form of writing *Ewe* instead of *Eʋe* and *Yeve* instead of *Yehwe*; the most frequent modifications have been to change ɔ to *o* and ʊ to *v* or *w*. *Dz* is generally pronounced as *j*. Dagbani spelling has suffered more seriously. Dagbani transliteration is still subject to interpretation, and for this book I have anglicized the spellings given me by Rev. Daniel A. Wumbee, the translator of the Bible. Readers should note that ŋ has been changed in various ways: to *ng* in *Bangumanga* (from *Baŋgumaŋa*), to *nw* as in *Nwundanyuli* (from *ŋun' da nyuli*), to *n* as in *yirin* (from *yiriŋ*). Also *g* is in some cases a gutteral, adapted from ɣ, as in *Lun-zhegu* (from *Lun-ʒɛɣu*), *Nagbiegu* (from *Naɣbiɛɣu*), and *moglo* (from *mɔɣlo*). In general, African words have been italicized only on the first occasion of their use.

Poets are bandleaders who have failed.

Ayi Kwei Armah
The Beautyful Ones Are Not Yet Born

Introduction:
Scholarship and Participation

At the crossing of two heartways stands no
    temple for Apollo.
Rilke, *Sonnets to Orpheus*

Those who dig won't fill their wig with all that
    blah blah blah.
Jon Hendricks and Count Basie, "The King"

During the two years I originally took to write
this book, what began as a detailed introduction
to African music became a focus for reexamining
many crucial concerns of my own life. The task of
interpreting my experiences of African musical
life raised for me certain questions regarding the
meaning of the very attempt to *understand* African music: African music does not require a
theoretical representation or an explicitly interpretive understanding. While I was having trouble
trying to begin my writing, I came across a book
by Friedrich Nietzsche, a book with the intriguing
title *The Birth of Tragedy out of the Spirit of
Music*. Ordinarily, a social scientist would avoid
beginning anything with a reference to as contro-
versial a philosopher as Nietzsche, but Nietzsche's
book was oddly appropriate to my situation. *The
Birth of Tragedy out of the Spirit of Music* is an
attempt to understand the significance of art in
a culture different from ours, not that of Africa
but that of ancient Greece.

   In a very funny preface entitled "A Critical
Backward Glance," written fifteen years after the
first publication, Nietzsche reflected on his earliest
book: "I was then beginning to take hold of a
dangerous problem—taking it by the horns, as it

were—not Old Nick himself, perhaps, but something almost as hot to handle, the problem of scholarly investigation."[1] Nietzsche had argued that music is beyond rational understanding: it is too close to the basic mysteries and contradictions of existence; it touches and conveys realities for which words or logic are inadequate; it is, in Nietzsche's words, "a realm of wisdom . . . from which logicians are excluded";[2] and it thus reminds us of the limitations of our power to understand the world. The purpose of scientific investigation and rational discourse, their "mission," Nietzsche claimed,

> is to make existence intelligible and thereby justified. . . . Socrates and his successors, down to our own day, have considered all moral and sentimental accomplishments—noble deeds, compassion, self-sacrifice, heroism, even that spiritual calm, so difficult of attainment, which the Apollonian Greek called *sophrosyne*—to be ultimately derived from the dialectic of knowledge, and therefore teachable. . . . This positive attitude toward existence must release itself in actions for the most part pedagogic, exercised upon noble youths, to the end of producing genius. But science, spurred on by its energetic notions, approaches irresistibly those outer limits where the optimism in its logic must collapse. . . . When the inquirer, having pushed to the circumference, realizes how logic in that place curls about itself and bites its own tail, he is struck with a new kind of perception: a tragic perception, which requires, to make it tolerable, the remedy of art.[3]

It was with such an awareness, Nietzsche maintained, that the ancient Greeks, who gave us our tradition of rational philosophy, also gave us our tradition of the tragic dramatic ritual. In Nietzsche's view, then, art is the fundamental and "necessary complement"[4] of our rational potential to confront life, and Nietzsche argued that upon such an awareness of ourselves and the role of understanding in life rests the balanced judgement of the world the Greeks called wisdom.

The Birth of Tragedy out of the Spirit of Music was an attempt to demonstrate the relationship of ritualized art forms and rational philosophy as they functioned in classical Greek culture. Nietzsche's response to the ironies of this relationship was to propose that scholarship look to music for intimations of the most profound realities as well as for inspiration in the search for vitality, that scholarship can help conceptualize the wisdom of music and in so doing balance itself in the perception of another kind of truth. Thus even while the young Nietzsche was speculating on the limitations of knowledge, he was trying, with his sympathy for the classical tradition and his keen sense of irony, to suggest his conception of the relevance of our intellectual potential. Nietzsche hoped that scholarly investigation might be seen as a process of opening our ways of thinking and talking to bring them closer to the vitality of life, and that the pursuit of knowledge might be seen not as something withdrawn from the world but as a style of discovery and involvement.[5] Simply, when we can more adequately portray that which has eluded us, we have broadened our capacity to respond to it. We may challenge and engage this capacity any time we meet something new, and sometimes, scholarship can lead us into a more fulfilling participation.

Nonetheless, Nietzsche raised the question of whether it is possible to comprehend music in a scholarly way; if we want to study the music of a different culture, the question is even more to the point. How can we bring something of a different order into our world of understanding and at the same time recognize and appreciate it on its own terms? Reading Nietzsche's book, however, I found myself encouraged by the feeling that there is a challenge and a potentially valuable confrontation in the mere attempt to write about music within the criteria of scholarship. The relevance of modern scholarship to the concerns of life has become increasingly perplexing, for modern scholarship is not a single path toward knowledge: it is a multiplicity of special perspectives and terminologies that we use to describe the world in various contexts of meaning. Among these perspectives, ideally, we must value those which might help us understand and describe our contacts with the people and the activities in another culture. In this respect, conveying my experiences with African music through the heritage of our traditions of understanding seemed to offer an opportunity not only to expand the relevance of what I had learned as an individual but also to indicate my sense of how those traditions can respond to the challenge of such an undertaking.[6] In such an investigation, we can learn as much about ourselves as about other people because we must see through our own eyes and we must find our own words to describe their world. And again, our eventual appreciation of African music will imply that African music has assumed an additional dimension of influence as our traditions of understanding stretch and adjust to encompass it.

What I learned during my study of African music has profoundly influenced me, and I feel it is important to note, in regard to some of the issues which writing this essay has raised for me, that it was the personal significance of my participation in actual social situations that made me think I understood what involvement with music means in Africa. In communicating my experiences and observations, therefore, I will use personal anecdotes and accounts of my African teachers as descriptive devices both to convey an impression of the social setting of African musical life and to document the influence which my own experiences had on how I arrived at my perspective. The virtues of expressive clarity and scholarly fidelity, however, do not always work in easy partnership. As a great prose stylist once observed, "It is probably always disastrous not to be a poet."[7] In this book, starting with a detailed description of some general characteristics of African music, we will reach an aesthetic appreciation that will refer us to a style of living and a sensibility toward life, revealing cultural patterns, ethical modes, and standards of judgement.[8] I am thus hoping to achieve several purposes. First, I want to provide a step-by-step introduction to help Western readers appreciate African music. Second, I would like to show how African music fits into the flow and rhythm of African culture generally. And third, I want to use music as the basis for a portrait of African culture that will have meaning and clarity for those people who have a personal or historical interest in the image of Africa.

Whatever systematic coherence this book might have, however, was by no means fully apparent to me when I was in Africa, involved in meeting the concerns of my everyday experience. I had been trained as a social scientist, but I did not go to Africa to understand, to help, or to profit. I was more without a reason for being there than any European or American I knew. For many years I had saved and planned to go to Africa, but when I did go, I went to fool around a bit and to see with my own eyes what was there, and I loved the music and wanted to learn to play the drums. The more I learned about the music, the more interested I became; still, in a performance in the Accra lorry park, with beggars and businessmen standing in the dust or on top of trucks to watch me play, or in the fetish cult ceremonies with dancing initiates singing in a secret language, I would sometimes smile and ask myself, "What am I doing here?" To an extent I have been asking the same question with regard to the pen in my hand and the rough draft of this book beside me.

I had, more significantly, asked this specific question right smack in the middle of the first year I spent in Africa. I was traveling in the north of Ghana from a very interesting little town, Bawku, to Bolgatanga and eventually to Tamale (tă′-mă-lē) to begin what I hoped would be my first serious and extended training in drumming. In all our traveling together during my first months in Ghana, the great Ewe (ĕ′-vĕ) drummer Gideon Folie Alorwoyie had not had time to show me much of master drumming, though we had certainly had a lot of fun. I decided that I might have better luck with the beautiful Dagomba drums,* shaped like hourglasses, with the skins over both mouths laced together with leather strings. By squeezing the drum, you can produce tones ranging more than an octave. But I liked Dagomba music for a different reason: the drumming was completely incomprehensible to me. I could never hear where the beats were or how the different parts fit together. When I had a chance to listen to these drums, I would become lost and disoriented. In short, they were wonderful in subjective complexity, and I was attracted.

Whereas the Ewes live in a coastal region of lush vegetation and cool breezes, the Dagombas live in the north of Ghana, which, after the forest ends, is savannah, a semiarid extension of the Sahara desert. Northern Ghana is part of a vast belt which runs across Africa from Senegal to Somalia and which was formerly all known as the Sudan, and anyone who travels there in any but the few months of the rainy season will realize that the appropriate adjective to describe most of the African landscape is not "steaming" but "baked." The Dagombas live in an area stretching between Yendi, their traditional capital, and the more populous Tamale, both of which are Dagomba towns. Most Dagombas are Muslims, and their bearing is restrained and careful.

Earlier, on my way to see Ouagadougou, capital of Upper Volta, I had stopped in Tamale to arrange for lessons to begin on my return. I went to the regional office of the National Cultural Center, now the Arts Council of Ghana, and asked for help. A secretary led me to the leader of the Takai group of dancers, whose drumming I wanted to learn. Under the shading of straw mats, a few men were weaving strips of cloth that would later be sewn into smocks. The lead dancer, an old man, was sitting at one side chewing kola nut, a mild stimulant people there use when they do not want to feel hungry or tired. The secretary introduced me, and I explained my business. Slowly the discussion progressed from greetings and inquiries of health. I told him that I admired the Takai music very much and that I wanted to study it so that I could learn more about it. The man spoke English passably, but we each spoke in our native tongue, and the secretary translated our speeches carefully while we waited and listened. Finally the old man said he would help me, and he sent another man to call the leader of the Takai drummers, Ibrahim

*Dagomba is how they have been called in English. They call themselves Dagbamba, occupy a traditional state called Dagbon, and speak a language called Dagbani.

Abdulai. While we waited, I tried my hand at the looms for everyone's amusement. With the drummer I spoke longer, repeating everything I had said, and we finally arrived at a price for the lessons and made arrangements to begin on my return from Ouagadougou.

In Ouagadougou, however, I fell sick; a doctor there diagnosed a rather serious problem, a temporary palsy. As it turned out, fortunately, he was mistaken, but in the meantime, demoralized and feeling poorly, I restricted my movements and isolated myself from most social intercourse. After a week of stoical detachment, urban wandering, and droll fantasizing, I returned to Ghana, immediately felt better, and made my way to Bawku, a short distance away on the northeastern border. On the Michelin map of West Africa, only two roads in Ghana are given a green stripe for scenery, and one is the stretch of road, some fifty miles long, that runs from Bolgatanga to Bawku. The characteristic brush gives way to rolling plains, broken irregularly by escarpments and dotted with complexes of round mud houses, which are painted red with bold, black, asymmetrical designs and are covered with thatched roofs. Before going to Tamale, I decided, I would stay in Bawku a bit.

I had good reason: Bawku is a remarkable place. At that time, the only electricity came from the generator which lit the big sign at the Mobil gas station at the main crossroads. Bawku, however, is by no means a village. It is unbelievably cosmopolitan, and people from almost every tribe in Ghana live there, even from those that are notoriously averse to travel. At night the main street is packed with friendly people strolling, conversing in many different languages. A few Roman Catholic priests, Protestant missionaries, and Peace Corps volunteers along with their Canadian and British counterparts round out a spectacle of activity. It is possible that the proximity of the border has had something to do with attracting so many people there; I have also been told simply that life is sweet in Bawku. Every third day the people from the surrounding countryside come to the market to buy and sell. The women, with their big straw hats to protect themselves from the sun, display neat piles of red peppers, tomatoes, onions, salt, ginger, beans, millet, corn, rice, and various flours and greens. The men bring crafted metalwork items such as farming implements and jewelry; several old, old men sit behind piles of medicines such as hides of wolf, lion, monkey and snake, powders of crushed birds' bones and dried plants, pieces of antelope's horns. In their accustomed place to one side sit the Mossi leather workers, fashioning and decorating wallets, machete cases, amulets. The tailors and the embroiderers sit at their places. Near them are the smock-makers, who sew together strips of beautifully striped hand-woven cloth into the fashion of the area, a loose-hanging garment flared with insets. In the Takai dance, the smocks swing and bell out as the men spin and turn.

Bawku was a fine place to spend a few days before going to Tamale to learn to play the drums. Accompanied recently by so many poignant experiences, I was feeling shy, and nice things kept happening. Jammed into a Bedford bus waiting to depart, I watched mundane incidents which seemed somehow to be especially dramatic. On the front of the bus was painted as a motto the popular saying, "Who Knows Tomorrow?" Following my unpleasant and lonely stay in Ouagadougou, and in a mood familiar to most Westerners who have ridden such buses, I was feeling very mortal. "Any minute now," I told myself, "you could be dead." I slowly realized I was indifferent. So what, I said back to my questioner, who continued, "Don't you want to write a book? Shouldn't you tell someone about this place?" The questioner became melodramatic: "And all your friends, wouldn't they like to know what thoughts you had before you died?" It seemed to me that lately most of the people I corresponded with had been asking me to write a book, and my education had taught me to assume that writing a book about a new thing one has learned is as natural as a reflex. My imagination ran to give details to the lives of all the people I had seen: who else would speak of them, and what have they themselves seen? Surely it is all of great interest and importance. And again I questioned myself: "What am I doing here?" In the fields, nobody bothered to look at the bus as it bumped past. With calm satisfaction I realized I had nothing to say.

We stopped. A small piece of the engine had fallen off onto the dusty road somewhere in the last twenty miles, and the driver wanted to go back to look for it. Most of us descended and spread newspapers on the ground beneath whatever shade was available. After an hour my attention was drawn to a group of secondary-school students who were having a conversation along lines similar to those I had heard so many times among high-school students in the United States: they were comparing the characters of students in different grades. A girl and boy were maintaining that the third form was very good, as was the fifth, but that the fourth form was a very bad group. The defender countered, "Yes, but you don't know them. If you knew them you would realize that they are very gentle. In fact, they are really the most gentle of all the students." I remembered that my students in the States had different concerns, and I smiled to think of them in that conversation there. The speaker elaborated several anecdotes of considerate gestures and sympathetic behavior. All this time, I watched and listened, saying nothing. I realized that I had come to a truly different place. My sense of isolation from the United States was a final sign that I had accepted a new home.

At that point, when it no longer made sense to think of writing about what I was doing there, I was moving into a level of involvement with African social life that went beyond the limited participation practiced in most ethnographic research orientations. Ordinarily, a social scientist is taught to try to keep a certain amount of emotional distance from whatever he is observing, and his detachment enables him to separate selected aspects of a situation in order to achieve a more objective perspective. However, when a researcher, in building his analysis, uses his own emotional responses to gain access to his material, he is using a research technique called participant-observation.[9] Among the repertoire of approaches that an investigator has available, participant-observation is particularly effective as a means of getting close to the experienced realities of social life and thus authenticating the importance of various factors within the research situation itself. By not abstracting his data too quickly, a participant-observer often obtains a better sense of how the elements of a given context blend together into a larger configuration. A researcher must make a choice of procedure based on the kind of insight he hopes his work will yield.[10] The peculiarities of the way I came to know African music gave me a different perspective on it from that which many other observers have had, and I am writing of my experience because I feel the reader needs to know something about the eyes through which I looked.

It is necessary to specify the method by which I arrived at my conclusions because people looking at the same phenomenon in different ways see different things. A social scientist, like a physicist, is interested in the relativity of understanding. Our relationship to an event determines what we can see of it, and a research method is a way of defining a style with which a researcher can relate to his data or participate in its recognition. As he discusses a particular religion, one person might define a world view and a cosmology, discovering an elaborate world of minor spirits and a somewhat aloof Father God; another person might find that most of that religion's practitioners are either ignorant of their pantheon or would never bother to locate the gods of their allegiance in any particular relationship, but rather attend rites generally for the purpose of exploiting the chance to meet a businessman or a potential lover. In a similar vein, we might think of the different analyses which would result from looking at the operation of a factory from the perspectives of management or workers.[11] The different facets of social reality which appear through different approaches to an event are actually complementary evidence of its complexity and vitality: each approach presents us with a certain truth regarding the world we wish to know. The complementarity of the various perspectives from which we may view a topic, as readers or as researchers, is basically another aspect of the relativity which limits our understanding. Yet the notion of complementarity is a notion of enrichment which may help us to acknowledge the validity of our own most personal and intimate relationship to what interests us. Since the days of the first social scientists, the search for ultimate validity in interpretation has become, to borrow a phrase, the banana peel under the feet of truth,[12] and I would not want to assert that my own interpretation of African music is more than one of many that are possible. The meaning of African music is indicated in everything that people say about it and do with it.

What is particularly suitable for a social scientist, though, is to try to present a coherent description of African music within its social and cultural context. Since this study is a product of my involvement with learning to play the drums myself, my hope is that it will complement those studies which analyze abstracted and formal musical structures. As my involvement with African musical forms deepened, my observations reflected more and more my relationship to the surrounding social environment. On a personal level, I still found myself abstracted and alienated from many situations, some of them mundane, like looking at my face in the mirror early in the morning, and some of them fantastic, like being asked to play for the paramount chief of Tamale during the Damba Festival, and getting tipped. But by the time I lost my desire to write anything about what I was learning, I had begun to appreciate the African way of life as a personal alternative. To arrive at the point where one sees the life of another culture as an alternative is to reach a fundamental notion of the humanistic perspective, and to accept the reality of one's actions to the people who live there is to understand that one has become part of their history. This insight can become a pathway to responsibility and an opening toward one's own human love. On that bus ride, when I felt that what I was doing in Ghana would probably have no consequence, academic, financial, or personal, if I returned to the United States, I was ready to begin the kind of education I wanted to get in African music. When there was no reason for me to be trying to learn the music except for my love of it, and when in my training I realized through my most personal self-consciousness that I could be socially and aesthetically criticized every moment for what I did, I began to understand what involvement with music means in Africa. We each move into situations in our own way, and some of us take longer than others. Generally we touch many apparent irrelevancies, and learning implies that at most times we will be at least partially confused. Just as one cannot think one's way into growth, there will be times when one is not aware, indeed cannot be aware, that what one is doing is providing the basis for significant work or discoveries.[13]

Thus there was in this research process an ironic element of forgetting of investigative procedures, as if my life in Africa were somehow put into brackets.[14] And if I admit that I did not try to give an academic coherence to my experience until I returned to the United States, I should add that the search to find the best way to present my data as scholarship made me realize more deeply that, whatever I had thought or was thinking, my "objectivity" is what I was when I was there, that part of Africa which I became, a fact in the lives and minds of those who knew me. As I still exist in that history, I am known by different names. To many Ewe people in Accra and in their villages, my name is *To dzro medea gbe o,* from an Ewe proverb meaning literally "still water makes no sound," or more loosely, "a calm sea does not move unless disturbed by wind or storm"; in other words, to quote one Ewe man, "Some people are quiet, and you cannot know them or what they can do unless they are approached or called." In Tamale and in the Dagomba towns of Ghana's Northern Region, I am known as *Lun-zhegu,* literally, "Red-skinned Drummer," the name of a man who lived about five centuries ago and who is taken as the grandfather of all Dagomba drummers. My teacher Ibrahim Abdulai told me, "Old, old Dagombas, those very old drummers, those who know about Lun-zhegu, they see you and they say that it is because you are very interested in drumming and because you were born in the same skin as Lun-zhegu. It is wonderful to them, and that is the reason why they are calling you our grandfather." In the streets and nightclubs of Accra, many people called me and knew me as "Psychedelic," or "Psyche" for short. If at first I thought that by *psychedelic*[15] they meant something new which made their minds change and that I had been given such an unusual name because I was carefree and always full of surprises, I later understood that they were defining the depth of my participation in the way that it defied and transcended the familiar categories into which I might have been easily placed. As I tried to live up to my names, I reflected that each was a way of telling me that I should try to consider myself as more than simply a student of their music present among them. As they welcomed me into their history, they indicated that they were ready to play upon the possibilities of a situation and to continue relating—and that I should be open to the experience. Now that I am reconstructing and remaking that experience as I write this essay, many dimensions of that experience are lost, and I understand that the main problem of participant-observation is the violence it does to the love which has motivated and sustained it.

The most important gap for the participant-observer, therefore, is not between what he sees and what is there, but between his experience and how he is going to communicate it. In attempting to do anthropological research, to translate the "structures" and "processes" which appear in another culture into the textual structures of his own, a social scientist must evaluate his own experience with flexibility. Finding the proper level of abstraction to portray with fidelity both the relativity of his own viewpoint and the reality of the world he has witnessed necessarily involves an act of interpretation.[16] He assigns a meaning to situations which were often extremely complex and ambiguous, and his interpretation of a given event balances the intimacy and depth of his appreciation of what happened with his explanation of what relevant factors provided the means for organizing that event's effectiveness. In the course of his work, he meets these concerns in ways he could not have imagined. To illustrate the cultural, personal, and musical themes of participation present in such an endeavor, I will describe at length a ritual which took place only a few weeks after my arrival in Ghana. Looking back now, I find my freshness at the time amusing and a bit embarrassing, yet also quite serviceable as a focus onto certain issues. In the town of Afiadenyigba in the Volta Region of Ghana, I was consecrated in the Yeve Cult of the Ewe tribe as an apprentice to Gideon Folie Alorwoyie. The ceremony differed in form but not in purpose from one described by A. M. Jones in *Studies in African Music*,[17] in which a young drummer "takes the arts" of the ancestral master drummers.

Basically the ceremony was to help me concentrate and learn better and faster. Gideon's uncle, an important fetish priest, was in charge. First, that afternoon, Gideon and I bought two white chickens, male and female for balance and harmony, and a bottle of gin. In the evening, after I had rested and bathed, we went to an open area by the priest's house. Eight drumsticks were selected from a bag containing the sacramental sticks of dead master drummers from more than a hundred years back and also from Gideon's own special bag of sticks, which had come to him from the same source, and these were laid on one of three beds of cowrie shells, also taken from the same bag as the sacred sticks. From left to right, there were Gideon's sticks, mine, and those of the dead master drummers. These sticks were the major focus of the ritual. They themselves were not for use except on ceremonial occasions; rather they held the spirits and skills of the dead master drummers who were asked to remain with the sticks which were to become mine. The libations, petitions, and sacrifice were done to formalize the continuity of the sticks.

We began pouring libations of various kinds onto the sticks: gin, corn soup, corn meal. Sometimes the priest poured the libation, sometimes Gideon, sometimes all three of us. Before most of the libations, four or eight cowrie shells would be thrown, particularly when the libation was not simply a matter of asking for help or recognition. Cowrie shells are shaped like turtle shells, rounded on one side and flat on the other, and a positive casting was indicated when the shells were either all up or all down or split evenly. They were consulted about such issues as whether my heart was pure—it was; whether I was honest—I was; or whether the ancestors accepted me—they did. I was blessed and the ancestors were asked to protect me. From time to time Gideon would explain what the priest was saying: "You cannot think bad toward any man. You can only play the drum. If someone should think bad toward you, the juju we have cast will make him so, when he is drinking water, he will drink his own blood."

Hearing these things, I began to think that what we were doing was very serious after all, and I tried to pay even closer attention. The problem was that the ceremony was so complicated: some libations we might touch to our mouths, offer twice to each pile, then take into our mouths and spit onto all three. I became confused trying to remember everything we were doing. To add to my difficulties, whenever the libation was gin, we would take a glass ourselves first. Thus, even as I was trying to remember the details, I began to think that if these things worked the way some anthropologists have maintained, perhaps it would be better to follow anthropological advice and allow my feelings to help make what I was doing more effective. After all, I did want to learn to play the drums.

Besides the effect of the gin, two other developments helped further my new orientation. One was that although Gideon explained a few points about the meaning of our actions, he did not try to influence me or impress me with esoterics. Instead, he told me that it really did not matter if I understood all the details, that if we went through the ceremony properly, it would work. The second development was that the shells kept turning up balanced at every question. This was unheard of, and people began to drift out of their houses to see just who I was that I was so pure and honest and acceptable. Since I was casting the shells a good part of the time, I did not think they were loaded, and besides, if a negative answer or two were to come out, it would only mean that we might have to go through a few more libations to satisfy the requirements of the ceremony. Too many bad castings, of course, might have spoiled the ceremony, but the only time the shells came out unbalanced was when we asked whether there was enough gin for the proceedings. I was among those who did not feel that this one mischance was a grave obstacle, and Gideon pulled some money from his pocket and sent a little boy to buy another bottle.

Needless to say, each time the shells came out balanced, I became a bit more excited. Consistent with my new purpose of letting the ceremony work on my feelings, I acquiesced to the gin, and during the many periods when Gideon and his uncle were performing their tasks without my assistance, I stopped watching and tried staring at the bright, full, tropical moon. Unfortunately, looking at the moon reminded me of the United States of America, toward which the moon had perceptibly moved in the course of the ceremony. Nobody I had grown up with, I reflected happily, had ever been involved in anything like this rite. Then I wondered if there might be a couple of men walking around on the moon at the moment. If they looked in my direction, they would never see me in that little clearing. There I was, having come all the way to Africa to learn the drums, and at this most crucial moment I was detached, skeptical, and a bit dreamy.

One important reason why my deeper feelings were not forthcoming was that I had fasted during the day and I was hungry. I noticed this fact every time we took a glass of gin. Thus as the ceremony progressed and I became less analytical, the many small details became less significant. Things began to make more sense in that I accepted what was happening to me and around me with a kind of nonchalance. I was then, it seemed, in the most appropriate mood to confront the supernatural. Everybody else seemed nonchalant, too. Gideon and a few spectators were joking around, and at one point a little baby tottered out into the circle and peed. The priest picked him up and put him to bed while Gideon filled in.

I was still, of course, more serious than anyone else. After about two and a half hours, though, I was more than ready when I was told to kneel before the sticks, putting the two chickens in front of me. I poured a gin libation on the three piles and then took a mouthful of gin and spat it on the piles too; then, corn soup. Eight shells were thrown: four up and four down. We proceeded. First the male chicken, for as Gideon mysteriously explained, "You must die before your wife." The fetish priest pulled the feathers from the neck and handed me a knife. He held the chicken while I cut its throat. The blood ran onto the three piles of sticks. Then with a quick twist he pulled off the head and laid it on my pile. Next I killed the female. The blood was shared onto the piles and the head went as before. After a few more libations, Gideon took over the service while the priest went aside to prepare the chickens for eating. One of the reasons for the fast was obvious. I was expected to eat a great deal, and I anticipated no problems: chicken was my favorite dish.

As the chicken stew was bubbling away, Gideon was busy pouring more libations and telling me what the ritual would accomplish. Everybody had been exceptionally pleased and astonished by the performance of the cowrie shells. After all the libations, the sticks were getting pretty gooey, and Gideon said he would clean them and place them with the shells into a special sack which I would put under my pillow when I went to sleep. The dead master drummers would come to me in my sleep and show me how to play. I would dream Ewe rhythms and beat my bed. If I were to play drums, the ancestral drummers would tell me what to do and would guide my hands. Their protection against enemies and their help in keeping my heart set on my purpose would mean that I would not mind or even notice mockery or criticism. They would tell me whom to trust. When I played the drums I would be strong: my arms would not tire and my hands would not hurt, and I would never feel any pain. I was very moved, and just at that point, the priest announced that the chicken was ready. He laid the breasts on the ancestors' pile. Then he gave me a big bowl and said, "Eat." In the bowl were those parts of the chicken which corresponded to those parts of myself that were to be protected: the two heads, the feet, the wings, the tails, the gizzards, and the hearts. I swallowed and ate. After that, there were a few more libations and I reeled off to bed.

Now, then, what really happened? From one point of view, it was an interesting way to spend an evening. It is obvious that in participant-observation research, as in travel, getting there is half the fun. Analytically, nevertheless, many attitudes toward the ritual are possible, and both then and now, the central problem is deciding how to approach the event. Academically, my understanding of the ceremony would be reflected through an interpretation.[18] For Gideon, however, who had told me not to worry so much about what everything meant, my understanding would be reflected musically. And to me as a participant, the most relevant question was, "What if it works?" Whether the ceremony had helped me learn to play the drums could be tested empirically, suggested another Ewe man to whom I spoke much later: I had merely to ask the priest to cancel the juju's effectiveness on a given occasion, and then I might see if my skills fell down or not when I tried to play. I have to admit that I was not ready to accept this challenge to my command of the drums. At the same time, it was evident that my participation had failed to provide me with any authentic feelings of belonging or under-standing; I was not in a position comparable to someone steeped in preparation and study for cult membership, and I did not attempt to achieve any further intimacy with cult esoterics. As a skeptic, I had taken the ceremony lightly, and I thought little of it afterwards. The bundle of sticks was too lumpy to bother putting them under my pillow.

My reflections on the ceremony became an issue because, though I am only an amateur musician, I managed to learn to play African drums.[19] Furthermore, if at the time of the ritual I could not consider myself properly assimilated or concerned, in the following months I was not even particularly dedicated to learning to beat drums. During my first months in Ghana, while Gideon was taking me around to display my skills, he spent only an afternoon or two teaching me a few support-ing rhythms. Yet whenever I played with Gideon in the cult, I seemed never to make a mistake.[20] Gideon would sometimes play rhythms to which I had never learned the responses, and still my playing would be correct. Cult drumming is fairly difficult, and I was a real novice at the time, yet nobody was surprised when I played well and nobody, not even Gideon, made suggestive reference to the ritual when they con-gratulated me. Practicing alone in my room, I could not maintain stead-ily even the responses I had learned.

In the cult I was usually as self-conscious as I had been the night I became an apprentice. Typically, as Gideon and I would arrive, the fetish priest would welcome us with spirits—double shots of gin, scotch, and local—and I was generally fairly drunk at any performance Gideon and I gave. As I stumbled out of the priest's house, a girl initiate with a shaven head might come up to me, slap my shoulder, and scream some-thing I could not understand. When we sat down, I would pick up drum-sticks for perhaps the first time that week and try to play properly while I looked around, in general satisfied if I could maintain my cool, avoid staring, and see my drum. When the ceremony ended, everyone would politely shake my hand and smile demurely. I understood very little on those occasions.

The whole matter of the ritual, however, goes beyond the issue of how one can talk seriously about something that was not very serious at the time.[21] If there was no solemnity in my early experiences in the cult, I again had reason to remember my ritual protection much later when I was living in Tamale studying the drumming of the Muslim Dagombas. By that time, after spending half a year running around Accra and traveling, I was beginning to wonder if I would ever take anything seriously. I had been in Tamale several weeks making rapid progress with the Takai dances, and my teacher Ibrahim Abdulai remarked that some people who had first laughed at my efforts had become afraid of me. What struck me was that prior to Ibrahim's comment I had not even noticed anyone mocking me, though I should have, since it had been so obvious. It was then that I recalled the cult's protection, and at this re-collection I began to wonder about and reconstruct the thoughts that I had had on the second morning of my instruction in Tamale. As a result of the first day's work, part of my right hand had swollen to twice its normal size and was so painful that I could not pick up a cup of coffee in the morning. I could not close it more than half way. On my way to my lesson, I was wondering how I would be able to play, but somehow I forgot to think about it when I reached Ibrahim's house. I picked up a stick and played for six hours. Of course, wondering about my in-volvement with rituals and juju was a kind of vanity, occasionally good for loosening up when I needed to relax, but I avoided thinking too much about what people felt was being accomplished by such things. I did not understand the whole issue and I thought that if I forced an inter-pretation on it, I would probably reduce the respect I was trying to give my teachers. If I had viewed their attention to these matters from the perspectives I had acquired in my native culture and, most unfortunately, even in my education, it would have been very difficult to keep myself low before them. Then, in a manner strikingly parallel to the way the Ewes had responded to my apprenticeship, the Dagombas gave me some of their own juju.

According to Ibrahim Abdulai, though I had progressed well, my wrist was still not "smart" enough to turn fast: when I played fast, my arm would become tense and I would tire. "Your wrist," he told me, "is not as smart as mine, and that is because you have grown up now and your bones are stretched and strong. I have been learning to beat drums from childhood up to this time, and that is why your wrist can't be fol-lowing mine all the time." I needed what he called a "cat's hand." "Did you ever see a cat catch a mouse?" he asked. He waved his hand in front of me. "You see," he said, "very flexible." If I liked, his "senior brother," Alhaji Adam Alhassan, an old and very great drummer, for-merly the leader of the Takai drummers, could give me a cat's hand. Of course I would have been happy to have it, but I delayed, thinking to wait a while until I could see how they would handle the situation. Later, when my problem saw no solution, Ibrahim asked me why I had not asked him what I had to do to get a cat's hand so that he in turn could ask Alhaji to make the juju for me. "It's not from a cat itself. It's medicine and it comes from juju. If you want to play, you put it on your arm and everything will be all right. You've come from far away. Everything you want, you must know. Everything you like, if it's there, I will try to get it for you. But as for you, when I call you, you don't answer. What can I do?" I dissembled. Suddenly I saw an opportunity to be a sociologist of religion. "O.K.," I said, "I agree, but please tell me something. You are a Muslim, yet you are telling me to do juju. Won't it trouble God?" He looked at me in amazement and said, "Trouble God?"

Alhaji Adam is one of those old people who are always happy. He had not been involved in my work, but we had a beautiful friendship. We liked each other very much, and whenever we met on the street, we were so happy that we would become confused: we would just be standing and greeting each other over and over again, laughing. When I visited him later and told him what I wanted from him, he asked me if I thought I could do a black man's juju. I said, "I don't know. What do you think?" Alhaji smiled. "I don't know either," he said. "Juju is like a small child: you can send him to get something for you; sometimes he will go and sometimes he will refuse." I asked him how it worked. "Everything is from God, and nobody knows God's work. Only God knows." He showed me his own amulet and told me how much he had enjoyed it in the old times. "If this is on my arm, even if the drummers are thousands, people will like me." When he was a little boy, his father had given the juju to him, and since then, many people had come to beg him to make the juju for them. He would do it for me because he liked me and because Ibrahim Abdulai had asked him. Otherwise he would have told me that he did not have the juju. There would be no charge, but if I liked it, I could give him something later. He instructed me to go into the bush and collect certain plants and then to go to the market and buy certain other things, including a white hen. Once everything were together, he would make the juju, and then I would take it to a cobbler who would use a white skin to sew it to fit my arm. "When you put it on, your wrist will become very soft, and as smart as a cat's."

That afternoon I went about ten miles outside of town and walked around in the bush until I found all the things Alhaji had asked me to get. He had told me that, once I was inside the bush and looking for a certain kind of grass, for example, I should stand and look around until I saw some growing; I would notice that one was taller than all the others, and I should go and pick that one by the roots. I had thought it sounded silly, but with everything he told me to find, there was always one which stood out according to his specifications. When I returned, I had just enough time to get to the market. Alhaji was playing with one of his great-grandchildren when I reached his house. He sent the child away and took parts of the plants I had collected, feathers from the chicken's back and right breast, and also the middle toenail from the chicken's left foot. He tied it all together and smeared it with some of the chicken's blood, collected from where we had cut its foot. While he was doing this work he was praying, telling his name and the name of the person who had given the juju to him, saying that he himself was giving it to me, and asking that it should work for me. He told me the name of the juju and told me to make charcoal from the remains of the plants, sprinkle some of it on the juju, and use the rest to cook the chicken. With the help of one of Ibrahim's sons, I prepared the charcoal and the juju. While the chicken was cooking, I visited the cobbler. Then I returned to another feast of wings, feet, and chicken head. By that time, however, I was learning to enjoy it. I sent some of the chicken to Alhaji, but he refused it, saying that if he ate any of the chicken, the juju would be undone. By then the cobbler had also finished his work, but Alhaji said we should not do the last part in the night. The next morning when I went to him, he put the juju on my arm and called its name. He took my middle finger and bent both it and my wrist inward until there was a loud crack at the base joint. He said it would now work with me. I plied him with questions. He had few answers and told me I need not ask so many questions. If I needed him for something else, I could come to him. "Too much of giving advice," he said, "will make me tell lies."

Having told the story, I nonetheless hesitate to say that the juju worked in a most uncanny way. When I tried it, I picked a very fast dance and increased my speed, noticing rather ambivalently that all I could feel of my arm was vibration, as if it had no bones. Such events are amazing, no doubt. When we focus on my musical training, the whole complex of activities surrounding the cult ritual and the cat's hand adds a possible dimension of interpretation completely different from the sociological and psychological considerations which will be advanced later in the discussion of aesthetic quality and creative influence. On a formal level, the traditional African interpretation does at least as adequate a job of accounting for things: there was no doubt in their minds as to why I was playing so well. At stake is more than a conflict of cultural perspectives from which we might choose the most plausible. In the situation, however, it was important not to choose. If someone were to ask me if I believe in juju, I would be tempted to dodge in the spirit of a Nigerian professor of sociology whom I asked a similar question about ghosts. "Well, you see," he joked, "nobody has ever been able to explain adequately to me that they do *not* exist." Ibrahim Abdulai himself never mentioned the juju until I asked him about it one day. He said, "Whether you believe it or you don't believe it, it doesn't matter. I asked you to go to Alhaji Adam for this juju. The juju that Adam has made for you is from the beginnings of his family, and it comes from his family. So this juju stands for the whole family, and since Adam has given it to you, then it should always be on your arm. But whether you put it on or you don't put it on is unto you. Perhaps you think it is useless for you, and if that is the case, you can leave it. No one can force anyone to put something on."

When I used the cat's hand and enjoyed it, behind the event was not an explanation but a background of social action, the context of participation and understanding. As I have said, our perception and interpretation of the basic elements and significant relationships of a situation can differ relative to different kinds of participation, and a participant-observer uses his participation to gain access to an alien context so that he may perceive its various aspects through the eyes of the people of the place. Thus, while I originally saw myself as merely trying to learn music, they saw something else, and the sense emerges that the Ewe and Dagomba rituals did not attain significance by being understood, either emotionally or esoterically, but that for me, they became relevant in Tamale only as an indication of my readiness to begin learning and my acceptance of the responsibilities and consequences of my participation. In that context, there was no need to interpret my relationship to the ancestors with any detailed clarity; understanding that relationship was to be something I would live through with the living. I was only one of several people involved in the rituals, and the rituals were there for them as much as for me. I could think about the rituals, just as on the bus I could think about my lack of desire to bridge my isolation from the United States in a literary way, without reflecting on these events as problems: they were only two aspects of the social context of my life.

The irrelevance of my reflections on the rituals, however, does exemplify an important aspect of participant-observation. If it is possible to be honest wth oneself, it is apparent that no matter how much one knows or how well one can control the potential analytic complexity of a research situation, at a certain level too much awareness makes it impossible to act or relate. My nonchalance toward events which might have been a key feature of any analysis of African music can be construed as part of a research strategy that allowed me to interpret a

situation only when I could judge my participation as effective and appropriate in that context. In participant-observation research, one's relationship to what one studies changes continuously. To recognize the
relativity of participation and understanding is to acknowledge that insight is dependent upon timing. As his perception of the configuration
of events changes, a researcher realizes that the process of learning
about and adapting to life in foreign cultures is as much a breaking
down of the categories and concepts he has brought with him as it is a
recognition and realization of the most meaningful perspectives he can
establish. The element of judgement in participant-observation research
means that its technique is difficult to teach and that its results are dependent on the temperament and circumstances of each individual researcher. Yet though participant-observation cannot claim the same *kind*
of scientific rigor as certain other methods of social research, it is especially well-suited to examine relationships of intimacy and differentia-
tion and processes of individuation and communal expression. In the
search for significant generalizations relevant to these central concerns
of the classical social scientific traditions, participant-observation has become a way to turn the limitations of many standard investigative methods to advantage through the uniqueness of a researcher who uses his
individuality to address social questions.

The character of participant-observation thus obliges some sort of
personal statement. My method of studying the music was to learn to
play it myself, and therefore on the crucial issue of judging the appropriateness of my participation in the context of my research, I could rely
on the judgement of my teachers. They had the problem of choosing and
organizing the basic rhythms of their music for me to learn, and as they
paced my exposure, they revealed their notions of difficulty and complexity. Most important, within this kind of formally structured relationship, I was able to look closely at the instances and ways I made
mistakes, and thus I acquired my awareness of African music not by
categorizing and abstracting its formal qualities but by noticing the ways
musical effectiveness could break down.[22] Something essential was usually missing when I played, and my teachers were pressed to engage
their critical and analytic sensibilities in a systematic demonstration of
the aesthetic requirements of proper playing. In this manner they presented a more authentic approach to the relevant issues of music-making
in the African context than I might have obtained arbitrarily or ethno-
centrically through my own observations. Also, any good performance I
witnessed brought musical qualities together so thoroughly that they
were difficult to distinguish; the incompleteness of my playing raised the

issues in a clear-cut fashion until I could eventually address the integrity of a successful musical event. As I became qualified and more in control of my drum-beating, I would deliberately make small mistakes to see if my teachers were paying attention, to test the possibilities and limits of variation and improvisation, and to learn how my teachers would further criticize my playing. While I cannot say I attained complete competence, I came close enough to recognize what would be involved.

In all this work, I learned music as if it constituted a kind of language. My instruction was, so to speak, directly and physically musical: I imitated what my teachers played, and I attempted to follow them through their changes by responding to their gestures and bodily cues.[23] I understood what to do before I learned how to think or talk about it. In many ways, their adeptness at mimetic techniques made their teaching perhaps less ambiguous than it might have been had they used words, and in fact, whenever I found one of my teachers trying to explain what I had to do, I knew he was at the last resort of his teaching capabilities. Words are problematic, of course, in any language. For example, if my drumming teacher listened to my playing and said, "You must be free," I might have nodded my head in agreement at the time, though it was not very evident what he meant. I would not try to think about what he had said until I was able to demonstrate to his satisfaction what he was talking about. To understand and translate the meaning of words like "freedom," it is necessary to examine the social context of their use, to look at what someone who talks of freedom does. In some respects, this particular interpretive orientation can characterize the social scientist's task, and the method of participant-observation is, as we have noted, a device for mediating the translation through the dimensions of social action.

Such an interpretation is an attempt to render the reality of a foreign culture in the world of our own understanding without absorbing or reducing the distinctiveness of that culture. Simply speaking, we describe and make sense of something different from us. I spoke earlier of the inherent violence in the work of giving a finished literary form to the love that obscures this difference. As the personal history of my research is sacrificed to recollection and to a final interpretation from across an ocean, the work of scholarship can still be seen as a gesture which may have value, particularly in its potential to affect the lives and destinies of the musicians who are striving for respectability and livelihood now. The prestige of scholarship extends into history by introducing or affirming ways of apprehending and describing the world. In that continuing history, there is always need for new mediation to help overcome boundaries in the name of love. In the plan of this essay, we first accept the different principles on which African music is based, then we learn to admire the way it achieves excellence, and finally we can appreciate its movement and cultural meaning.

In that appreciation, a reader may find a basis for relating to a different style of life. I would hope, therefore, that the validity of this work be measured by its openness to new applications, not necessarily in conventional scholarly terms, but in the practical and mundane situations which others may encounter. I would hope that someone who goes to a performance of a national dance troupe from Africa might understand and appreciate more of the sense behind what he sees and hears, that an anthropological field-worker who lacks training in music or aesthetics might see more when he looks at an event of which music is a part, that someone who stumbles across a group of conga players in a park might be able to judge why he likes or dislikes their drumming even though they appear to know what they are doing, that an aficionado of any genre of music might find a fresh way of thinking about his tastes, that someone might find a framework for assessing the authenticity of an American group which uses African musical instruments or the historical self-consciousness of an African group which uses Western ones, that a seeker or a musician who works or finds himself in an African musical idiom might discover new criteria for evaluating his purpose.

In informing the judgements with which we view the world, scholarship can help us to be more receptive to what is new. If we can accept the complexity and openness of history, we will meet the issues of our interest in the present. There are those who can find African genius only in the past, who seek an image of Africa in the arts and wisdom of traditional societies; in the meantime, new styles of music and dance sweep the continent, signs of a tremendous creative vitality. Both the Highlife music of the city and the drumming music of the cult, each within its own form, raise certain cultural themes to a unique resolution and display. Before we mourn the passing of the old forms of music and hurry to grasp our last chance to know them, we should heed the advice of a famous art critic who wrote that "a 'dead' style is one that is defined solely by what it is *not*; a style that has come to be negatively felt."[24] And whether we listen to the music of the tribes or the music of the cities, we might heed another critic who reminds us that "the dead convention can be restructured and revived, as it is in all authentic art. We recover its nature by an act of historical or artistic sympathy."[25] Understanding the relevance of African music involves an engagement with a tradition of artistic genius, and in the continuity of that tradition there is an element of renewal.

In this context, scholarship becomes a celebration of the uniqueness and variety of humankind. A study of African music must tell you something about what it means "to live" in Africa. An understanding of African music may lead to an understanding of the amorphous background of cultural forms, but it should also tell you something about how to find a friend or what to do at a dance or how to behave on a street. If you play a recording of American jazz for an African friend, even though all the formal characteristics of African music are there, he may say, as he sits fidgeting in his chair, "What are we supposed to do with this?" He is expressing perhaps the most fundamental aesthetic in Africa: without participation, there is no meaning. When you ask an African friend whether or not he "understands" a certain type of music, he will say yes if he knows the dance that goes with it. The music of Africa invites us to participate in the making of a community. In the words of Léopold Sédar Senghor:

> Cette force ordinatrice qui fait le style nègre est le *rythme*. C'est la chose la plus sensible et la moins matérielle. . . . Même dans les quotidiens tams-tams du soir, [la musique nègre] n'est pas pure manifestation esthétique, mais fait communier, plus intimement, ses fidèles au rythme de la communauté dansante: du Monde dansant.[26]

> [This organizing force which makes the black style is *rhythm*. It is the most perceptible and the least material thing. Even in the nightly drumming, black music is not a purely aesthetic manifestation, but brings its faithful into communion, more intimately, to the rhythm of the community which dances, of the World which dances.] (Translation mine.)

Rhythm is the most perceptible and the least material thing.

Glistening bodies and furious hands, . . . the language of the drums is one of disturbance, . . . a basic message capable of producing strong unexpected reactions in listeners, . . . the immense stimulation of the always approaching climax. . . . Here we are face to face with a sure manipulation of an elemental human instinct.
Liner Notes
Drums of Trinidad, Cook Records

The equilibrium and poetic structure of the traditional dances of the Yoruba in Western Nigeria, as well as the frozen facial expressions worn by those who perform these dances, express a philosophy of the cool, an ancient indigenous ideal: Patience and collectedness of mind. . . . Ask a traditional member of this populous African society, "What is love?" and he may tell you, as one told me, "Coolness."
Robert F. Thompson
"An Aesthetic of the Cool"

1

The Study of Music in Africa

If you ask people what African music is like, most will with little hesitation and great confidence tell you that African music is all drumming: Africans are famous for their drumming. It is exactly this mass impression that ethnomusicologists, those people who study the music academically, love to correct. Anyone reasonably well-informed about music-making in Africa will immediately react against such a naive notion by citing a wealth of musical instruments: xylophones, flutes, harps, horns, bells. Regarding drums, he might further report that almost every tribe, and sometimes even specific groups within a tribe, has its own different kinds of drums, beaten in a special way, or he might say that there are a few tribes which have no drums at all.[1] Yet the popular conception persists, and it is perhaps understandable that after several months in Ghana as a music student I was surprised to hear an old man gleefully welcome the approach of some drummers by saying, "Ah, music!" Most Westerners cannot find anything particularly musical about a group of drums, and their judgements, therefore, seem only to demonstrate their ethnocentric biases.

People from Western cultures historically have had a difficult time understanding anything African. Those who dislike African music respond to it in several ways. Some say that they are bored, that the music is so monotonously repetitive that it just dulls the senses. Others, alternatively, say that the music is so complicated rhythmically that they get confused and cannot make any sense of it. These people are likely to add that because they cannot figure out any pattern, they feel threatened that either the monotony or the confusion might take them over, and they do their best to ignore the unpleasantness. Less tolerant people have felt their sanity or their morals challenged, and in the past some of them even took the truly remarkable step of forbidding Africans to make music.[2] Those with an open mind wish the music were more quiet.

Yet there are many Westerners who love African music. To them it seems to translate, they might say, into visual patterns or physical movement. Such Westerners overcome their frustration by eliminating the need to find the beat: they express themselves any way they like, they say, and appreciate the feeling. A dancer I know told me how she had practiced very hard to African music until she was finally able, as she said, to let herself go and move freely. African music, like other African arts, is admired mostly as a spontaneous and emotional creation, an uninhibited, dynamic expression of vitality, and Picasso himself found such inspiration in African masks early in his revolutionary career. We may note that, in a sense, those who accept African music affirm the feelings of those who reject it: neither admirers nor detractors can relate to the music by making distinctions among the rhythms. Popular Western attitudes toward African music, whether affirmative or negative, are alike in emphasizing an awesome distance between Western and African sensibilities and in involving the topic of African music with the extremely ambivalent connotations of the word "primitive."

Understandably, the work of many ethnomusicologists derives from an attempt to confound any generalization about African music which might wander close to the swamp of racial prototypes. The detailed and esoterically specific studies of Western academicians, though serving to deprive Westerners of their myths, have reinforced the sense of distance between continents. It is almost as if African music gains in respectability by remaining beyond the facile and patronizing understanding of Westerners: both admirers and detractors find that one should not think of Africa as a single place, for to do so would be to ignore its diversity of cultures. African poets and politicians may speak of African unity; Western students avoid the dangers of racist simplification by stressing African complexity. It is probably safe to say that many ethnomusicologists, though hoping to demonstrate a wider usefulness for their knowledge, consider their main purpose to witness, record, preserve, and thus enrich the world's musical heritage. As a science, ethnomusicology is still at a "data-gathering" stage, and its most immediate applicability seems to be to augment music theory. Moreover, the appearance of a specialized branch of academic inquiry has discouraged many social and cultural anthropologists from their former practice of discussing art in their monographs.[3] Though the study of art is a valid tool for historians and philosophers, it is reasonable and quite common for an anthropologist to discuss a social event without any analysis of the music which might have been played at the time: in most views music is only an accompaniment to something more important. Two major gaps in the academic study of African music, then, are the lack of a unifying framework for evaluating the information collected about African music and the lack of a theoretical perspective for integrating musical analysis with social analysis. Given the undisciplined prejudices of many Westerners, the difficulty and dryness of most academic studies is commendable, but such work often does not touch our capacity to feel the reality of our common humanity or to recognize our most wonderful potentials in the genius of a strange person.[4]

From another perspective, though, music seems to offer one way of thinking about what unities may exist among African cultures. Certainly there is a musical continuity which reaches in an easily distinguishable way into the Americas,[5] and music continues to carry a message of solidarity to African peoples throughout the world. You can hear Soul and Latin music almost anywhere in Africa; you can hear African and West Indian music on the radio at various times in most large cities in the United States; you can sit in a bar in Ghana, Togo, or the Ivory Coast and hear music from Zaïre and Congo, from Nigeria, from South Africa, from Jamaica, Puerto Rico, Colombia, and the United States; great drummers, aficionados, and scholars can trace the rhythms of the Latin dance halls of New York to Cuban and Brazilian cults and then to West Africa.[6] In Haiti, I demonstrated for some drummers several Yeve Cult rhythms which were familiar enough to have Haitian names, and while I would not consider the rhythms to be identical if I transcribed them, my friends there said they knew the rhythms well.[7] That there exists a basis for thinking about an "African" musical style seems obvious and is unquestioned by those most directly involved. If they consider all this music to be their own, then it is. And interestingly enough, even the inability of most Western listeners to move beyond a simplified response or to make rhythmic distinctions at a basic level is balanced by their ability to say, with surprising accuracy, "That sounds African."

What, then, is "African" about all this music? This academic problem is as well a political and historical problem. "Africa" is a concept, a broad generalization we may use for various reasons, yet the academic stand against simple reductions is not without foundation. Among the metaphors of African unity, racial ones are spurious; geographical ones omit the African peoples spread throughout the Americas; historical, political, and economic ones are unrealized; and cultural ones are often vague or inaccurate. Discussing "African" music, therefore, we must recognize that, academically, we are examining music as potential evidence for a conception of Africa.[8] What so many people accept is that there is an essential African style which can be perceived in the different musics of African peoples. While a social scientist understands such an identification as an indication that a unity exists, it remains important to characterize what it is. Although to discuss "African" music, or "African" anything, will involve the looseness and possible distortion that comes with generalization, we realize that without a feeling for the general meaning and order of what we may see and hear at an African musical event, it would be difficult to sense the significance of the variety of specific details we may experience.[9] Although our interest is usually aroused by the particular character of the people and places we know, we can nonetheless make good use of a flexible and unifying orientation. As a first step to familiarity, therefore, we must build a model, an abstracted and composite description of those features of the music which appear *more or less in common* in the various musics of African cultures. A social scientist might call such a model an "ideal type" and use the relative limitations of its applicability as a basis for making comparisons.[10]

With this model, however, we can only begin to describe the African musical style. To refine our sensitivity, we must ask aesthetic questions: Why is a certain piece of music good? Why are people moved or bored when I play? What is the purpose of the music? The quality of a specific performance cannot be judged by whether the music conforms to an abstracted formal model of "musical" properties or structures as defined by the Western tradition. These properties may serve as a basis for an academic description of diverse African musical idioms, but people do not relate to the music on such a basis. The variations from formal and familiar structures in an actual performance are what count most in distinguishing and appreciating artistic quality within a certain type of music. To clarify this point, we might think of a joke which we have heard before, maybe often: a good comedian could still make us laugh at it. We would miss the point if we analyzed or thought of the joke as merely an arrangement of words about a particular theme or of the music as merely a structure of sounds.[11] In other words, we can clearly perceive African musical forms only if we understand how they achieve their effectiveness within African social situations.[12] Ethnomusicologists working in foreign cultures consider themselves social scientists rather than humanistic critics because they are aware that the best way to begin to appreciate another culture's music is to try to understand the people who make it and its place in their society.

This issue is a bit more subtle than it appears, and it may seem perhaps too academic to some readers until we have carried through the substantive discussion of African musical form in the next chapter. On the most obvious level, of course, we understand that music's effectiveness and meaning are dependent upon its context because aesthetic standards of judgement, taste, and perception are relative. This perspective is basic and simple: anyone who has ever traveled or lived among different types of people knows how the whole feeling of life, down to the smallest detail, can change from place to place. In my introductory discussion of participation and understanding, I said that a person's relationship to an event determines what he can see of it, and similarly, people listening to the same music will hear different things. Philosophically, there is no logical connection between music and an individual listener's response.[13] Though some people still like to argue the point, it is difficult to maintain that a certain piece of music is inherently and universally religious or warlike, filled with love or anger.[14] The history of Western music is full of stories about how certain works were first reviled then loved, and for different reasons; even in the course of one's own life, one may find that music which once moved one to tears can seem boring or trite. When we try to understand the music of a different culture or historical period, we must be prepared to open our minds not only to the certainty that people will have different standards for judging musical quality but also to the possibility that they may have an entirely different conception of what music itself is.

More significantly, then, our attitudes about what art is can influence our notions about how art works. As Westerners, we habitually look at art as something specific and removed from the everyday world, something to appreciate or contemplate, something to which we must pay attention in a concert hall, a museum, a theater, a quiet room. The fact that we have, at least since Plato, developed an impressive tradition of philosophical, moral, and critical literature regarding the problems and possibilities of our relationship to art is evidence that we see art as in many ways something separate and distinct. Learning to appreciate an "artwork" usually involves developing an awareness of its place within a tradition of influence and innovation among other artworks. In other words, we isolate the work of art from the social situation in which it was produced in order to concentrate on our main aesthetic concern,

those qualities which give it integrity as art.[15] Whatever gives the artwork its unity becomes a symbol for the art's communicative effectiveness as the purest representation of an idea or the most expressive
condensation of an emotion. From such a perspective, art *reflects* the
social and psychological realities of its context, restating and representing them through the artistic medium which transforms or, some would
say, distorts them. While we admit that the meaning of an artwork may
have been different in its original context and while we can certainly be
interested in deepening our understanding of that meaning, what we generally consider most wonderful about art is its enduring ability to affect
us, to withstand the test of time, as the saying goes, and to transcend
the limitations of its particular historical and cultural location.

Even music, toward which among the arts we are perhaps least inclined to be analytical, remains somewhat beyond our daily lives, having
little direct relationship to what we are doing most of the time. We
speak of a musical diversion, interlude, or distraction. We must stop in
order to listen, and we might say that someone who talks or moves
around during a musical performance is not "really" listening. Yet we
respect music as a profound art because it enriches our lives. Those
people who take music seriously say that it beautifully expresses and
communicates ideals and emotions and that they return again and again
to music to find again the fulfillment and revitalization they may have
found at a concert, in church, or wherever they as individuals were
touched and moved to a different feeling about life. According to our
conception of a music-making situation, the conditions of musical enjoyment are those that enable us to focus exclusively on the greatness
that is in the music itself, greatness that a virtuoso musician can elicit.[16]
In a well-built concert hall, people will forget that they are in the second
balcony, and after a particularly fine performance of a work, the whole
audience may be moved to a standing ovation. But if you begin clapping
your hands in time with a symphony, people will tell you that you are
disturbing them. The effectiveness of music, for Westerners, is its power
to express or communicate directly to individuals, and we would defend
our right to a personal aesthetic judgement independent of the tastes of
everyone else.[17]

What is aesthetically significant for a social scientist looking at such a
situation, however, is not so much our preferences for Mozart or Beethoven or Prokofiev or Bartok but rather the way we orient ourselves
to music in the first place and our consequent approaches to the potential experiences we might have. This is the crucial issue, of course, which
confronts Westerners who find themselves alienated when they listen

to African music. Expressing oneself "spontaneously," without a sense
of appropriateness or control, being able to hear only a single, mo-
notonous beat, or trying to put the music out of one's mind, these responses are indications that the difficulties in perceiving the complexities
in the rhythms are also difficulties in recognizing the meaning and purpose of one's relationship to the music as an event. To put the matter
another way, we might characterize these responses as an initial anxiety
followed by privatization and simplification,[18] and suggest that this with-
drawal from a sense of intimacy with African music stems from different
assumptions about the conditions of involvement and communication.
Like institutions, the different musical styles which different cultures
evolve require and focus different kinds of participation, and to a social
scientist the nature of this participation is the key to the music's effectiveness. When a Western friend for whom you might play some African
music says in disgust, as he sits fidgeting in his chair, "That's not music,"
he is ironically both right and wrong. African music is not just different
music but is something that is different from "music." For a Westerner
to understand the artistry and purpose of an African musical event, it
is necessary for him to sidestep his normal listening tendencies, slow
down his aesthetic response, and glide past his initial judgement. The
reason why it is a mistake "to listen" to African music is that African
music is not set apart from its social and cultural context. Perhaps more
than the novelty or the strangeness of the sounds, the different meaning
of a music which is integrated into cultural activities presents difficulties
to the Western listener and undermines his efforts to appreciate and
understand African music. A Westerner who wishes to understand African music must begin with a recognition of his own fundamental attitudes about music so that he may adjust to a fundamentally different
conception. The study of African music can thus also become a focus
for understanding the meaning of cultural differences.

There are so many ways to recognize and describe what scholars call
the "functional integration" of music and culture in Africa that this
integration can be considered a formal and general musical characteristic in its own right. This community dimension is perhaps the essential
aspect of African music. For instance, several authorities cite hand-
clapping as the most prevalent means of musical expression in Africa
because they do not want to distinguish the audience from the musicians
at a musical event.[19] From a similar perspective, others have maintained
that Africans have not developed systematic and critical traditions of
the philosophy of art and aesthetics and that people who do not perceive "art" as a conceptual problem do not distinguish or separate art

forms from their context.[20] Furthermore, the traditional arts of Africa are not easily distinguished from each other: witnessing a ritual involving masked dancers, a Western observer might wonder whether sculpture, dance, music, or drama was the dominant art, and if he could understand the language of the drums or the words of the songs, he might have to consider poetry as well. To these notions of musical and cultural integration, one might add the simple fact of the sheer amount of musical activity in African cultures. There are very few important things which happen without music, and the range and diversity of specific kinds of music can astound a Westerner. Ashanti children sing special songs to cure a bedwetter; in the Republic of Benin there are special songs sung when a child cuts its first teeth; among the Hausas of Nigeria, young people pay musicians to compose songs to help them court lovers or insult rivals; men working in a field may consider it essential to appoint some of their number to work by making music instead of putting their hands to the hoe; among the Hutus, men paddling a canoe will sing a different song depending on whether they are going with or against the current.[21] The reader can find dozens of similar examples in ethnographies and travelogues, but the central point remains that, compared to Western societies, African societies have many more people who participate in making music, and they do so within specific groups and specific situations.

The extent to which music-making is a group activity points to another dimension of the integration of music and culture, that is, as an institution. The rich repertoire of music in many African cultures, in focusing people's activity on many specific occasions, speaks of a concern to develop a means of recognizing the important moments of an individual's life and referring them to a common tradition. This quality music shares with myths, proverbs, and folklore. Moreover, as a group activity, music is a means for tradition itself to be organized and communicated. In many African tribes, different social groups have rights and privileges with respect to different types of songs. People organize themselves into musical associations and clubs. In the cities these groups are important not only as embodiments of tribal loyalties and continuities but often as organizations for political and economic action;[22] in the villages, creative effort in musical competitions becomes a way of discriminating status, obligations, and identity. The stability and continuity of musical forms and associations suggest that music in Africa can be considered a formal institution: both a rich man who is a patron of a musical club and a member who counts on his club playing for free at his funeral certainly think so. All societies, in varying degrees, have institutions which channel and bind activity in a similar way, but it is particularly in Africa that music so often serves as a foundation. Like language, kinship, or occupation, music helps people to distinguish themselves from each other. In many parts of Africa, one need not be a sociologist to determine someone's social background from the music he dances to or plays. Thus, music serves as one of the important mediators between a person's activity and his community. Finally, as an institution, music itself provides a basis for thinking about and ensuring the integrity of a group, like a symbolic characterization of a person's heritage. So it was, legend has it, that a long time ago some African stevedores, who had their own songs for their work of loading and unloading boats, first understood a machine to be the white man's music. In many African cultures, musicians are the acknowledged authorities on history and myth,[23] and formerly in the great centralized kingdoms like Dahomey, Benin, and Ashanti, if a drummer made a mistake when drumming the names of the chief's lineage, it could be a capital offense;[24] among the Dagombas, a chief will not go anywhere unless he is accompanied by a drummer to signify his status. In Africa it is a drum and not a scepter which is the symbol of the king and the voice of the ancestors.[25]

One feature which African musical traditions seem to have in common, therefore, is the depth of their integration into the various patterns of social, economic, and political life. In its own way the astounding diversity of musical situations and musical activity seems to offer support for a unified conception of African music. The aesthetic principles of African music are to an extent dependent on how the music can become socially relevant. In fact, these principles are more uniform than the apparent and culturally idiosyncratic differences in such "musical" factors as scales, vocal and song styles, and instrumentation. Therefore I have begun with a consideration of the general concerns and problems of musical meaning and cultural differences because these issues touch the dominant themes of my interpretation of aesthetic effectiveness. There was a very brief period during my stay in Ghana when I thought it would be a good idea to ask various people I met, "What is music?" Most looked at me as if I had said something funny or strange, and a few simply laughed and said, "Don't you know?" I had slightly better luck when I asked what difference it makes to have music. When I asked Ibrahim Abdulai, he said, "Music is something which does not conceal things about us, and so it adds to us." In general, while many people were surprised at my question, more than one person said something like, "Music is essential to our life," and elaborated in various ways on a theme on which J. H. Kwabena Nketia, perhaps the foremost African musicologist, has written: "A village that has no organized music or neglects community singing, drumming, or dancing is said to be dead."[26] And in his detailed study of Dan music, Hugo Zemp uses as an epigram a Dan proverb which says, "The village where there is no musician is not a place where man can stay."[27] Such statements begin to relate music, in the same way Senghor's words did,[28] to a sense of community and a recognition that African music, if it can be discussed at all, has something to do with the continued workings of people's relationship to society.

The fact that most people in Africa do not conceive of music apart from its community setting and cultural context means that the aesthetics of the music, the way it works to establish a framework for communal integrity, offers a superb approach to understanding Africans' attitudes about what their relationship to each other is and should be. The judgements of competence which people make and the standards of quality of which a musician is aware are elaborations of their own conceptions about the nature of their social life, elaborations which are particularly more evident in musical activity than in many other institutionalized relationships because these artistic standards involve explicit judgements on the potential of the communities within which people live.[29] The study of African music, therefore, can reveal a great deal about the nature of culture and community life. From such a perspective, a culture may perhaps best be considered not as an abstract idea or as a basic formal structure but rather as a dynamic style with which people organize and orient themselves to act through various mediators —institutions such as language, production, marriage, folklore, religion, and of course, art. African music is a cultural activity which reveals a group of people organizing and involving themselves with their own communal relationships—a participant-observer's comment, so to speak, on the processes of living together.[30] The aesthetic point of this exercise is not to reflect a reality which *stands behind* it but to ritualize a reality that is *within* it. The African integration of art and context and the absence of a literary philosophical tradition do not in any way preclude a lively critical atmosphere, as I certainly knew whenever I played poorly. Criticism is presented every moment: it is a part of the context and a part of the art. In an African musical context, criticism is seen and offered as an act of participation and a gesture of support to help the artistic effort achieve its communal purpose, and to systematize the criticism would destroy the integrity of the event. Criticism in Africa is a measure of people's concern that the quality of their art is intimately connected with the quality of their lives. Africans use music and the other arts to articulate and objectify their philosophical and moral systems, systems which they do not abstract but which they build into the music-making situation itself, systems which we can understand if we make an effort.

African music is indeed different from what we ordinarily consider music to be, and as we examine the way African music becomes a focus for values as it mediates the life of a community, we will find that our assumptions about tribal communities are similarly challenged. Our history teaches us to consider the relationship of individual identity and communal unity to be a matter of common faith and common feelings, and we may be surprised to discover different conceptions concerning the nature of character and individuality, understanding and communication, participation and group involvement, and freedom and discipline. The basic plan of this book will be to approach these dimensions of social action through an examination of *how* Africans use *rhythms* in their music to achieve an integration of music and community. Because of our tendency to perceive musical qualities as distinct from their social and cultural context, we must first discuss African musical forms as we perceive them, and because of our inability to respond effectively to African rhythms, we must begin with a step-by-step exposition of just what a complex rhythm is.

2

Music in Africa

At the beginning of each year, the *harmattan* winds blow a fine dust from the Sahara Desert across the Sudan and over the coastal areas of the Gulf of Guinea. In Bamako, capital of Mali, you might observe the evening traffic as if through a reddish-brown filter which softens and mutes the sights and sounds of the crowded streets. The atmosphere is tranquil, and standing on the long bridge over the Niger River, with cars passing just a few feet behind you, you might look at a lone fisherman in his graceful canoe and feel that only the lovely melodies of the harp-like *kora* could capture and convey the unity of the scene. At night the temperature drops until you might wonder why you ever thought you missed winter, and if by chance you found yourself in an isolated village at the right time and you looked up at the multitude of clearly visible stars, you might hear the music of xylophones through the crisp air and believe that the clarity of the music was perhaps more than superficially appropriate to the stillness of the night. In a big coastal city like Accra, Ghana, or Lagos, Nigeria, you would probably feel quite different. At rush hours, the taxi drivers talk to each other with their horns, and every pedestrian is going his way at a different speed. Later the richness of heat and color is still apparent, cooled down and mellowed in the Highlife dance music of the nightclubs.

If you valued those moments when you felt that you had more deeply seen a particular place because of its music, you might possibly be reluctant to simplify your experiences to a level which obscured the way each was special. Understandably, those fortunate people who pursue such moments within their professional lives would sympathize with you, but they would have an obligation to be prepared if someone were to ask them to describe African music in a short essay. Among the Western authorities on African music, some would flatly refuse, but others, after a cautionary phrase about the problems of diversity and generalization, would probably mention the social importance of music and then list several musical elements centering around the notion of rhythmic complexity. In this chapter we will examine some of the general characteristics of African music, and we will draw heavily on the work of a few scholars who have made an effort to condense their broad experience into brief summaries. To illustrate these characteristics I will rely mainly on my own greater familiarity with Dagomba and Ewe drumming, though I might easily have chosen, and my readers might easily find, examples from the wide variety of recordings and scholarly sources available.[1]

Just as the African integration of music with its social context establishes a basic sociological perspective in the face of the diversity of cultures and musical situations, so does the notion of rhythm form the basis for discussing, on a musical level, the general characteristics of the various African musical traditions which are otherwise so distinct in terms of instruments, tonal organization, and vocal styles. If the rhythmic systems used by different African peoples are not the same (though they are often surprisingly similar), they at least have in common the fact that they are complex, and the greater complexity of West African rhythmic systems supplies us with a more thorough and intelligible analytic tool. Senghor says that rhythm is the basis of all African art, and regarding music, A. M. Jones writes, "Rhythm is to the African what harmony is to the Europeans, and it is in the complex interweaving of contrasting rhythmic patterns that he finds his greatest aesthetic satisfaction."[2]

Before we attempt to examine what a complex African rhythm is like, it will be valuable to review the organizing principles of our own music. Western music, in general, is based on the harmonic potential of tones. Through an elaborate system of fixed intonations of exact intervals, the music moves by chords or melodies or by both, and the rhythm is basically the duration of time behind each progressive step. In effect, the tones are sounded simultaneously to produce the harmony or in succession to produce the melody, and harmony and melody are what count most. We can make a visual representation of our music, writing it down in a standardized system of symbols for musical notation. Notes

spaced vertically on a five-lined musical staff represent the pitch of the
tones, and we represent time by using different types of notes. Various
other symbols can indicate accentuation, increasing or decreasing intensity, instrumental techniques, or tempo, the relative speed of the
music. We assign a time signature to indicate a meter, the basic measure
of time which we separate by placing bar lines on the staff; to quote a
popular dictionary of music: "3/4 meter (or 3/4 time) means that the
basic beats are [represented as] quarter notes (lower figure) and that
there are three (upper figure) of these in each measure, the first receiv-
ing an accent."[3] For metrical accuracy, we sometimes rely on a metronome, a mechanical or electrical device which can be adjusted to mark
the interval of time between basic beats. Thus, for example, Western
music might be written as is this Beethoven piano sonatina:[4]

Both parts are in the same meter, and a good musician could play the
piece immediately and at the proper speed. (He would set his metronome at 60.) If he did not have a piano, he could imagine the melody
at the correct pitch.

Our approach to rhythm is called divisive because we divide the
music into standard units of time. As we mark the time by tapping a
foot or clapping our hands, we are separating the music into easily
comprehensible units of time and indicating when the next note or
chord is likely to come. A Western rhythm marks time at an even pace
with a recurrent main beat, generally with a major pulse every two,
three, or four beats. What is most noticeable about the rhythm is that
it serves to link the different notes to each other. We say, for instance,
that a piece of music has a certain rhythm, and as we count out the
beats, we will notice certain things. First, most of the instruments play
their notes at the same time, and second, if we have a sequence of notes
that runs into a phrase or a melody, the whole thing will start when
we count "One." It is this fact, that Western musicians count together
from the same starting point, which enables a conductor to stand in

front of more than a hundred men and women playing in an orchestra and keep them together with his baton.[5] Rhythm is something we *follow,* and it is largely determined in reference to the melody or even actually defined as an aspect of the melody. Our approach to rhythm is obvious in most popular or folk music, but it is no less evident in a fugue in which the melody may start at different points. What is important is that the rhythm is counted evenly and stressed on the main beat, and we have the special word "syncopation" to refer to a shifting of the "normal" accents to produce an uneven or irregular rhythm. Even composers in the Western classical tradition who used complex rhythms, like Bee-thoven or Brahms, or twentieth-century composers who were influenced by African musical idioms, like Stravinsky,[6] manifest this basic orienta-tion. In the popular or folk idioms of Western music, the more "ar-tistic" complexities rarely arise.

In Western music, then, rhythm is most definitely secondary in em-phasis and complexity to harmony and melody. It is the progression of sound through a series of chords or tones that we recognize as beautiful. In African music this sensibility is almost reversed. African melodies are clear enough, even if African conceptions of tonal relationships are sometimes strange to us, but more important is the fact that in African music *there are always at least two rhythms going on.* We consider the rhythms complex because often we simply do not know what "the" rhythm of a piece is. There seems to be no unifying or main beat. The situation is uncomfortable because if the basic meter is not evident, we cannot understand how two or more people can play together or, even more uncomfortably, how anyone can play at all. On a superficial level, we might get away with describing the beating as "fanatical"[7] or by re-ferring to the "rhythmic genius" of African people, but such comments explain very little, and they are, of course, inaccurate because they only indicate our sense of what African music seems to require or bring out of us. Since we are used to hearing one set of tones move through "time," we do not expect any distractions from a musician who plays "out of time" or "misses the beat." Exposed to the music of an African drum ensemble, even the most accomplished Western musicians have expressed bafflement.

Before we discuss the issues involved in these differences of rhythmic sensibility, I wish to introduce the Ewe and Dagomba instruments which will figure in my illustrations so that readers might have concrete images in mind. The Ewes use straight sticks to play drums which are made like barrels and painted in red, blue, and green or in green and white bands.[8] The strong hide of a small bush antelope serves as the drumhead. The hide is sewn onto a hoop around the rim of the mouth, leaving loops of string which fit into notched pegs that are driven into holes on the side of the drum and secured by friction. You can tune an Ewe drum by knocking the pegs deeper to raise the pitch or by striking the drumhead with the butt of your hand to release the pegs somewhat and lower the pitch. To get the best resonance, the Ewes prepare their drums by letting them stand upside down with water inside for a few minutes, moistening the drumhead and allowing the wood to "drink" so that the seams will close more thoroughly. Various drums are used depending on the type of dance. An Ewe drummer sits behind the drum he is playing, but the largest of the drums, Atsimewu, is between four and five feet tall and is propped up at an angle so that the drummer may stand beside it. Either Atsimewu or Sogo, a large fat drum which sits on the ground, serves as a "master drum," whose rhythmic patterns stand out in timbre, voice, and complexity. Master drums are often beaten with hands or with one hand and one stick. Among the other drums, Kagan is slim and high-pitched, and Kidi is slightly larger than Kagan and pitched lower. Two small, deep-voiced drums, Totogi and Kroboto, also figure in our study. On these various drums, Ewe drummers can play several kinds of beats. Striking the drumhead freely so that the stick bounces up gives a resonant and stressed beat, but secondary notes are played by pressing the stick onto the drumhead to produce a muted beat several intervals higher than a free stick beat. In addition to the drums, there are two time-keeping instruments, a flange-welded double bell called Gankogui and a rattle called Axatse which is made from a calabash covered with a net of beads and which gives a sharp, high-pitched sound. The Ewes sometimes think of their drums as a family. The bell is like the heartbeat which keeps things steady. Kagan is the baby brother; Kidi is the mother; Sogo is the elder brother; Kroboto and Totogi, when they are played, are the twin brothers; Atsimewu, the master drum, is the father, who, according to their tradition, is in charge of everything.

The Dagombas mainly use a drum commonly called "dondon" in West Africa. As I mentioned in my Introduction, it is a tension drum, carved in the shape of an hourglass, with two mouths; the two skins, thinned almost to parchment and sewn onto rings of bound reeds, are laced together with leather strings. A Dagomba drummer fits his dondon under his arm, securing it with a scarf or a strip of cloth looped over his shoulder. Wrapping his arm around the drum and hooking his thumb through several strings, the drummer turns his wrist outwards to push his forearm against the strings and thus vary or resonate the notes he

can produce.[9] Besides dondon, the Dagombas use a large tom-tom with
a snare of hide stretched across the top section of each of the two large
circular drumheads. The drumheads are set over the drum with loops
of rope and laced with heavy strings of cowhide; leather straps around
these strings are pulled to tighten the drumhead before use. Called
"gongon," the drum hangs like dondon from one shoulder, and the
drummers can walk around or dance when they play. The gongon
drummer rests his arm so that his hand extends over the edge of the
drum and his fingers rest lightly on the skin. Both dondon and gongon
are beaten with a special stick which curves more than ninety degrees
and which has a bell-shaped knob on the end. The drummer holds this
stick across the palm of his hand and beats the drum by flicking his
wrist. He mutes a beat by turning his stick slightly so that the edge of
the bell-shaped knob "stops" against the drumhead. The gongon player
can also beat with his hand and his stick along the upper edge of the
drumhead, getting a higher-pitched buzzing sound, or he can press his
fingers against the skin to alter the quality of his main beats. The Dagomba drums "fear" water, for the skins would be ruined if beaten
when wet. Drums are often warmed in the sun before they are played.

As we examine some of the rhythms which are played on these drums,
it will be important for some readers to remember that the brief series
of notations I will provide are only one part of the broader discussion
of African music and social life. The notations will, I hope, help clarify
certain aspects of the music, but they will not provide the major focus
of our discussion, and they may be approached merely as rough pictures
of musical structure. It would certainly be possible to design or modify
a notation system which could accurately represent the sounds of an
African musical performance, but rather than try to overcome the limitations of Western notation, I want to use these limitations to help clarify
some of the differences between Western and African music. Though
some readers, I suspect, will find the notations either too simple or too
difficult, I have tried to strike a balance so that more readers will be
encouraged to examine the illustrations closely for the sake of the
broader discussion.[10] In this chapter I am not trying so much to present specific data on either Ewe or Dagomba drumming as to describe
general features of African music, and we will begin directly by discussing the central issue: what is music based on multiple rhythms like and
how do Africans orient themselves to play and appreciate such music?

Let us first reflect on a dance from the Republic of Benin which I
saw performed by various groups on several occasions in Accra. The

dance is called Adzogbo, and it belongs to the Fon people, whose culture and whose music are closely related to Ewe culture and music. I studied the drumming with Freeman Donkor, a great Ewe dancer and drummer who is a knowledgeable master of the music of many African cultures and who was most responsible for my eventual training in Ewe drumming. Though I did not see the dance in Benin, what I heard and learned in Accra offers a good illustration of what musicologists call *polymeter* or *multiple meter,* the simultaneous use of different meters. African music is often characterized as polymetric because, in contrast to most Western music, African music cannot be notated without assigning different meters to the different instruments of an ensemble. In the notation below, it is sufficient to notice that the musicians do not find their entrances by counting from a main beat, but rather, they must find their entrances in relation to the other instruments. Without discussing yet the complicated playing of the master drum or the possibilities of variation and improvisation in the drumming, we will just look at the bell, Kagan, and Kidi. In the introductory Kadodo section of Adzogbo, the bell plays a simple rhythm throughout. Kidi also plays a simple rhythm, consisting of three beats hit freely so that the stick bounces from the drumhead, alternating or broken with three beats which are muted by pressing the stick against the drumhead. (In the notation, the heavier notes with the stems up are freely struck beats.) Kagan improvises away from and back to a basic rhythm which converses with Kidi. It should be apparent that to assign either bar lines or time signatures would be rather arbitrary, and if we follow our tendency to place bar lines at the beginnings of the different phrases, we may become confused about the main beat. (I have marked the actual main beat with an *X*.)*

Adzogbo (Kadodo section)

The most significant point is that while each of the rhythms is simple, in combination their relationship is a bit complicated. Besides the independent entrances, the bell (which we might write in 4/4 time) plays its pattern three times while Kidi (which we might write in 6/8 time) plays her pattern four times. In the Kadodo section of Adzogbo, Kidi will also respond to the very complicated patterns of the master drum, Atsimewu, whose phrases have independence of entrance and variable lengths.*

A Dagomba dance called Zhem offers another good illustration. Zhem is one of the most important of the Dagomba dances, for it is played during the installation or funeral of high chiefs. I knew Ibrahim Abdulai for four years before he told me the significance of Zhem, and my instruction was accompanied not only by the observance of several ritual obligations, including the sacrifice of a sheep, but also by long lectures on morality and correct living. In Zhem, a lead dondon and any number of supporting dondons play two independent rhythms which are interlocked with great precision to make a tight and intriguing combination. Again, one could not try to play either rhythm by counting the music in a single meter: the rhythms do not meet at any point, and the lead dondon gives a feeling of 3/4 time, while the supporting dondons play to a count of four. *

Zhem (dondon parts)

Lead dondon   etc.

Supporting dondons

In such music, the conflicting rhythmic patterns and accents are called *cross-rhythms*. The diverse rhythms establish themselves in intricate and changing relationships to each other analogously to the way that tones establish harmony in Western music. The effect of polymetric music is as if the different rhythms were competing for our attention. No sooner do we grasp one rhythm than we lose track of it and hear another. In something like Adzogbo or Zhem it is not easy to find any constant beat at all. The Western conception of a main beat or pulse seems to disappear, and a Westerner who cannot appreciate the rhythmic complications and who maintains his habitual listening orientation quite simply gets lost. The first impression given by much African music has been described by S. D. Cudjoe: "The changing configuration of Ewe drumming . . . is so well exploited by the greatest master-drummers that one gets the notion of a movable bar contracting or expanding in time signature according to the inspiration of the moment."[11] Actually, if we try to apply Western notions of bars and time signatures, the music seems much more complicated than it really is. Adzogbo and Zhem offer clear visual illustrations of polymeter: the individual rhythms are simple, but the way they are combined can be confusing to Westerners. In spite of what we think, most African music is in some common variety of duple or triple time (like 4/4 or 12/8) and not in the 7/4 or 5/4 that many Westerners have thought they might have heard.[12] Music in 7/4 time would be very difficult to dance to.

Africans who are qualified to play such music as Adzogbo or Zhem and who like to dance to it, however, avoid becoming confused by concentrating each on his own part. The Kidi player in Adzogbo does not try to count over the twenty-four beats it takes to reach a recurrent cycle of unity with the bell; rather, he thinks in terms of three or six beats. If you are just starting to learn to play African drums, you will be told to concentrate on what you yourself are doing, for if you should listen too closely to the others, you will become confused and lose your place. The use of "staggered,"[13] independent entrances into the cross-rhythmic relationships of the music indicates an important characteristic of African music, what Robert F. Thompson has called "apart-playing,"[14] the separation of parts. Each musician contributes his own part in the total polymetric fabric, and there are never two or more playing the same thing unless their specific drums are the same. If the drummers played in unison, there would, obviously, be no polymeter.

Polymeter and apart-playing are complementary notions which we use to describe music which we find to be rhythmically complex. Both notions suggest the same thing, that as A. M. Jones has emphasized in his writings, the cardinal principle of African music is the clash and conflict of rhythms.[15] But after all, nobody could play the music unless there were some kind of beat, and for the time being it is still fair for us to ask what happens to the beat or, rather, where we can locate a main beat. The answer seems to be in direct contrast to our music: whenever we would want to mark the beat is when the least is heard. Ask almost any Westerner to snap his fingers to any piece of African music, and he will mark the first and perhaps the third beats, as is the tendency in our music. But go to a jazz club, and you will notice that people snap their fingers and the drummer taps his cymbal on the second and fourth beats. In fact, none of the musicians seems to want to play a note on the first beat. Asked to supply a second rhythm to a piece of music in either 3/4 or 4/4 time, a Westerner and an African would respond in quite different manners:

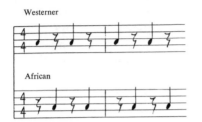

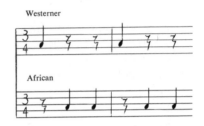

Generally, in African musical idioms most of the notes seem to fall on what we would call the "off-beat." In Bawku one night, I passed a house where a group of small children were trying to dance to music from a portable phonograph. The smallest of all was so young she could hardly keep from missing her hands while she clapped them and bounced, but significantly, even she clapped on the second and fourth beats.

To illustrate further the relationship of "main beat" to "off-beat," let us look at a notation of the basic drumming of an Ewe dance called Agbekor,* a spectacular dance which is played in a number of towns along the southeastern coast of Ghana, most notably Anyako, Afiadenyigba, Aflao, and Kedzi. Agbekor can be played in both slow and fast variations, and the clubs which have been formed to preserve and to perform this dance will change from one variation to the other in the course of their arrangements. Omitting the master drum part and the muted beats, we get a very simplified picture of the slow form of Agbekor, to which we might assign the time signature 12/8. The four beats of the rattle pattern are the basic beats for the singers and spectators to clap their hands; likewise, the master drummer's playing and the dancers' basic stepping are to this steady beat. But if we look at the notation, we find that none of the drums plays a dominant free beat on the first and third rattle beats, and that only Kidi's last beat marks the second and fourth rattle beat. The rhythm that might be considered the main beat of the music is not emphasized.

We can say that the musicians play "around" the beat, or that they play on the off-beat, but actually it is precisely the ability to identify the

*The final "r" is not pronounced.

Slow Agbekor (supporting drums)

beat that enables someone to appreciate the music.[16] We begin to "understand" African music by being able to maintain, in our minds or our bodies, an *additional* rhythm to the ones we hear. Hearing another rhythm to fit alongside the rhythms of an ensemble is basically the same kind of orientation for a listener that apart-playing is for a musician—a way of being steady within a context of multiple rhythms. Just over twenty-five years ago, Richard Waterman, in a paper which was a real breakthrough for Westerners interested in African music, supplied the term "metronome sense" to describe the musical sensibility necessary to play or listen to such rhythmic music, a sensibility which need not be developed for European music.

> From the point of view of the listener, it [metronome sense] entails habits of conceiving any music as structured along a theoretical framework of beats regularly spaced in time and of co-operating in

terms of overt or inhibited motor behavior with the pulses of this
rhythmic pattern whether or not the beats are expressed in actual
melodic or percussive tones. Essentially, this simply means that African music, with few exceptions, is to be regarded as music for the
dance, although the "dance" involved may be entirely a mental one.[17]

Recalling the African who could claim to understand a certain piece of
music by knowing the dance that goes with it, we might begin to perceive a dancer's feet, to which in fact there might often be rattles attached, as a part of the music: if a dancer with rattles tied onto his feet
made a mistake, we would hear it. In African music, it is the listener or
dancer who has to supply the beat: the listener must be *actively engaged*
in making sense of the music; the music itself does not become the concentrated focus of an event, as at a concert. It is for this fundamental
reason that African music should not be studied out of its context or as
"music": the African orchestra is not complete without a participant on
the other side. The full drum ensemble is an accompaniment, a music-
to-find-the-beat-by.

In his article, Waterman went on to talk about what he called the
"subjective beat."

> The assumption by an African musician that his audience is supplying
> these fundamental beats permits him to elaborate his rhythms with
> these as a base, whereas the European tradition requires such close
> attention to their concrete expression that rhythmic elaboration
> is limited for the most part to mere ornament.[18]

The musicians themselves maintain an additional beat, as has often been
observed, by moving some part of their body while they play, not in the
rhapsodic manner of a violinist but in a solid regular way. Those people
who have said that drummers dance while they play were right in the
sense that the drummers keep the beat in this way so that their off-beat
drumming will be precise. The point is that a drummer plays only some
of the things he hears. Abraham Adzenyah of the University of Ghana
Dance Ensemble and Wesleyan University, a Fanti master drummer and
an expert of many different tribal styles, says that he always listens to
or keeps in mind what he calls a "hidden rhythm" within his improvisations. In many ensembles, one instrument in particular may be desig-
nated as the time-keeper, and all the musicians depend on hearing their
relationship to this one. If you ask a Kagan player to demonstrate what
he does during Agbekor, he will click his tongue against the roof of his
mouth between his two strokes, and the master drummer will often
click the bell pattern while he plays his complicated phrases. The hand-

clapping that accompanies so much African music is "metronome sense" in action, and Jones maintains that the clapping "is not beating time in the European sense, but is an undercurrent providing the free rhythms of the song with a metrical basis."[19]

In short, musicians must keep their time steady by perceiving rhythmic relationships rather than by following a stressed beat. When you begin to learn drumming, as I have said, you mind only your beat, lest you lose it; nevertheless, you will hear the other ones. Eventually, when your playing becomes stronger so that, as some Africans say, "Drum beats himself,"[20] then you can listen to the whole music. In this sense, though the rhythms are played apart, the music is unified by the way the separate parts fit together into a cross-rhythmic fabric.[21] Only through the combined rhythms does the music emerge, and the only way to hear the music properly, to find the beat, and to develop and exercise "metronome sense," is to *listen to at least two rhythms at once.* You should attempt to hear as many rhythms as possible working together yet remaining distinct, and you can judge or train yourself by counting how many rhythms you can hear while holding on perhaps a bit more closely to one in particular.

Still, some teachers of African music discourage students from tapping their feet because often the students tend to find a main pulse that eliminates the real rhythmic tension and conflict in the music. What the African drum teachers are afraid of is that their students are approaching the music by marking time from their own beats instead of from a beat which serves as their unsounded beat. Hewitt Pantaleoni and Moses Serwadda, beginning an innovative attempt to design a notational system for African drumming, maintain that

> The African learns the whole simultaneously with the parts, which
> is why he has never depended on stress for rhythmical precision. He
> is not "thrown off" by hearing misaccentuation, but by the failure
> of some other part of the ensemble to occur at the right time. The
> Westerner taps his foot to give himself a regular stress on which to
> hang his part; the African taps his foot to mime the motion of the
> dancers, or any other part of the ensemble he wishes to add par-
> ticularly strongly to his own.[22]

Russell Hartenberger, an American percussionist, told me that one night when he was in a bar in the north of Ghana, in Bawku actually, he was tapping his foot to some music, and people in the bar started pointing at his toe and laughing. Eventually someone came up to him and said, "Oh, so you are trying to dance. Fine!"

The inadequacy of Western efforts at notation and the clumsiness of Western efforts at participation reflect the basic problem: we can choose any of several rhythmic approaches, yet we have no way to judge the proper one. To a more sensitive ear, the flexible and dynamic relationships of various rhythms actually help distinguish one rhythm from another, and on a basic level, *one rhythm defines another.* One drum played alone gives an impression of a rhythm tripping along clumsily or senselessly accented; however, a second rhythm can make sense of the first.* To illustrate this point, we can take a rhythm very common in Africa, a rhythm which we have encountered as the bell pattern of Agbekor: by crossing it in different ways, ways which I have heard in various dances, we can completely alter its character—and how we might hear it or try to dance to it. The different points of unity which the other rhythms share with the first rhythm suggest different accents and possibilities for further combinations.*

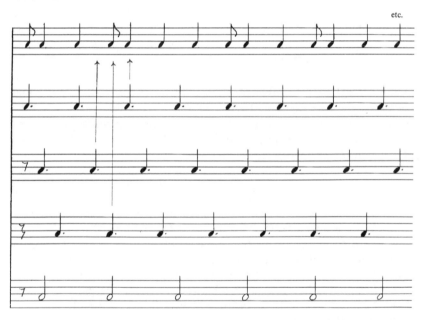

The establishment of multiple cross-rhythms as a background in almost all African music is what permits a stable base to seem fluid. Stable rhythmic patterns are broken up and seemingly rearranged by the shifting accents and emphases of other patterns. The same processes of relationship are at work among the drums of Agbekor or in any piece of music based on multiple rhythms, and the *basic organization of rhythms is the essential composition,* what an African might call the *beat,* of a piece of music. The coherence of the conflicting rhythms is thus based upon a kind of tension which gives the music its dynamic power. The accents of a singer or a master drummer will engage and highlight various rhythms in order to increase the effect. Most significantly, then, once you are playing the music properly, it becomes extremely difficult to play your part unless the whole ensemble is playing; you depend on the other rhythms for your time.

An interesting illustration of this point occurred while I was trying to record separately the many stylistic variations the lead dondon can play in some of the Dagomba dances because I did not want to forget what I had learned. Ibrahim Abdulai, as the leader of the Takai drummers in Tamale, was to play. The Takai dances are a series of several different dances, of which the first one proper is called Takai. The supporting dondon part for each dance, which is generally a single stable pattern that cuts across the leader's part, was not to be included so that I could hear the leader's variations clearly. The example below shows the two dondon parts for the Takai dance, with Ibrahim's main beat on the off-beat of the rhythm of the second dondons.[23] *

Ibrahim, however, complained that he could not "hear" his variations when he played without a second dondon. He regarded the counter-rhythm which would tend to throw Westerners off the beat as the only thing that kept him on time and enabled him to hear what he was playing and to be creative. It may have been the first time he had ever played the Takai drumming by himself. Jones notes that an Ewe master drummer can often have trouble remembering his variations without the other drums,[24] and I experienced the same dependence in the later stages of my training in Ewe drumming. Freeman Donkor would tell me to listen to Kroboto or to the bell or to some other instrument to help my timing when I played different variations.

A contrasting illustration to Ibrahim's predicament is just as interesting. I have a cousin who trained as a pianist to the point that she contemplated a professional career. During a discussion we had about African music, I asked her to beat a steady rhythm on a table top, and she of course did so quite well until I added the off-beats between her beats. She became so erratic in her beating, speeding up and slowing down, that she accused me, incorrectly, I would think, of deliberately syncopating my beats in an effort to confuse her. I replied that she should have been able to maintain her rhythm anyway. That such an apparently simple task should have presented her with such difficulties is an indication, particularly in view of her specialization, that the Western and African orientations to rhythm are almost opposite.

When I began my training, I often had to count through rhythms very slowly until I had figured them out and could get started on them, but generally, if I could hear the entire rhythm, I tried to play it immediately without thinking about it. After I returned to the United States, I tried to teach several people to play the Dagomba drums, and I found that if I tried to demonstrate how to enter with one drum by counting from another drum's beat, I could not do it. The only way to begin correctly was to listen a moment and then start right in. Ibrahim had trained me effectively by at first always directing me to begin playing the part I was learning, after which the other drums would enter. When I protested that I wanted to try entering music already in progress, he said that I should have patience, that at that stage of my training I would only become confused, and that later it would not be a problem. He was right. But later in my own efforts to teach other Westerners to play, I discovered that I could no longer hear the music as they did and that, if they could not grasp a rhythm, I had to learn at that time to break it down for them by counting. As I watched myself struggling with this problem, I reflected that the music is not very complicated in terms of the generative principles which form the basis of performance and appreciation, but that even on a basic level a Westerner can find it easier to think about this sensibility than to exercise it. Almost always, the critical factor which determined a student's progress was not so much his former musical experience as his acquisition of the ability to pay attention to a second rhythm while playing, and this problem was solved at a basic level with simple rhythms or not at all. Unlike Ibrahim and like my cousin, the students could play one rhythm well but they lost it when I added another rhythm.

We can think about this difference in sensibilities as the difference between perceiving a rhythm as something to "get with" or as something to "respond to." Rhythms which cut across each other are also dynamically coherent. Ibrahim felt that his isolated beating was meaningless without a second rhythm, but more than that, he could not even think of the full range of stylistic variations he might play without the beating of a second drum. There was no *conversation,* and this kind of responsiveness is given another, fuller expression in African musical arrangements. From our discussion of multiple meter and apart-playing, of hand-clapping and "metronome sense," we might tend to conceive of the basic rhythm of a piece of music as the fastest pulse on which all the beats could be located or as the slowest pulse which unites all the patterns.[25] But while certain rhythms may establish a background beat, in almost all African music there is a dominant point of repetition developed from a dominant conversation with a clearly defined alternation, a swinging back and forth from solo to chorus or from solo to an emphatic instrumental reply. Call-and-response, as this kind of arrangement is generally known to ethnomusicologists, is a major characteristic of African musical idioms. This characteristic is not particularly difficult to understand, for we are familiar with this standard format in Afro-American music. When James Brown sings "Get up!", Bobby Byrd answers "Get on up!"; when Kool sings "Get down," the Gang's horns answer. In African music, the chorus or response is a rhythmic phrase which recurs regularly; the rhythms of a lead singer or musician vary and are cast against the steady repetition of the response. In essence, if rhythmic complexity is the African alternative to harmonic complexity, the repetition of responsive rhythms is the African alternative to the development of a melodic line. Jones writes that an African "would find our broad changes of melody coarse and inartistic. . . . He knows the artistic value of a good repetitive pattern."[26]

We are not yet prepared to understand how people can find beauty in repetition, and for the moment we must gain a better notion of how rhythms work in a conversational mode. Because we are not dealing with song texts, I will give examples from the drumming of various dances. In some Ewe drumming, the musician playing the master drum has an opportunity to display his skill in various improvisational figures called "rolling," when he plays with two sticks instead of the hand-and-stick technique he usually employs. In Sohu, a dance of the Yeve Cult, Sogo plays figures over the response of Kidi. In the notation, observe how each Sogo figure ends during the pause just before Kidi's doubled sixteenth notes.*

Sohu

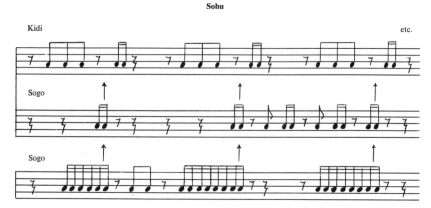

What is important is that if Sogo ends his figure anywhere but at the correct point, he may be in time with all the instruments, but he has nonetheless missed the beat. Once a responsive relationship of one rhythm to a counter-rhythm has been established, the leader may extend his phrases over one or more responses until he ends up on the beat again, and the music will show a particular complexity when the soloist's rhythm overlaps the response. While the responsive rhythm is basically stable, the soloist is free to place his variations on not only his phrasing but also his entrance. All that is important is that he come out on time. In Western music, the lead singer or instrumentalist starts on the main beat; in African music the situation is reversed: *the musician unifies his time with the last beat he plays rather than the first one.*[27] *

In African music, then, the main beat coincides with the entrance of the chorus and not the soloist, and in particular contrast to our music, the main beat comes at the end of a dynamic phrase and not at the beginning. Part of the power and drive of African music derives from the way that African musicians play *forward* toward the beat. Thus, although Waterman's notion of "metronome sense" is very useful in some respects, an African musician is not so much moving along with a pulsation as he is *pushing* the beat to make it more dynamic. The forceful quality of this orientation had led some people to speak of African musicians as playing their instruments, whether drums, flutes, guitars, or even fiddles and harps, with "percussive attack," staying "on top" of the beat and imparting a rhythmic momentum to even the sweetest melodies. Within the framework of call-and-response, the rhythmic variations of a soloist become different avenues of approach to the emphatic statement repeated by the chorus. Thus, while we might tend to focus on the lead musician's rhythms as the key to the music, actually it is the chorus which is more important. The tendency, in notating African music, to assign compound meters or changing time signatures based on the complex beating of a master drummer has been criticized by Marius Schneider, who accurately points out:

> Even if one lets the "strictly organized" structure of [an Ewe rhythm played on] Atsimewu in $5+5+2+5+5+1$ pass as an individual form, its actual dynamics still grow out of its being embedded in the rhythm of the whole, the 12/8 measure. This is because the Atsimewu and Sogo formulas, which are shorter or longer than the 12/8 measures of the main pattern, continuously change their accents until they return to their initial pattern.[28]

Though a formally structured arrangement of leader and chorus may not always be present in African music, the conversational mode is usually inherent within the cross-rhythmic fabric. Thus in the Kadodo of Adzogbo, when Kidi has not changed her beat to respond to Atsimewu (and in the notation it was the endings of Atsimewu's phrases which I marked with an X), Kagan, as we have noted, is permitted to weave in and out to improvise a conversation with his mother, Kidi.[29]* If a piece of music is tightly composed, there can be any number of possibilities for rhythmic communication and dialogue, and of course, you will enjoy the music more if you can hear them. In Takai, the basic rhythms fit together into several clearly responsive relationships. The lead dondon and a lead gongon converse, and there is a second gongon part which responds to the first gongon's improvisations.*

Takai

The kinds of rhythmic relationships in the Takai ensemble, once established in a piece of music, both suggest the possibilities and define the limits of improvisation. A drummer will cut across the other rhythms, but at the same time he cannot step too far outside a responsive relationship without destroying the basic character of the beat; since drummers depend on each other to stay on the beat, he might even get everybody so confused that they would have to stop playing and start again. If a drummer strays too far from his rhythm, he will misaccentuate or overemphasize the beat and thus ruin the intriguing balance, and if he moves into too close a synchrony with another drum, he negates the potential effect of both rhythms. The rhythms must be clearly distinguishable from each other because one rhythm determines the way we can apprehend another rhythm. Changing the part of one drum in a composition, therefore, would alter the effect of the total rhythmic fabric.

The supporting drums, particularly, will vary only within the boundaries determined by their place in the ensemble. To clarify this point, we can examine the way the Kidi player might improvise during the Agbekor dance. Kidi's pattern, we recall, consists of three freely struck beats followed by three muted beats.[30] To enrich his part, the drummer playing Kidi may add beats only within the time span covered by Kidi's freely struck beats, and these beats must also be in Kidi's original meter. In short, beats may be either dropped or doubled. Kidi's part may not be extended into areas which are more properly reserved for other drums, particularly the master drum to which the dancers need to pay close attention. By staying within his assigned framework, the Kidi player ensures not only that he will not undercut the effectiveness of the master drummer but also that the responsive potential of Kidi's rhythm will remain stable enough for effective exploitation by the master drummer. Thus the improvisational possibilities for the Kidi player in Agbekor are basically limited to the rhythms shown on the following page.*

These phrases, however, will be employed most discreetly: a drummer will establish them singly or in pairs throughout a section of the music, perhaps selecting them in response to specific master-drum patterns, and always returning to the basic. Once established, they will not be changed rapidly. Without any embellishment, however, the music could seem uninspired, or as one Nigerian friend was fond of saying, "Beautiful—but dull." How a drummer judges the appropriate variations is a matter of more complexity which we will discuss in the next chapter when we examine the master drummer's improvisational styles. For the moment, we may note first that a drummer's freedom is limited

by the organization of the music, and second that the coherence of an ensemble is chiefly dependent on the maintenance of the rhythmic relationships which emerge from the basic composition. The "beat" which these relationships establish serves to guide a drummer's sensibility. Different drums may have more or less freedom within a particular dance, and in different dances the music may call for more or less embellishment of the beat.[31] For example, in Agbekor, Kroboto's stylistic variations are much less limited than Kidi's, yet they always keep in time with the bell, they always continue and enhance a conversation with Totogi, and they never stay away from Kroboto's basic pattern for very long.*

Basically, if a drummer is going to vary his beating, he must be aware of what changes are happening in the ensemble. Naturally, any variation will stand out, bringing into sharper focus a particular rhythm and its corresponding relationships, but since the music is built from many rhythms, such a concentration of emphasis, if continued, would limit the dimensions of the other rhythms to one rhythmic perspective. The major improvisational considerations for the supporting drums in particular are dependent on a recognition of the fact that a drum in an African ensemble derives its power and becomes meaningful not only as it cuts and focuses the other drums *but also as it is cut and called into focus by them*. Rhythmic dialogues are reciprocal, and in a way that might seem paradoxical to a Westerner, a good drummer restrains himself from emphasizing his rhythm *in order that he may be heard better*. Just as the beat of an ensemble is made interesting by the master drummer, so a rhythm is interesting in terms of its potential to be affected by other rhythms.

In general, African drummers will adhere rather strictly to the various cross-rhythmic and conversational relationships, and highly accomplished musicians will often play an extremely simple rhythm throughout a dance without introducing any changes. When my students had learned their parts and wanted to express themselves, they never tried to improvise on a pattern by dropping notes out of it; the more "expressive" they became, the louder the music became. Apart from simply learning to maintain their rhythms, the most difficult task the students faced was learning to continue to maintain their rhythms. A rhythm which cuts and defines another rhythm must leave room for the other rhythm to be heard clearly, and *the African drummer concerns himself as much with the notes he does not play as with the accents he delivers*. Though to a Western ear a piece of music may seem complex and confusing, to an African ear it may seem extremely open and clear. In traditional African music, compositions have been developed and refined over the years, and superfluous beating has been eliminated so that the rhythms do not encroach on each other. A master drummer's varied improvisations will isolate or draw attention to parts of the ensemble more than they seek to emphasize their own rhythmic lines, and a musician must always play with a mind to communicative effectiveness.

This preliminary discussion of a drummer's sensibility should, I hope, qualify our notions of improvisation. African music is improvised, but most of it is not, as many Westerners think, made up on the spot, nor is it particularly loosely structured. We do well to remember at this point that most African musical expression has a place within the framework of tradition. Almost anyone would have a difficult time understanding the rhythmic relationships of a certain piece of African music during the few minutes he or she hears it at a concert hall where a national dance troupe is performing; in an African society, one is brought up with essentially the same music being played on each appropriate occasion, and most master drummers may have spent several years playing the simple rhythms of each of the supporting drums while they developed their understanding of the beat and its potential. A drummer also hears other drummers playing and builds up a "vocabulary" of rhythms before trying to take the lead. In the Dagomba area, for example, only once did I see a man younger than thirty playing lead dondon, yet most drummers start training and accompanying musicians to functions while still small boys.

People can hear the music for years and always find it fresh and lively because of the extent to which an African musical performance is integrated into its specific social situation. In traditional African music-making situations, the music is basically familiar, and people can follow with informed interest the efforts of the musicians to add an additional dimension of excitement or depth to a performance. Relatively minor variations stand out clearly and assume increased importance in making the occasion successful. Thus while artistic activity reaffirms and revitalizes tradition, people expect their traditional arts to be continuously vital forms. A "traditional" piece of music can therefore still be open to innovation, and Africans who love to celebrate and recollect the great events and personages of their past remain curiously indifferent to what is an important concern of Western culture, the issue of artistic origins, because for them, each new situation is the fundamental setting of artistic creativity. Ibrahim Abdulai lectured me on the many dimensions of their seemingly paradoxical orientation when I was questioning him on the history of Takai. We can use Ibrahim's lengthy comments to reflect more deeply on how a style of music can be both traditional and improvised. At this point, too, as we begin our efforts to see beyond the purely "musical" side of drumming, it will be worthwhile to pause to gain a more vivid picture of the historical setting of the music we have been studying. For these purposes Takai can serve as a good and fairly typical example.[32]

"Every Dagomba has grown up to meet Takai," he began. "You want to know who introduced the beating, and I can tell you that no one introduced Takai. Any time you hear a dondon beater beating, and someone is dancing, then you must know that the dondon beater introduced the playing. He is the one who introduced the beating of the drum."

"The man himself?" I asked.

"Yes. The dondon beater himself: he introduced the playing. You see, dondon beaters usually introduce more styles into the drumming, so they are the people who introduced it. During the olden days, there were not many styles like today. They were just playing one way throughout, without changing. Now in these modern times, everything has got more styles in it. So now we have put many styles into Takai. Takai is standing as the Dagomba dance which is more popular than all the others: it is the one which can be played and everyone will be happy. It can be called for funerals or weddings, or the chief or anyone else can call it. We are after money, so anyone can call us to come and play."

I asked him if there are many regional differences.

"Takai is played all throughout Dagbon, but there are differences. Those living in the towns and those living in the villages have different styles. Take this as an example: you have a pair of trousers and someone living in Savelugu may also have one made with the same material, but when you see him, you find that his trousers are very dirty compared to yours, even though they are the same material. Those living in the towns play Takai much better than those in the villages because they have more styles in it. It is not all Dagombas who know how to play Takai: they must learn it. Some of them learn it and some do not. Among the Dagomba dances, Takai is a special dance, and it is not played all the time. In the towns, there are weddings, funerals, and festivals. But in the villages, the people are not many, and they are always farming. It can be a long time before they can have a chance to call a Takai dance. If you know something and you don't do it, a time will come when you will forget what you know. So the beating of drums wants today and tomorrow. As for the playing of Takai, those living in the towns have more experience. They know much more than those living in the villages. In Tamale there is a special group for those who play Takai very nicely, without any confusion in it. They are the right people to play it because they learned it very well."

"Is Tamale the best group?"

"Yes. We have been making practice all the time, and we have been going around all the nine regions of Ghana because we know it better than the other people. Even in the colonial days, before Nkrumah came to power, the government used to call this Takai group to come to Accra and play. Anytime the government invites groups to come for the Takai dance, we are chosen as the best. We are always bringing more styles, and we keep on changing the beat to make the music more lovely. It is the village playing that people won't like because the styles don't change. Any time we are to play Takai, you will see that the villagers have come to watch, and they are just standing there, studying our playing and trying to pick our styles."

The original Takai consisted of four dances: Takai proper, Nyagboli, Dibsa-ata, and Kondalia. These four dances are the ones usually played in the villages throughout the Dagomba area, but the Tamale people have added several others. Ibrahim Abdulai continued by telling me how they adapted a dance called Nwundanyuli to the Takai dance, elaborating in detail on the context of their innovation.

"As for Nwundanyuli, we drummers in Tamale are the ones who decided to put it into the Takai dance. When we want to put anything into
a dance, we decide what we want to do and then we play it and compare it, asking, 'If I put this in, will it be nice or not?' For everything we
want to put into the dance, we sit together and decide whether it will be
following the drumming or not. We felt that if we added Nwundanyuli
into the Takai dance, it would be good because Takai has got a steady
beat and so does Nwundanyuli."

"Were you among the ones who did it?" I asked.

"If not me, no one can decide to put Nwundanyuli inside Takai. I sat
with those who are playing now. You know many of them: Fuseini, Alhassan Abukari, Salifu the singer, and others were among. Have you
heard Nwundanyuli outside? It is Nwundanyuli that the women dance
as Tora, you know, when they are jumping about, knocking their bottoms. Nwundanyuli is from Tora, and the Tora people got it from the
Baamaya people, who formed it and who also play it. Nyagboli too is
also inside Baamaya dancing, and the Baamaya people took it from
Takai. But you should know that the Baamaya people formed Nwundanyuli, but we decided to put it into the Takai dance."

"Did you take it straight?" I asked.

"We never came to imitate someone. When we imitate you, it won't
be the same as you are playing. When Baamaya people are playing, you
won't see many dondons; rather, only gongons are playing with one dondon and making the beat without styles. When we decided to put Nwundanyuli into Takai, we sat down and discussed it and afterwards we
made practice. During the time we were practicing, some knew how to
drum and others did not, so we continued teaching them until they became perfect. It took twenty days. Then we called Amadu [the leader
of the dancers] and the dancers and asked them how they could dance
to it. They practiced it, and now they are also perfect in it. And we got
it well before we started going around with it."

"When was this?"

"In 1966. The Arts Council had not even been formed at the time.
Up to that time we were only playing the first four dances. Nwundanyuli
is still a new dance and not everyone knows how to dance it, so even
now we don't always play it. Among all the dances, Takai is the most
professional, so we don't have to be displaying it all the time unless we
are called. Sometimes we are called often. Sometimes it can reach five
months and we don't play Takai. We can practice, but we won't go to
play it. Someone may get married, but he has no money to call Takai;
somebody's father or mother may die, but he has no money to call the
dance. And we will never go to play free for them. There is no time that

we will be playing the other Dagomba dances and someone will just come out and say, 'Play Takai for me to dance.'[33] If a chief is chosen and he has got his elders, the elders may decide to call the Takai people to come and dance for one week. We will start by five o'clock in the evening and play until the sun falls. When we go we start with Takai itself and sometimes we will beat Takai to the end, and we never reach Nyagboli or the others. When the government calls us to play Takai, sometimes they ask us to beat through all the different dances of Takai in some few minutes' time. We have learned to do it both slowly and fast. Each can be nice, but I prefer the slow one so that people will hear it and the dancers will dance well. It is good for one dance to be played for a long time before we change to another. We usually play Nwunda-nyuli when we have enough time. Unless we have enough time to play, we usually don't bring Nwundanyuli into Takai because it might spoil our dance."

"When you add a style or you add a dance," I asked, "how do you feel about the fact that you are changing the dance?"

"People like it. We have a word *m-pahiya* for when we bring styles. It is a big word for which we have many explanations. It can be for music or anything. For example, if you send a child to buy five ciga-rettes and you give him the exact money to pay for them and he comes back with six cigarettes, it is m-pahiya because he has come back with one more above the amount your money can get. He has increased it by one. We can call this increase m-pahiya. So when you make some music and you add something to it, it means you have increased the whole music: you have added something which was not in the original music in order to keep up the music. So it is m-pahiya when you bring styles.

"But if you are shaking your body when drumming or dancing, if you are making some action or just bluffing as a kind of display, we call it *golsigu*. Do you remember when you saw the students dancing Takai at the Arts Council? They are still learning and they dance it roughly. So they can make rough actions but they can't add anything to the dance. It is because they don't know it. So as the Takai dancers who are dancing now are becoming old, they will train another set after them, and another set, and when some of these young people are coming up to middle size, maybe they will not learn it well and they will continue to dance it in a rough way. And maybe they will also add some styles to it. No one knows the original beat of Takai, and by that time the beat we take as Takai will die. It may be a new one altogether. By that time, I and the others will not be there. And those people who will be there at that time, they will think that they are dancing the real thing because they will not know the original beat as before. Before me, Alhaji was leading the Takai group. I grew up and saw Alhaji drumming and I followed him. Alhaji was beating the dondon and I was beating the gongon, just as my son Alhassan is following me now. But Alhaji has now given it over to me. At present if we are drumming and he comes there, he says that we have changed the beat so much that we have spoiled it. And whatever happens, in the future it will also change. Even in our time it is not the original beat. That is what will keep on happening."

"So how do you feel about the fact that they will be changing the Takai beat?"

"To me, I feel it is better. The change is better because I have come to the stage that I feel that what we are drumming is good. If an old man says that at the time they were drumming, the beat was good, I don't know what the beat was at that time, so I feel that what we are doing at present is good. And in the future they will feel that what they are doing is better than what we have been doing now. That is what will keep on happening."

"And what will you tell them?"

"I won't tell them anything because by that time I will not be there."

"But if you are there," I asked, "what will you say?"

"I'll tell them that they are spoiling it."

Ibrahim's lecture conveys much of the detailed background of musical creativity in traditional African contexts. Musicians and musical associations introduce slight innovations with the idea of doing something a bit new with the same thing. Among the Ewes, a similar flexibility and variety in the presentation of traditional forms is also encouraged. Gideon, for example, has organized and trained several Agbekor troupes in his home town, for whom he created whole new styles of drumming and dancing. A spirit of rivalry exists among the various towns where Agbekor is danced, and one of the most easily noticeable functions of this competitive spirit is to raise the standards of performance. Both the personal style which a musician brings to his playing and the particular style with which a traditional piece of music is presented enhance a performance by making it, quite literally, special. African musicians create in a balance through which they draw upon the depth of a tradition while they revitalize it and adapt it to new situations.

Africans who pay informed attention to the distinctive quality or style of a musical performance are concerned with the distinctive quality of its social setting, and they will even judge the music in terms of the success of the occasion.[34] They expect the music to be responsive to the development of a situation, and they expect a musician to rely not only on his virtuousity but also on his mood and sense of appropriateness. Particularly in types of music that are less classical than Takai or Agbekor, a musician orders or extends his rhythmic variations to suit the movement of a crowd of spectators or dancers. Ibrahim Abdulai chose an indirect way of telling me to be alert when I played. During practice one very hot day, sweat was running into my eyes and I closed them so that I could play on without being distracted by the stinging. I heard Ibrahim calling me, "John, John, are you sleeping? Look at me when I play. Am I sleeping?" I laughed and told him that maybe he found the practice easy, but it was work for me. He shook his head. "Still, you are not lying in bed. If you want to sleep, you shouldn't be beating dondon. You should go to bed." A drummer must be able to listen to and respond to the crowd.

S. D. Cudjoe describes the essential point in a discussion of drumming for Ewe dances in which specific dance steps correspond to specific drum rhythms: "The real art of master drumming does not consist merely in playing beautiful contrasting themes, but in the drummer's ability to introject his themes before the dancer shows obvious signs of waning vigor. A true master must time his utterances to replenish the dancer's physical and aesthetic energy at the right psychological moment."[35] In other words, the drummer must make his music in reference to how tired or disaffected the dancers are becoming, giving them time to rest as well as inspiration. As Gideon explained it one day, "If the dancers are looking very happy and you are rather squeezing your face, people will become confused and say, 'Why? This man is not giving better face. What is wrong?' You have to mind the dancers." In Takai, the drummers are inside the circle of the dancers. "Takai should not be played when you are standing in one place," Ibrahim told me. "It is the kind of dance in which the drum beaters should be following the dancers so that the body will be getting strong. Sometimes you can be following them round, round, round, and the sound of the dondon will beat somebody so that he will move inside, and you can follow him and beat the drum through to him and then he will be happy and dance very well."

The "action" in an African context is thus a kind of social manifestation of what Waterman was getting at with his discussion of "metronome sense" and his reference to the audience's "subjective beat" on which the drummer relies. As the dancers mark a different rhythm with their feet, they contribute to the music, and a poor dancer can jeopardize the quality of the music just as a good dancer can inspire musical perfection. On occasions when I played poorly for dancers, they *danced* their criticism by executing their steps in an obviously half-hearted way, or they helped me by simplifying their steps to emphasize a more consistently responsive rhythm. This kind of reciprocal responsibility for "making the occasion sweet" is hard to describe but easy to perceive as a participant within a musical situation. It is difficult to dance to bad music, of course, yet if there is trouble at a nightclub, the musicians will become confused and the quality of their music will fall.

Beyond the innovations with which African musicians refine and sophisticate their traditional rhythms, therefore, African music is improvised in the sense that a musician's responsibility extends from the music itself into the movement of its social setting. From our earlier discussion of some of the artistic implications of cross-rhythms, responsive rhythms, and the interdependence of musicians, of course, it is easy to understand how musical forms can lend themselves to social considerations. But in African music there is a more direct relationship. When you ask an African how he enjoyed certain music, he may very well respond by saying, "It was a beautiful scene." He understands that the music is important only in respect to the overall success of a social occasion, and he does not focus on the music but rather on the way the situation is picked up by the music. In the West, when someone is making music, people will listen, but in Africa something else is always going on when music is being made. People pay attention in a special way, and a master musician uses his music to comment upon and influence the situation in much the same way that he comments on the rhythms of a supporting ensemble. Beyond the obvious comparison of a concert hall and a dance floor, we can compare a folksinger in a coffee house and a jazz combo in a bar. In the latter, even a great artist will not stop the action and the conversation; rather the artist will help the scene move.

The intimacy of this communication means that a musician's creative contribution will stem from his continuing reflection on the progress of the situation as both a musical and a social event, and just as the music will tell a participant what to do, so will the situation provide a musician with an index of how well he may be doing. In an African musical event, everyone present plays a part, and from a musician's standpoint, making music is never simply a matter of creating fresh improvisations but a matter of expressing the sense of an occasion, the appropriateness at that moment of the part the music is contributing to the rest.[36] Just as anyone present must behave properly, so does the music become something which *behaves,* and the master drummer fulfills a complex social role. In effect, the drummer must integrate the social situation *into* his music, and the situation itself can make the music different. Gahu, an Ewe social dance, starts out as the drum asks all girls with big bottoms to come out and start shaking; by continuing his beating in a certain way, the drummer can make the shaking continue or not, depending on his sense of just how much shaking offers the most appealing spectacle. One of the many examples of Akan drumming texts which J. H. Kwabena Nketia has compiled is an amusing responsive dialogue played when carrying a chief: one drum beats, "I carry father, I carry father; he is too heavy for me," and the other replies, "Can't cut bits off him to make him lighter."[37] Similarly, when Dagomba drummers are going to follow a chief somewhere, the rhythms they beat change completely when the chief appears at his door, when he walks to his horse, and when he rides.

The way that African musical expressions follow the movement of their social contexts thus extends from a general sense of the occasion to the very rhythms that the musicians play, and as we become more familiar with any particular type of African musical situation, we will recognize this tendency working in various ways and on various levels. In exemplifying this point, we can take the opportunity to describe an important genre of African musical expression. In the Dagomba culture, as in many of the Muslim cultures of Africa, people often focus their involvement in musical situations around traditions of "praise-singing" and "praise-drumming." Ibrahim Abdulai explained how the Dagomba drummer fulfills his social role on such occasions. "In Dagbon here, we drummers know the family; we know the names of people's fathers and grandfathers, and we call the names. And all the names that drummers are calling, they all have histories, and it is drummers who know them. These names are like proverbs; we don't call names like Fuseini or Ibrahim or Alhassan. If you are someone here, sometime you can say something which is very sweet, and people will take it and praise you. Or someone can say something and it will fall into your heart, and you will take it as a name. As you call a name for yourself, you call with sense. If you give birth to children or grandchildren, when we see them, the name you called is the name we will use to call them. We will take your name to praise your children, and even if you are dead for a hundred years, we will see your grandchild and call him by your name.

"If we go to a wedding house and the women are standing or sitting there, you will see a drummer go up to a woman and be singing and beating his drum. He is calling the names of her grandfathers who are dead. He can call them to the extent of his knowledge. Someone can know two, someone else can know six, and someone else can know ten. And as the drummer is calling their names, when the woman knows that it is her grandfathers' names he is calling, sometimes it is sweet for her, and she laughs. And at that time she will come out and start dancing. And all the money she has brought, she will give it out. And someone can be there: you will call the grandfather's name and she will be crying. And as she is crying, you run away and leave her. So this is what we do. Sometimes someone is there and you will not call the name of the grandfather, and the friends standing there will say, 'Does this mean that person has no forefathers?" The wedding we last went to, we were sitting down and the Nyohini-lana Pakpon [the title of the eldest daughter of the chief of Nyohini, a village near Tamale] came there. And we didn't know her. And one woman came and said, 'Nyohini-lana Pakpon is sitting there, and she says: don't you know her?' And at that time we didn't know this woman's name. But we knew her father's name and her grandfather's name. And we changed our playing and the woman came out and made us play for her to dance.

"When people meet at a festival or a wedding house or a funeral house, everyone wants people to know that he or she has a father and a grandfather. It means that as the person is there, he is standing inside a family, and his family is this or that family. Someone's grandfather was a chief and the father was a chief's son but not a chief, and someone's grandfather was a drummer, and someone's grandfather was an elder, and it is we drummers who know and who show them their standing place. So it is at a meeting place that people get to know one another. Sometimes they themselves don't know all their grandfathers and great-grandfathers, and we show them. And sometimes two people are there and they are Dagombas of the same family, but they don't know they are related. Let's say that their great-grandfather was a chief of Savelugu and was called Alhassan. We take Savelugu Chief Alhassan's name to praise the first one and then we take Savelugu Chief Alhassan's name to praise the other. And at that time, if they have sense, they will know that they are related to each other. And have the drummers not brought the family together? So that is how it is. That is what we do and they come out and dance."[38]

To complement Ibrahim's discussion, we can look at the role of the master drummer at an Ewe musical event. A fine description of the Ewe master drummer's role has been given by Hewitt Pantaleoni and S. Kobla Ladzekpo, whose brother C. K. Ladzekpo helped me with timing when I learned Agbekor. In an article about Takada, an Ewe social club dance, they write about the master drummer:

He has an audience, consisting of players and dancers as well as spectators, and he creates for them as well as for himself. He is a master of ceremonies in a way, whose responsibility is that everyone have a good time. He will invite honored guests to dance; he will drum compliments and comments on his instrument, and use it to call someone up to shake his hand; he times the length of the movements, sets the tempo of the dance drumming and keeps his musicians up to the mark, reminding them of patterns if they forget. In dances in which, unlike takada [Agbekor, for instance], the patterns of the lead drum determine the choreography, this musician controls *every* aspect of performance. In takada, the success of the occasion rests largely in his hands.[39]

In the nightclubs of African cities, the pop musicians do the same thing as the traditional master drummers. Watching the Ghanaian star Nana P. S. K. Ampadu of the African Brothers Band moving dancers by playing his electric guitar, you would realize that in spite of his Western instruments, his music is fundamentally "traditional." In the world of African pop music, a singer will tell the dancers how to do a certain new dance, coaching them in their movements. Popular Nigerian Juju musicians make up verses praising a particular person who is present or who has organized the event at which they are entertaining. The great Nigerian musician and composer Fela Anikulapo Kuti, inventor of Afro-Beat, may inspire the ladies to dance and then tease them:

> You dance too much. Why?
> Maybe it's the rhythm; maybe it's the music.
> You know what it is.
> You dance too much: your wig has fallen on
>   the ground and somebody stole it.
> You dance too much: your underwear cuffs
>   are now showing under your dress.[40]

In a more serious vein, because people expect their music to be made in reference to the social situation, music-making provides an effective way of focusing attention and commenting on issues of social concern and importance and thus rendering certain perspectives with a more forceful expression. In general, African song lyrics, as Robert Thompson has pointed out,[41] are especially concerned with moral and ethical questions and attack pride and pretension in whatever form these unsociable qualities appear. Countless examples have been recorded of this well-recognized characteristic of African music, and one point worthy of note about "songs of allusion" or "songs of derision" is that such songs serve as vehicles for the mobilization of authoritative com-

munity values. In many African societies, someone with a grievance
may hire a songwriter to prepare a song which states the problem: a
song may exceed the boundaries of social propriety without giving un-
due offense, and at the same time, people attracted to the song will be
more accessible to its argument and may help induce a miscreant to
make amends. Alan Merriam has documented a particularly interesting
situation, in which workers on a plantation presented, over several days,
their demands for higher wages through five progressively explicit
songs.[42]

In African musical idioms, one aspect of the musician's specialization,
as we shall see, involves insight into deep issues and the consequent
fulfillment of certain moral roles which our society delegates to other
professions. Musicians are often the guardians of esoteric knowledge;
in less formal contexts, it is their duty to lend the power of music to
the support of civil behavior. The "griots" of the Western Sudan, for
example, are a hereditary caste of musicians whose political duty it is
to preserve and recite the great historical traditions. As I mentioned in
the first chapter, the court historians of the centralized kingdoms are
drummers, and musicians accompany the chiefs and dignitaries at of-
ficial functions.[43] One of the most beautiful records I own, from the
Republic of Guinea, almost always gives friends who hear it spiritual
or romantic inspiration; it is actually a song of praise to the political
leader of the country, Ahmed Sékou Touré.[44] Surprisingly many of the
popular Highlife songs deal with philosophical and ethical themes: the
nature of the family, the necessity of providing for your children after
you die, the sorrow of children whose mother has died.[45] For Westerners used to the words of yearning lovers, it may seem surprising that
the sexy Highlife dancers are dancing to lyrics that say God never
sleeps.[46] Indeed, the proverbs which provide the lyrics for many Highlife songs are often so obscure that on several occasions when I asked
the meaning of a given song, I unwittingly provoked philosophical
arguments among my friends, who continued their debates long after
I lost interest.

Even the most satirical criticism, rather than being malicious or arbitrary, will be directed in the service of indigenous values and wisdom.
In the nightclubs, people trying to show off on the dance floor, if they
are doing it for the wrong reasons, are likely to find other dancers
imitating and satirizing their movements; yet an awkward dancer who
is nonetheless trying is unlikely to suffer this experience, and people
may merely say, "A bad dance does not kill the Earth."[47] A satirical
imitation will exaggerate aesthetic inadequacies in order to shame vanity,

and a song will be composed or extemporized with the same intent. In Nigeria the Eastern Star Dance Band sings in Pidgin English about ladies who like to make up their faces too much:

> O Baby Pancake,
> She dey love pancake,
> She too love pancake.
> When she say she going for market,
> She dey rub pancake.
> When she say she go for cinema,
> She dey look for mirror,
> She dey shake her waist,
> And make like-a-dis like-a-dat,
> And rub, and rub, and rub.
> O Baby Pancake.[48]

And even Africa's most modern musicians often sing deep proverbs. In "Water No Get Enemy,"[49] Fela Anikulapo Kuti and the Africa '70 Band touch a theme which, it will become evident, is highly relevant to our study:

> *T'o ba fe lo we omi l'o ma'lo,*
> If you want to wash, na water you go use.
> *T'o ba fe se'be omi l'o ma'lo,*
> If you want cook soup, na water you go use.
> *T'o ri ba n'gbona o omi l'ero re,*
> If your head dey hot, na water go cool am.
> *T'omo ba n'dogba omi l'o ma'lo,*
> If your child dey grow, na water he go use.
> *T'omi ba p'omo e o omi na l'o ma'lo,*
> If water kill your child, na water you go use.
> *T'omi ba p'omo re o omi na no,*
> *Ko s'ohum to'le se k'o ma lo'mi o.*
>
> *Omi o l'ota o,* nothing without water.
> *Chorus:* Water him no get enemy.
> *Omi o l'ota.*
> *Chorus:* Water him no get enemy.
> I say water no get enemy.
> *Chorus:* Water him no get enemy.
> If you fight am unless you want die.
> *Chorus:* Water him no get enemy.
> If you fight am unless you want die.
> *Chorus:* Water him no get enemy.
> I dey talk of Black man power.

> *Chorus:* Water him no get enemy.
> I dey talk of Black man power.
> *Chorus:* Water him no get enemy.
> I dey talk of Black man power, I say.
> *Chorus:* Water him no get enemy.
> *Omi o l'ota o.*
> *Chorus:* Water him no get enemy.
> *Ira, la, la,* etc.

The tradition of using songs to express philosophical, ethical, or satirical themes is so much a part of African musical idioms that it has continued, along with many rhythmic characteristics, within the development of Afro-American styles, and songs continue to serve as guides in practical philosophy to the people who listen to them.[50] "So Them Bad Minded,"[51] a Calypso tune, addresses the question of affirmative and negative ways of viewing the world:

> In every home that you can find,
> There are people who have bad mind. (*Repeated*)
> *Chorus:*
> Certain bad mind in a certain line,
> Saying criticize the people who pass. (*Repeated*)
>
> You meek and you looking thin,
> They say consumption in your skin. (*Repeated*)
> *Chorus:*
> Certain bad mind in a certain line,
> Saying criticize the people who pass. (*Repeated*)
>
> You rosy and you big and fat,
> They say dropsy in your skin.   (*Repeated*)
> *Chorus:*
> Certain bad mind in a certain line,
> Saying criticize the people who pass. (*Repeated*)
>
> You kneel in your home to pray,
> They say a hypocrite you did play.   (*Repeated*)
> *Chorus:*
> Certain bad mind in a certain line,
> Saying criticize the people who pass. (*Repeated*)

In the United States, too, popular singers like Bobby Womack, the Isley Brothers, and James Brown often give moral and philosophical advice in their songs, and James Brown has even released an album called *Reality*.[52] To an Accra "guy" like Stephen Evans, alias Sartana the Angel of Death,[53] James Brown's lyrics in particular are "thick proverbs" comparable to the most philosophical Highlife songs. In fact, many of my friends who were most eager to help me understand their Highlife songs were just as eager for my help in translating James Brown's slang, which they interpreted with no end of enjoyment and wonder. In a recent album, *The Payback*,[54] James Brown sings a song entitled "Shoot Your Shot (Before You Get the Shot Shot out of You)," which is about the ability to act with clarity and confidence at the right moment, and his bandsmen demonstrate the point musically with their solos as he cues each in turn, calling, "Shoot your shot!" "Mind Power," from the same album, with the main lyric being "What it is is what it is," is a discourse on a mental attitude, and the degree to which, in the music itself, it is also a demonstration of the power of mind will become apparent in the next chapter.

Many Westerners who like African music would nonetheless be unable or reluctant to perceive the philosophical dimensions of James Brown's music. One reason, of course, is that most Westerners are simply not familiar enough with African musical idioms even to imagine how African music can serve as a medium for articulating philosophical and religious traditions. For the moment, however, we should note that the difficulty Westerners have in bridging the gap in cultural sensibilities about rhythms is often paralleled by an ethnocentric inability to attribute complexity to, or even to recognize, the more intellectual aspects of an alien culture's expressions. When it is music we are confronting, this inability is compounded by our own habitual aesthetic orientation. In the Introduction, I discussed some of the difficulties of translation and interpretation of cultural differences: it is usually easier for people from different cultures to understand their relationship if it is limited to clearly positive or negative feelings or to a practical task. Feelings or work can be shared or lived with in a meeting at the margins of two cultural worlds, and the broad range of cultural points of view and interpretive possibilities that each person brings is often not relevant to the reasons which have brought them together. As a Ghanaian seaman phrased it when discussing how to relate to people from other cultures, "Live with them; move with them; observe them; but never judge them." In such a context of communication, one may keep the full dimensions of one's perceptions to oneself and mistakenly assume that the other does not act with the same kind of restraint or think with the same kind of mind. While we are not yet ready to examine the particular way in which intellectual and emotional faculties are oriented in African musical styles, we can begin to recognize that the interrelationship of musical and social expressions will require that a musician be both observant and self-conscious in order to bring about the full effectiveness of the music, and in the context of this chapter we can elaborate on one striking way in which the content and the form of African music are integrated and set into a dynamic relationship.

While in Western music, certain kinds of musical themes may suggest images or feelings, the astounding fact is that in traditional African music, the rhythms themselves are a specific text. When the earliest European travelers described drum-signaling between villages, they assumed that the beating was a kind of code. In reality, the drums actually speak the language of the tribe. During my first day practicing with Gideon, I was following him well until he suddenly performed a rather complicated series of rhythms and then went back to the basic rhythm he was showing me. A few minutes later a man who had passed at that moment returned with two bottles of beer. The way that Africans can talk with their drums has been investigated and described numerous times,[55] but the notion of "talking drums" has lost none of its fascination for Westerners, and no general discussion of African music would be complete without a description of how a drum can speak. And the use of "drum language" has, as well, many implications regarding the musical and social qualities we are considering in this chapter.[56]

Basically, there are two reasons why Africans can talk with their drums. First, African languages are what are called "tonal" languages. In tonal languages, the pitch of a spoken word is important in determining its meaning, and the "same" sound pronounced at different pitches can mean entirely different things.* Second, a drum is not just an instrument to play rhythms: it plays a melody. By using two drums or by striking a drum in different ways, a drummer can duplicate the speech patterns of his language: African music is derived from language. Working among the Jabo people of Eastern Liberia, the linguist George Herzog concluded that "Drum-signaling in Eastern Liberia may be said to render the tonal and length factors of speech accurately enough. It reflects quite faithfully the essential structural pattern of the language, including some of the more intricate details of the constitution of the . . . syllable."[57]

Of course, there is a high degree of specialization necessary to be able to render an exact duplication of speech, yet the phenomenon is present to varying degrees in almost all African cultures, and few villages are without people who can do it. How exact the communication is varies from tribe to tribe. Similarly, the ability to understand drum language is not universal, but neither is it uncommon. Large sections of the drum histories I mentioned are actually recited on the drums. I also mentioned songs which a young Hausa man may have composed to declare love or to ridicule rivals, or a young Hausa woman may have composed to praise her beauty or to mock easily available women: these songs are actually rhythms which drumming groups play for a fee.[58] Even in Highlife music, conga drummers or dondon beaters may talk with their beats. According to the interpretation of several people I know, in one song by Jerry Hansen's Ramblers International Band, the bass guitarist plays the Twi: *Hwe ne nante, hwe na to* ("Look at her walking; look at her buttocks").[59] Regarding a trumpet solo in a popular tune in Zaïre, J. F. Carrington, an expert on talking drums, observed: "Such two-toned playing was immediately felt by the hearers to suggest a linguistic basis and such a basis was indeed supplied by some of them."[60]

Ibrahim Abdulai's son Alhassan, who was assisting in my instruction, displayed great ingenuity during an extended prank in which he tried to confuse me in my work by inventing false meanings to fit many rhythms in Takai. Many of the rhythmic styles a Takai drummer beats are played only to make the music more interesting, but the language Alhassan supplied matched the rhythms so perfectly that I began to think Ibrahim was withholding the meanings. When I persisted in my questions, he said, "We have a general name for the whole Takai drumming, but only a few of the rhythms have names. In Zhem, all the drummers will be making speeches, but in Takai the rhythms are mainly to make the dancers strong. The name given Takai is for the different rhythms combined together, and all the rhythms are equal. Anyone who wants to tell you words for these rhythms is lying. Anytime I want, I can just listen to the sound of the dondon or gondon and compare the music to something in Dagbani language, but it is not the same as making speeches. As for the styles you have been learning, I am the one who has been bringing all these styles when drumming Takai, and I am the right person to give them meaning, but I have no name for them. So how can another person give them meaning or say that this style says this or that style says that while I was not making speeches when I got those very styles?" Alhassan had simply used his imagination to give what Ibrahim called "false" meanings. For some dances like Zhem, the drum language is a secret, and drummers may be able to beat the rhythm without knowing the meaning. Ibrahim Abdulai did not know the meaning himself until, out of fidelity to his sense of responsibility in directing my research efforts, he traveled to Yendi to consult the chief drummer of the Paramount Chief of the Dagbon State. There he observed the same ritual obligations and received the same complement of moral advice that I later received from him. He told me that one of the other secret dances he taught me, Bangumanga, has a false meaning which is widely accepted by junior drummers.[61]

All that is really necessary to speak on a drum or any instrument is the knowledgeable use of notes of at least two pitches. Among drums, this potential is most obviously exemplified, of course, by the dondons: tension on the leather strings can tighten or release the drumheads and thus raise or lower the pitch.[62] In Tamale, when I arrived for lessons each morning, I would beat the drum for Alhassan: *Alhassani Dagomba, be boon' a* ("Alhassan Dagomba, someone is calling you"). I have taken liberties with the representation below: the pitch intervals, which would vary with different-sized drums, are somewhat approximate; the timing, which would vary with my impatience, is shown spatially rather than with notational values; and the arrows indicate pitch movement achieved by working the leather strings while the note resounds.

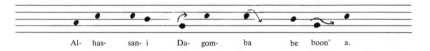

Al- has- san- i   Da- gom- ba   be boon' a.

Westerners thinking about African talking drums often think of dondons, but another way of talking with drums is to use two drums of different pitch, as the Ashantis generally do. In a legendary incident from the colonial wars, Ashanti warriors besieging a British fort broke into the cellars and trapped the British soldiers upstairs. The Ashantis pulled in their drums and danced to music based on the phrase *Oburoni bewu abansoro* ("The white man will die upstairs"). The pitch intervals in my notation will indicate the two drums.

O-   buro- ni be- wu a- ban-so-   ro.   O-   buro- ni be- wu a- ban-so-   ro.

It is quite possible, moreover, to speak on a single drum by striking it in different ways. A Dagomba gongon beater can speak basic phrases by using the muted beats he makes when he turns his wrist and "stops" his stick in the center of the drumhead. But we can look to the Ewe drums for a more detailed example. Jones gives nine basic types of notes which can be produced on Atsimewu, and he points out that the range in pitch falls "within the range of the adult male's *speaking voice*."[63]* Each type of beat can be mimicked by an onomatopoeic syllable which has no meaning except in reference to drumming.[64] Freeman Donkor used the nonsense syllables extensively when he was teaching me to play Atsimewu. I would often learn to say the rhythm before I learned to beat it, and if Freeman was busy playing the bell pattern on the side of the drum we used, he would correct my mistakes by speaking the proper rhythm. Similarly, if one drummer in an ensemble forgets his part, another will be able to prompt him without having to stop his own playing. The following representation is adapted from Jones and offers the syllables as I was taught to pronounce them by my teachers.[65]

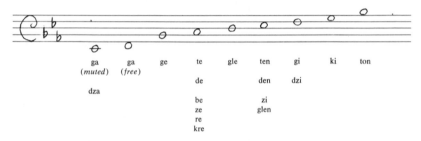

ga	ga	ge	te	gle	ten	gi	ki	ton
(muted)	(free)							
			de		den	dzi		
dza								
			be		zi			
			ze		glen			
			re					
			kre					

For example, my name, *To dzro medea gbe o*, is played *Gadenton dzadzadza*:

To dzro   me-dea gbe o

Whether by intention or coincidence, my name is similar to Gideon's, *Gadenton dzidzidzi* for *Gabla godogo* ("Rolled-iron strap" [for packing cases]—it can tie so many things together well). If I or any drummer played *Gadenton dzidzidzi*, Gideon's head would snap up, and he would immediately stop whatever he was doing to come and shake the drummer's hand.

Without reference to accentuation or volume, the basic notes of Atsimewu can be produced in the following way. The highest pitch is produced by pressing the drumhead with the hand and striking the center with the stick: *ton*. A free stick beat on the center is *te*. By hitting the drumhead freely with the stick and then stopping the sound

with the fingers, you get *ten*. Sliding the stick across the drumhead
gives *zi*. By hitting the center of the drum with a flat hand, you get
ga. Hitting the edge of the drumhead with the hand and letting the
beat sound is *ge*. Hitting the edge of the drumhead with open fingers
and muting the beat by not letting your hand bounce is *gi*. Playing
ga while you simultaneously strike the side of the drum with the stick
gives *dza*. Playing *gi* while simultaneously striking the side of the drum
with the stick gives *dzi*. Rolling with one stick or both gives *re*. Striking
the center of the drum with a stick just after you strike an open beat on
the edge with your hand and then muting the beat with your fingers
gives *glen*, or *gle* if you do not mute the beat. Hitting the edge of the
drumhead freely just after you strike a free stick beat in the center gives
kre. Even all these beats do not exhaust the possibilities. For instance,
depending on how you hit *te*, the quality of the beat can be changed to
give *de*, *be*, or *ze*. A note like *ki* is produced in the phrase *ki-ton*, when
the center is hit with the hand and followed by *ton*. And muting a stick
beat raises the pitch by not allowing the drumhead to vibrate freely,
thus limiting the depth of the vibration. A similarly broad range of
sounds can be produced if a drummer plays with two hands, with the
hands held in different shapes and the fingers variously employed, and
by striking the center, the area around the center, or the edge of the
drumhead. When Sogo is played with both hands, it has as much range
as Atsimewu. A representation like ours, of course, is approximate, as
even Jones admits, for the tuning of the drums is relative and never
exactly fixed. In addition, because the drumhead is soft, a note like *ton*
can extend over an interval of a third and will vary depending on the
particular phrase.[66]

At any rate, African music can hardly be described as "monoto-
nous." A drummer must have a highly developed sense of pitch.[67] From
tribe to tribe and from dance to dance, the role which language plays
may vary greatly. Sometimes it is only the basic rhythmic phrase which
has specific meaning; other times everything each drummer does is
rigidly prescribed.[68] The proper use of tonal qualities while playing
reflects more than a concern for eliciting an instrument's richest voice;
because of the conversational and linguistic clarity required in much
African music-making, this aspect of drumming is a central focus of
communication.

For a Westerner, however, perceiving the "melody" of a drum rhythm
is often more difficult than perceiving cross-rhythmic relationships. In
African ensembles, the different drums are tuned so that the contrast

of their rhythms will be enhanced by the contrast of their pitches, and
in a traditional musical arrangement, two supporting drums may even
be doing some talking. As Nketia points out:

> The use of cross rhythms without the addition of tone contrasts is
> not often successful. If you had four drums of the same size and
> pitch playing different rhythms at the same level of pitch, the im-
> pression of crossing would be very slight or indeed confused. Hence
> whenever a number of drums are played together, you will find
> that they are graded in size and pitch. When drums of approximately
> the same size are used they may be tuned differently or assigned
> rhythm and tone patterns which can be clearly contrasted.[69]

Even a Highlife band, for example, might be tuned so that the pitch
of the lower of the two bongo drums, if they are used, is matched with
the higher of the conga drums, while the pitch of the lower conga drum
will match one of the jazz drummer's tom-toms. Westerners listening
to African drumming should try to hear all the properties of tones—
pitch, duration, intensity, and timbre—even while they focus on rhythmic relationships.[70] Farel Johnson, musical director and lead drummer
for the Afro-American Dance Ensemble and an expert on many styles
of African and Afro-American drumming, told me that he insists that
his students learn to get the proper sounds from a drum even before
they begin to learn rhythmic variations. And in his article on Ewe
drumming, Cudjoe goes so far as to maintain that the different high
and low sounds of a master drum are clearly associated with different
types of dance movement.[71]

   It can safely be said that in general both rhythms and melodies
are constrained by the dimensions of language. A composer will find
it difficult to write a rising melody when the words have a falling intona-
tion,[72] and similarly, an African rhythmic pattern is more properly considered as a phrase than as a series of notes. Naturally, compromises
are made in the interest of expression, but still they are compromises
and cannot go too far. Musicians, of course, do not conform to these
constraints out of a respect for "rules." Their language is a fundamental
dimension of their lives which they bring to their music, and people
associate melodies and rhythms with speaking because their speech has
meaning in terms of its melodic and rhythmic character. If you play
gagedega instead of *gagedegi* when executing a phrase on Atsimewu, or
if you miss the pitch when beating a dondon, you may have made a
more serious mistake than you think. Indeed, one of the reasons why
repetition is so important in African music is that repetition of a rhythm
often serves to clarify its meaning. When rhythms change too abruptly,

the music can lose some of its meaning, and similarly, although tonal relationships may be extremely important, the harmonic chordal progression which we appreciate in musical expression would, quite simply, not make sense.

The relationship of drumming to language is one of the most important factors in limiting the freedom of improvisation. On one hand, linguistic expressions help the African drummer to create fresh rhythms; in most cases, on the other hand, because of the interweaving of musical and linguistic considerations, a drummer cannot move too far either from the rhythmic potential of a particular pattern or from the meaning that the pattern may have as a comprehensible phrase. In essence, a good drummer must integrate his comments musically, but when a drummer speaks, he must make music as well. Ewe drummers sometimes engage in competitions, hurtling insults at each other on their drums or trying to duplicate each other's improvisations and body movements. Often, when Gideon was going to be around, other drummers would not even appear: they were afraid to go up against Gideon. Gideon could always invent witty remarks which could be clearly understood, which involved extremely subtle beating, and which always fit perfectly into the rhythms of the ensemble. He stumped everybody, and when he wanted to, he completely stupefied them. (Gideon could play three drums while he rolled backwards into a head-and-shoulder stand, clapping his feet together and singing at the same time.) In Dagbon, many popular dances originate from the rhythms of praise-names, and when a chief dances, the drummers all gather around him and take turns beating their dondons. All very nice music, a Westerner might say, but more than that, the drummers are talking to the chief, praising him or his dancing and trying to get him to do something spectacular. Both the music and the comments are necessary to inspire the chief, who as a connoisseur is probably not easy to please. Similarly, in their discussion of Ewe dance drumming, Ladzekpo and Pantaleoni write:

> For example, part of the dance to takada music may involve bending the torso toward the ground. A lazy dancer is apt not to bend very much. When the drummer notices this he might comment, "Those who do not bend down are hunchbacks," which in Anlo-Evegbe is "Amesí ke me bòbòwò dzime kpékpé." With the negating suffix "-wo" elided smoothly into the preceding vowel in normal speech, the sentence can be played on atsimevu as "Ga Ze Gí Ke (Re) Be Gà Gà Ke Re (S) Tó Tó."[73]

The proper use of language by a master drummer is therefore one of the ways in which the specific situation can be brought into focus and thus become more tightly integrated with the music. And the fact that a musician is talking means that different drummers will distinguish themselves by the special style of their touch on the drum. While many connoisseurs of Western music possess a remarkable sensitivity that enables them to say, after hearing only a few notes, whether it is Rubinstein or Horowitz playing the piano, such discrimination rarely can be applied beyond a select group of virtuosos. I found this sensitivity regarding their own musicians extremely widespread among my African friends, who were quick to point out that they admired how a certain musician had his own "way" with his instrument. In Tamale one day, Alhassan easily identified all the members of a distant party of drummers from "the way they talked." When an African responds to you because of "how you say something," he may mean it literally and not in reference to the particular words you chose: style of speech is more important to him than to us. Readers familiar with both African and Western musical idioms will recognize that even in American music, distinctions of musical touch are perhaps more readily apparent among Afro-American musicians, particularly jazz players, than among Western musicians.*

In Africa, as we have noted, people are interested in the special quality of a given performance, and they pay attention to the distinctive touch of a musician who through his central role in the event characterizes it with his personality. Africans cultivate this kind of critical refinement because the style of a performance is such a significant issue. Improvisation for the master drummer, as we shall see, lies not so much in the genesis of new rhythms as in the organization and form given to the already existing rhythms, and a musician's *style* of organizing his playing will indicate the way he approaches from his own mind the responsibility of his role toward making the occasion a success. The musician who can add an extra dimension of excitement, the cutting edge, to a performance will demonstrate both his mastery of all the elements of the music and his involvement with the progress of the social event. In the next chapter, we will examine in detail how he makes his judgements, but to complete the discussion of this chapter, we will examine two pieces of music which I have chosen with the purpose of showing how all the considerations of ensemble-playing, language, dance, and social meaning are brought together in an African musical event.

First we will look at Zhem. Ibrahim Abdulai told me, "Zhem is the first dance of all the Dagomba dances. Zhem signifies chieftaincy, and when the Dagomba tradition was formed, they formed it with chieftaincy. Zhem was used in installing the first Ya-Naa, the Paramount Chief of the Dagomba people. When a Ya-Naa is installed, he is given many presents [the sacred regalia of office] to show that he is a chief—smock, hat, sandals, walking stick. All the time they give him these things, Zhem is the first drumming they will be beating, and they will continue to play Zhem throughout. And it has become a custom that Zhem must be played when a new Ya-Naa is installed, and it has also come down to all chiefs who are being installed, especially the powerful ones—at Yendi, Savelugu, Karaga, Mion, Gushiegu, and a few others." For the Dagombas, the installation ceremony is extremely complicated and important, and in recent Dagomba political history one attempt to remove a Paramount Chief was legitimated on grounds of irregularities in the installation proceedings.

Zhem is also played when a chief dies. Ibrahim said, "Zhem is only beaten in serious cases. We can play Takai for final funerals [well after the burial], but by the time they are to perform the funeral there is no dead body lying in the house. By that time everyone is somehow happy. It seems to be a happy day. But we can never beat Takai for a dead man lying in his house. Zhem shows both death and happiness, but Takai is only happiness. Zhem is for our most serious things; it is a big thing in our culture, and we only use it when we need to force something important. Because you have been with me for a long time, I am showing it to you, and if you are going to show someone this dance, you should charge or require something great from that person. Or if you write a book about it, you can write about it to show that when you came here, you met some people who knew and who have shown you the great secrets of the Dagomba culture." During the installation ceremony, the new chief does not usually dance Zhem; rather, his children dance, joined by his wives and the elders. The language of the drumming to which the chief's family dances is appropriate to the responsibility he now holds: "He who does evil, it is unto him, it will wait for his children." The gongon and the lead dondon beat *Nun tum ka di bie* ("He who does evil"), and the supporting dondons beat *Di be la o sani* ("It is with him"), *Din gul' o bia* ("It will wait for his children"). The notation is given on the following page.*

Agbekor is a highly standardized dance based on traditional Ewe dance movements combined with stylizations of movements from warfare: it tells the story of how the Ewes fought their way to the place where they now live. In various towns along the Ewe coastal region, it is performed at funerals and festivals and preserved by musical associations organized specifically for this purpose. There is competition among

the groups, and new parts to the dance are added and new arrangements tried. In Agbekor, the drum patterns are specifically related to the dance steps, and consequently the master drummer's beating is standardized to the language which calls and describes the dance steps. The main step of Agbekor is called the "turning," and a shortened form of the step is referred to as the "half-turning."[74] The basic meaning of the turning phrase is "Turn around. Stop and turn around, and be sure. We are going far away. Be sure. We are going far away. You must go carefully." Both the turning and the half-turning phrases begin with *Ton*. Thus when the dancers hear *Ton*, they immediately begin the turning step which follows the drum language. Most of the different steps are separated by either the turning or the half-turning, and the master drummer's variations will consist of isolating and elaborating various parts of the basic turning and half-turning rhythms. The alternation of the basic step with the other steps provides a coherence to the dance and a unity to the drum beating.

We have already looked at the basic rhythms of the ensemble, and all the Agbekor drums orient themselves to the theme of war. The baby Kagan cries *Mitso, mitso* ("You stand up; you stand up"). But the mother, Kidi, does not want to see war, and she says, *Kpo afe godzi* ("Turn to see homeward; let's go back home"). The twin brothers pay her no mind and encourage each other to go on: Kroboto says, *Gbedzi ko ma do* ("I will die [sleep] in the bush, at the battlefield"), and Totogi supports him with *Koko dzi* ("For sure!"). The dancers follow the father's words and carry through the fight.

Let us look at an example of the music of the master drum. The half-turning phrase is generally played with the hand-and-stick technique,

Slow Agbekor (supporting drums)

and in the slow version of the dance, one way the half-turning is played runs *Tonten, gazegi, tenten, gedega gedegi, gagedegi, kre kre kre, gagedegi gedega.** In the transcription on page 86, *ka* is a stick beat on the side of the drum with which the drummer keeps his time during pauses. The drum language is *Tso tso avawovi, mitso ne mia bla alidzi, kple dzidodo; tso, tso, tso, avagbedzi nya de dzo.* ("Stand up, stand up, warriors! You stand up and gird your waists. With courage, stand up, stand up, stand up! Hear of the battlefield; something has happened.") Looking musically at the notation of the half-turning, we may notice first what a difference it makes to assign pitch to the different drum beats and how important this dimension is when we want to listen to African music. The higher notes will relate to the higher drums and the lower notes to the deep-voiced twins. A second point recalls our discussions of conversations and the unifying character of the last beat: as the master drummer and the dancers finish the half-turning and before they begin the next step, the ensemble has a chance to respond. Third, Atsimewu's entrance with *Ton* coincides with the rattle's third beat, and if we look at the rhythms of the ensemble, we realize that neither the bell nor any of the supporting drums has a freely struck beat at this point. When the master drummer strikes *Ton*, he dramatically fills a gap in the middle of the music and he will as well be heard clearly by the dancers. Fourth, we can notice the complexity of the accentuation: the half-turning phrase involves shifts in timing, and it also runs against the 12/8 beating of the ensemble. Furthermore, *ten, de, ze,* and *kre,* the stick beats, which are more noticeable, are all off-beats. Compared to many other patterns, the half-turning is not even particularly difficult to play because it fits with the rattle on the note *gi:* some patterns are set completely on the rattle's off-beat. Finally, we notice that there are pauses in the pattern during which the other drums may be heard. The half-turning pattern breaks up the background and cuts the other rhythms in its own way. Other patterns will highlight the ensemble in other ways, and the complexity of the ways in which the master drum cuts the ensemble and converses with the rhythms is what makes the music interesting.

Slow Agbekor (half-turning)

The artistic depth of an Agbekor performance is the product of intentional design. The process of composition was described to me by Freeman Donkor. Several dancers try to describe the situations of war: "Get down and be ready" or "Go forward slowly; stop and watch right and left, and go forward again" or "If I get you, I'll cut your neck."

The dancers stylize the motions in keeping with the form and meaning of the dance. A drummer is called to contribute the descriptive poetry in such a way that the drumming will be appropriate to the music. As with Zhem and Agbekor, the integration of all these artistic and social concerns into a single unified event is the essential inspiration of an African musical performance. In the depth of this integration, we can recognize the expression of a profoundly humanistic sensibility and one of the great artistic achievements of humankind. The most successful performance will involve everyone present on various levels of participation and appreciation, and their enjoyment is the chief criterion of excellence; Westerners fortunate enough to witness African music-making in an African context will by all means be included, and their admiration and understanding will contribute to the overall success. In Africa, the power of music is a social fact. In the next chapter we will broaden our capacity to appreciate its power.

In this chapter we have discussed the form and the structure of a complete musical system based on rhythm. The general features of this system appear, more or less, in almost all of the diverse idioms of African music. As we introduced new ideas, each should have served to extend and reinforce the meaning of other ideas, until finally they all combined to reflect a particular balance and organization. We described the formal components of a complex rhythmic system built around cross-rhythms and responsive rhythms, and in the notions of apart-playing and off-beat accentuation we began to indicate a particular appreciative mode. As we thought about how rhythms work together, cutting and conversing with each other, we began to sense the distinctiveness of the African approach to music. Locating the main beat at the end of phrases, marking it with movement or dance, and thus relying on other beats to find our own, we began to isolate an aesthetic perspective quite different from ours. In the "behavior" of the music as interlocutor and pacesetter and in the relationship of language to melody and rhythm, we found an interweaving of musical elements and social expressions. The model we have built in this chapter should help us as Westerners to *recognize* the relevant relationships, processes, and dimensions of music-making in Africa, and in our brief references to the kinds of judgements which must inform the improvisational activities of supporting drummers, we began to examine the dynamics of interaction which bring life to the organizational system of the music.

But our model does not show how an African musician might think about or orient himself to the potential of his musical system: while it is evident that the integration of African music with its social context is the basic movement and concern of a musical occasion, the model does not reveal in depth the particular ways this integrative potential reaches its greatest effectiveness. The potential of the various musical elements we have discussed is realized through the establishment of a special style of involvement which is based on more fundamental attitudes about relationships. The master musician's skills are founded on a knowledge of how to exploit all these relationships and thus bring the formal potential of the music to life; a master musician's aesthetic command will be for us a manifestation of those qualities of engagement which make for the best contribution to social living. As we begin to exercise our new appreciative capacity in order to examine more closely the ways in which a musician relates to his musical system, we will eventually be able to *characterize* African attitudes about relationships in terms of a style of living and the aesthetic philosophy this style defines. To comprehend these attitudes, we must focus in greater detail on the dimensions of intentional design and creative purpose within a musical event. Thus, in the next chapter, we will continue our discussion of the techniques of improvisation.

3

Style in Africa

Westerners who learn to appreciate African music may easily forget the problems they may have experienced at their first exposure to it. The difficulties of hearing or distinguishing several rhythms or of tapping out even the simplest rhythms will not remain an obstacle. Once a Westerner understands the organizing principles of African music, he is prepared to relate to many of the artistic dimensions within which an African musician creates. At such a point, a Westerner might consider himself to be a receptive listener, an adequate participant, or a knowledgeable critic. Yet at that point still, a traveler in even a very limited area of Africa may meet so many different kinds of marvelous musical situations and performers that he might feel his awareness is actually superficial. The music in different places would also feel different, for the interweaving of rhythms by various types of instruments and ensembles would produce music of quite distinct textures. The various formal characteristics would be readily noticeable, but such analytic considerations would seem not to reach into those subtle aspects of a performance which make for great music. Beyond being able to recognize the formal dimensions of African music, a traveler moving from place to place would feel the need for a general sense of standards of musical excellence.

As Westerners, we would be forced to depend on all our observational capacities because Africans have not developed their musical traditions with us in mind. Readers who are still having trouble relating to rhythms can take consolation from the facts that in Africa very few villagers can themselves play the drums and that most "drummers" rarely progress beyond the lesser drums. The villagers, of course, like to listen and dance to their music, and most would probably be quite willing to talk about their traditions with a visitor from a foreign land. There are many connoisseurs with whom one might discuss fine points, and with well-asked questions, the traveler might perhaps become a party to more privileged information about the music, unknown even to many members of the community. And although for various reasons there are no systematic aesthetic philosophies to guide us, the fact that music plays such an integral role in African life means that if comparatively many people are artistic participants, many are also what we might call "informal" critics. Indeed, the absence of scholastic criticism is perhaps due in part to the fact that most people are too actively involved discussing what is going on to allow any specialist to tell them what to appreciate. There will be any number of complementary perspectives available at a musical event, and we may as well simply observe the "scene" as as index to musical quality: if someone executes an especially wonderful dance step and everybody watching smiles or cheers, we can be sure that the music has also reached a high point. All in all, then, we would not be without resources in our efforts to distinguish musical quality.

Above all, though, we must beware of misinterpreting the meaning of what we are told or what we see and hear according to our own ways of thinking about music and enjoyment. If four untrained Westerners were given drums and asked to make some African music, they would not hesitate to start pounding away. On the other hand, if a Westerner who has learned all the possible variations for a master drum is put in front of a fired-up group of musicians, everybody might still become bored. In either case, two little African boys playing on bottles could probably do much better. Obviously there is a special kind of sophistication to the ways that rhythms work in African music. What would be at issue would be a difference of sensibility, the whole orientation to music and to life which defines the significant dimensions of excellence within the total configuration of a musical event. In this chapter, as we try to think our way into an appropriate aesthetic perspective, our foremost concern will be to attempt to judge the music on its own terms, to try to get an idea of what dimensions of musical performance and participation will make the occasion "very, very sweet."

With such a goal, we will think again about rhythms: this time, however, we will not think about rhythms as Westerners who are orienting themselves to African music for the first time; rather, we will try to see the rhythms working within the formal structures established in the context of African musical expression. Now that we have an idea of the basic organizing principles of the music, we can use our awareness to see what actually happens when musicians and a crowd of people get together, and we will look more closely at the people who make the music. In the process of selecting and judging the rhythms that he plays, an African musician must have some creative purpose which, if we can understand it, will both give us some idea of what an African would want to experience through the music and as well help us explain the existence of some of the striking social dimensions of the music. In view of the fact that rhythmic complexity is the heart of African music, an understanding of the way in which African rhythms are structured is our best analytic tool.[1]

In the Introduction and in the first chapter, I discussed some of the ways a social scientist might approach a study of African music. First, of course, it would be important to understand the music within its own context, and we thus take the organizing principles of African music as the starting point for an analysis. Second, a social scientist would be interested in music as an institution which mediates and focuses certain distinct types of interaction and behavior. Since African music is not abstracted from its social setting as an "art form" but rather is directly integrated into social activities, it is particularly accessible to a social scientific approach. From such a perspective, the "aesthetic effect" of the music would appear in the particular way the music "functions" to involve people in a specific social event. A social scientific perspective should therefore be useful on the one hand for analyzing how the music works as an integrative force within its context and, on the other hand, for describing the music in terms of those qualities of social interaction and participation which the music elicits. And in the depth of the interrelationship of music and social life, we may find a basic vantage point from which to look at African cultures.

Whether or not one is looking from the point of view of a social scientist, one of the most noticeable features of African cultures is that many activities—paddling a canoe, chopping a tree, pounding grain, smashing up the yams for dinner, or simply moving—seem set within a rhythmic framework which can and often does serve as the basis for music and songs. On one of my first afternoons in Accra I went to the airport to fill out the many forms I needed to clear my tape recorder, which had been sent as unaccompanied baggage, through the bureaucratic tangle of customs. After I had become quite familiar with the view from in front of all the different desks in the office, I had an opportunity to study the filing system in great detail while I helped a clerk search for the record of the shipment I was expecting. Eventually one of the chief inspectors, with whom I had by that time become friends, called another clerk to prepare typed copies of the invoices and other papers. The two of us went to a little desk in one corner, and then the man began typing. I flipped. Using the capitalization shift key with his little fingers to pop in accents between words, he beat out fantastic rhythms. Even when he looked at the rough copies to find his next sentence, he continued his rhythms on the shift key. He finished up each form with a splendid flourish on the date and port of entry. I thanked him for his display, and though I regretted having to leave the customs office, I was eager to go out and begin my work, for I realized that I was in a good country to study drumming.

"We have to grasp the fact," writes A. M. Jones, "that if from childhood you are brought up to regard beating 3 against 2 as being just as normal as beating in synchrony, then you develop a two-dimensional attitude to rhythm which we in the West do not share."[2] A crying African child is attracted and soothed by lullabies with rhythms that cut across the rhythm of the arms which rock and comfort him. African children play games and sing songs displaying a rhythmic character quite different from that of the games and songs of Western children, and African children learn to speak languages in which proper rhythmic accentuation and phrasing is essential to meaning. On religious occasions, they hear drums instead of an organ. At a musical event, a young boy may sit beside his father who is drumming, and the boy may tap out rhythms on the side of the drum; a shy little girl may get down off her bench and tentatively try a dance step that the adults are doing, until she sees she is being watched and, giggling, runs back to her place. Facility with rhythms is something people learn as they grow up in an African culture, one of the many cultural acquisitions that make someone seem familiar to people who have also learned the same things. Rhythms are built into the way people relate to each other. When women pound cooked yams, the woman who turns the yams while her friends are rhythmically smashing them with heavy wooden poles converses most amiably, as if the safety of her fingers were of no concern. Obviously she does not have to try very hard to maintain a simple rhythm, and she counts on her friends to be just as steady. These women, however, will probably not consider pounding yams for dinner to be a kind of music: they will want to hear something a bit more complicated. On the other hand, Eshu, a Yoruba trickster god who is full of contradictions, has a praise-name that asserts: "He knows dancing well. He doesn't join in singing. If there are no drums, he will dance to the pounding of the mortars."[3]

We should be able to see, by this point, the validity of Waterman's conception of musical "metronome sense" as a cultural index. Certainly, the African rhythmic orientation is quite different from our own. The fundamental characteristic of African music is the way the music works with time in the dynamic clash and interplay of cross-rhythms. As we might phrase it, there is more than one "time" in the music. We tend to think of "time" as a single, objective phenomenon, moving quite steadily (as our philosophical heritage tells us) toward some distant moment (as our religious heritage tells us). Our music, of course, is above all a way of ordering sound through time, and Western music imposes a rather strict order to time. From one note to the next in the most beautifully changing melodies and harmonies, we follow the rhythm of the music. If we found ourselves thinking about something besides what we were hearing, we would assume that we did not like the music. In contrast, one of the central themes that emerged in the preceding chapter stressed the importance, in the African context, for both the musician and the spectator to maintain an additional rhythm in order to give coherence to the ensemble; otherwise he or she would become confused by the multiplicity of conflicting rhythms and accents. The essential point is the notion of an ability and a need to *mediate the rhythms actively*. In the Western context, when we hear several different tones together, we hear them as a unity, and we have the word "harmony" (or "chord," if there are three or more tones) to express the oneness of the sound. Most significantly, we have no names for specific rhythms, and our words for describing the relationship of beats separated in time—accelerando, ritardando, rubato, syncopation—refer to the speed of a rhythm, its tempo, or to the irregular accentuation of its steady progression, its meter. In Africa, different "beats" have specific names and specific rhythmic variations which can "fit inside the beat"; in an African musical event, one participates by integrating the various rhythms to perceive the "beat," and the "beat" of the music comes from the whole relationship of the rhythms rather than from any particular part. If one is habituated to this kind of music, this integrative task of "getting the beat" is not very difficult—it might even be fun.

From our discussions of the structure of African music and of common Western responses to it, the most evident dynamic feature of African music is that the way the rhythms are established in relationship creates a *tension in time*. This tension is built into the *formal organization* of the different parts of the ensemble. If we remember that the integrity of the ensemble is always the critical issue and that this integrity proceeds from a combination of distinct and separate parts, then we realize that relating to the music depends particularly on resisting the tendency to fuse the parts. The music is engaging because the tension must be comprehended without undermining the power and vitality that come from the conflict of the rhythms. The Western composer who observed that "composing is essentially a problem of capturing force with form"[4] was perhaps more accurately describing the African approach than any other. As we proceed through the musical notations and examples in this chapter, we will elaborate on these concerns bit by bit.

In his landmark article, Richard Waterman recognized and wrote about dynamic tension in the off-beat accentuation patterns of African music. Despite his rather abstruse and circuitous language, we shall quote Waterman at length here to give full credit to his analytic insight.

Melodic tones, and particularly accented ones, occur between the sounded or implied beats of the measure with great frequency. The beat is, so to speak, temporarily suspended, i.e., delayed or advanced in melodic execution, sometimes for single notes (syncopation), sometimes for long series of notes. . . . The maintenance of a subjective meter, in terms of the metronome sense, requires effort and, more particularly, a series of efforts regularly spaced in time. The regular recurrences of these "rhythmic awarenesses" involves the expectancy, at the moment of any beat, that the next beat will occur precisely at some succeeding moment determined by the tempo. Subjectively, the beat does occur. If it is reinforced by an objective stimulus in the form of a percussive or melodic tone, the metronome sense is reassured, and the effort involved in the subjective beat is masked by the effort of perceiving the objective impulse. [Not really too much effort there, I would say.] If the objective beat is omitted, however, the co-operating auditor becomes very much aware of the subjective beat, which thus attains for him greatly increased significance [like missing a step on a staircase]. If the objective beat occurs ahead of time, the auditor, unprepared for it, perceives it and assigns to it the additional importance always accorded the unexpected, further reinforcing it with his subjective pulse which occurs at the "proper" time according to his experience [like stubbing a toe]. If the objective beat is delayed, the period of suspense between subjective and objective beats likewise increases the auditor's awareness of the rhythm [like getting hit on the back of the head]. When the objective, audible beat occurs halfway between the two subjective pulsations, as is frequently the case, both mechanisms operate to give the off-beat tone heightened significance.[5]

Waterman was on to one of the key ways in which African rhythms put pressure on time. Of course, when the listener (or "co-operating auditor") hears a drumbeat (or "objective stimulus"), it is not entirely a matter of being surprised or kept in suspense. What Waterman was getting at with his oddly chosen mechanical metaphor of the "subjective pulsations" of a "metronome" was first the notion we have stressed, that to appreciate African music requires an active engagement, and second the fact that, compared to us, Africans acquire a rather exact sense of time as they learn to relate to the rhythmic potential of what goes on around them. Jones comments in the same vein: "When we Europeans imagine we are beating strict time, the African will merely smile at the 'roughness' of our beating."[6] An African has had a more comprehensive education in rhythm.

One way for us to perceive this dynamic rhythmic tension with clarity is to look again at the dondon parts of Takai. Recalling our discussion of how one rhythm defines another by crossing and cutting it, we should ideally try to listen to the leader's part by focusing on the stable second dondon. Ibrahim Abdulai often had me play the second dondon for long periods during our practices. He would say, "Play the second dondon so that you can listen well. Play it and listen to me; then you can play to resemble me." Yet if we draw vertical lines at each note, at first glance the even beating of the lead dondon begins to look uneven because of the way the second dondon part cuts it.[7]

Takai (dondon parts)

Lead dondon   etc.

Supporting dondons

In effect, the irregular rhythm of the second dondon exerts a kind of pressure that seems to pull two notes together or push them apart, and this pressure accounts for our tendency to hear the two rhythms as a single rhythm. The tension of the rhythms works to make time seem to speed up or slow down,[8] as if the rhythms, which are founded on recurrence, were somehow knocking on their own foundation. The question of aesthetics is whether this time foundation is supposed to withstand the test or to collapse.

Waterman had continued his discussion thus:

> If a whole tune were to be sung in such a way that each note occurred a half-beat ahead of a corresponding beat established by the subjective metronome on the basis of cues from, say, the initial beats of a percussion instrument, the subjective beats would sooner or later, depending on the degree of intransigence of the metronome sense of the auditor, come to be interpreted as off-beats, and hence would be realigned so as to coincide with the new beat pattern.
>
> In other words, complete "off-beating" has the same effect as complete lack of off-beat patterns. . . . The off-beat phrasing of accents, then, must threaten, but never quite destroy, the orientation of the listener's subjective metronome.[9]

In other words, a musician should deliver not too many and not too few off-beat accents because people can get thrown off the beat, and at a certain point either their orientation to the rhythms will shift or they will begin hearing the separate rhythms as a single rhythm. In either case, the tension has been lost and the music becomes dull. The lead drummer, however, balances his beating so that the cross-rhythms will remain distinct, and the point of balance, as Waterman recognized,[10] reflects the level of rhythmic sophistication in the audience.

Waterman's discussion of African music certainly contained many valuable notions, and at the time it was written, no Western scholar had even come close to describing the dynamic tension on which the power of African music is based.[11] Waterman's article was significant because he was the first Western scholar to define an African musical situation with such a notion of *deliberate* pressure on the continuity of time. The off-beat accentuation Waterman discussed is somewhat like syncopation and involves accents or notes thrown in at special times to threaten or affirm an effort to maintain rhythmic continuity. Such a situation seems comparable to what is happening in an Ewe dance like Agbekor, in which the accents of a master drum highlight the rhythms of an ensemble that is itself strictly organized on the recurrent pattern of the bell. Further on in his article, however, Waterman qualified his own argument about off-beat accentuation and polymeter. Referring to Afro-American jazz, he wrote: "The off-beat phrasing of melodic accents is a stylistic trait which functions in jazz in unusually clearcut fashion perhaps because of the absence of polymetric formulations, *which tend to make the off-beats equivocal.*" [Emphasis mine.][12]

The Dagomba drumming, in its polymetric structure, seems to put pressure on the continuity of time in a different way from the one Waterman described. If we look at the complete Takai ensemble, we are dealing not so much with the intriguing accents of a dominant drum as with a kind of movement through time of seemingly isolated strands of rhythm. These rhythms reinforce each other, more or less, at the well-spaced recurrence of the metal rods which the dancers click, but both the lead dondon and the lead gongon will be continually changing their parts by playing any of their many stylistic variations. *

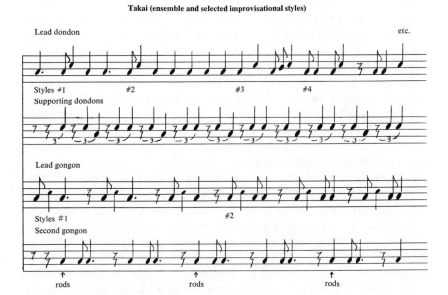

Takai (ensemble and selected improvisational styles)

Off-beat phrasing is one matter, but this kind of metric tension constitutes a real frontal assault on the subjective pulsations of the cooperating auditor's metronome. Several rhythms, each with shifting metric potentials, create an instability in combination and are not so much dependent on accentuation for effect. There is a rhythmic movement which is perhaps too complex to be grasped in its individual parts. To perceive the ensemble as a whole, a listener should hold on to the supporting dondon part and follow the relationship of lead dondon and lead gongon, much in the way he might listen to the rhythm guitar in African popular music in order to focus on the lead and bass guitars. Certainly the listener will maintain his equilibrium, but also he can allow his perception of the rhythms to be transformed as the drummers shift from one style to another.

How does the Takai music change and what are the techniques of improvisation? Unlike the Ewe master drum patterns, which are long, complicated, and frequently dependent on what the dancers are doing, the patterns of the lead dondon are short and not particularly complex. A Dagomba drummer has the choice of moving to any stylistic variation he wants and playing it for as long as he wishes. When I had learned to play many of these variations and could change from one to another, I might have considered myself qualified to play, except that I could not "feel" how to vary the variations. As I became more and more familiar with the music, I listened very closely to Ibrahim Abdulai and to other drummers. In my notation of Takai, I presented four dondon styles. One might imagine that the lead drummer would proceed directly through many styles in order to display his skill and make the music interesting with accentuation. Instead, those drummers considered to be the best do just the opposite. *They take their time.* Once into a style, even the second one I showed, which consisted only of "single" notes, the lead drummer will continue to play that style for a long time. It is the duration of time that a drummer plays a particular rhythm, *the amount of repetition and the way the rhythms change,* to which the drummers pay attention, and not so much any particular rhythmic invention. The aesthetic decision which constitutes excellence will be the *timing* of the change and the choice of a new pattern. This choice will ideally reflect upon the way the gongon beater is developing his styles in relation to the characteristic movement of the particular beat. A radical shift in accentuation may or may not be appropriate. Thus, the dondon beater keeps the tension in the music at its maximum point. In other words, he keeps the music interesting by maintaining the music's continuing potential for engagement. When the lead drummer finally changes his style, it may seem as if the entire music has changed, even though the other drums continue as before. Similarly, within the polymetric framework of Dagomba music, if the gongon is changing, there is less need for the lead drummer to elaborate many styles, and he will hold his changes to a minimum. With the dynamic potential of the beat as a foundation, the changes put pressure on the existing rhythms, and those rhythms become transformed in the sense that the musician, as we might say, "renders his interpretation" of the beat; the new style will cut the music differently and maintain the tension from a different rhythmic perspective, often introducing new tensions to support or go against the perspective which a spectator, or a dancer, had been trying to maintain. But the way a drummer changes, above all, is to be prized for a kind of *smoothness and fluidity,* for the music must both move forward and be steady in order to be interesting and danceable.[13]*

Ibrahim eventually lectured me in depth about the techniques of improvisation. I had been asking him how he learned drumming and how I could learn to improve my playing. I had been with him for some time and I had confidence in my observations of how the music changes, but I was still hoping for more detailed instructions and I wanted to know the way he thought about musical quality. He told me he would talk to me about my questions, and the scope of his discussion went far beyond my hopes. He moved from a broad overview of the meaning of drumming to an intricate critical appraisal of my playing. His ability to articulate his knowledge so thoroughly reflected both his own insight and also, to an extent, the greater degree of professionalism among certain musicians in many of Africa's Muslim cultures as compared to some musicians in other African contexts. Yet in his artistic attitudes, what he said rings true for all that I in my experience have seen or been told or heard played among drummers of integrity elsewhere.

"Drumming has no end," he said. "And to talk of drumming, you cannot talk of it and finish. As we are drumming, every drumming has got its name, and again, every drumming has got its dance. Every playing is different, and in drumming everyone has got his hand. So no one can know everything about drumming; everyone knows only to his extent. If you want to know everything, what are you going to do and know it? The knowledge you have today and you are taking to bluff, there is someone somewhere who knows more than that. So in our drumming way, no one blames another. If someone doesn't know, you don't say, 'This man doesn't know.' If you say that, you have demeaned yourself. Maybe as you say you know, someone too knows better than you, and as you are bending down looking at someone's anus, someone is also bending down looking at yours.

"And again, if you want to learn drumming, it has many types. If a villager comes to dance, how we are going to play will be different from what we will play for a townsman. The men's dancing is different, and the women's dancing is also different. As the dancing is different, the village drummers have also got their way of playing. If a village drum-

mer comes to the town, he has to forget about his village playing and
follow the town people's playing, because if he brings his village playing
into the town, no one will look at him. But when you see a villager
coming to dance, and his village drummer is there, his village drummer
will know the way his leg will go. And that drummer will let you stop,
and he will change to the way he has been playing for that fellow to
dance at home. Those of you who have been playing in the town, at that
time you will stop and look at the village drummer. It's sweet: you look
at him; it's not sweet: you look at him. Because if it is not sweet, it is
sweet for the villager, and that is why he is dancing. And a townsman
will go to a village and cannot dance. At that time you will hear him
blaming the village drummers that they don't know how to play. It
means that his town's drummer is not there, and he has learned his way
of dancing in his town. Everyone and what he has learned at his place.

"And the different tribes that are here, their way of playing is also
different. This Zamandunia you have been learning to beat, it is for the
Kotokolis, and the Hausas have collected it and called it Zamandunia.
The Kotokolis call it Gabati. And the Dagombas have also heard it, and
we call it Ayiko. The styles of beating Zamandunia are so many that if
you say you will know all of them, you will be learning until you are
tired and you run away and leave it. There are some ways I can play
Zamandunia and you will hear it and not think that it is Zamandunia I
am playing. Some day you will see us beating it and you will say you
have never heard Zamandunia played in that way. But we are playing it.
When the Dagombas come out to dance it, we know how to play it for
them; when the Kotokolis come out, they are for the dance, and we
change it and they hear it from the gongon. When you see them you will
know that truly, it is their dance. It is one dance but it has three names,
and the playing is one but those who beat it differ. If you have not gone
round and watched and asked, will you know? The one who has not
watched and asked, when he is going to play it, he will group all of them
together. And the Mossis, their way of playing the gongon is different.
If I am going to play for a Mossi to dance, how I will hold the gongon
and press it is quite different from the Dagomba way. So in drumming,
you learn how to move your hand, and you ask the tribes how they
play it.

"So it's not only in your town that you learn to drum. If you want
your eyes to be open in drumming, you have to be traveling. As you are
going round, you will see all the different types of drumming, and if you
are watchful, you will learn. When you go to a different town, if you
have sense, whatever they are doing in that town, you will put your

heart into it, and if your heart is bright, you will learn it. When I was a small child, every time I heard a drummer drumming, my heart would get up. I would want to try and play like him. I was born at Voggo and I learned drumming there until I went to Nanton. It was at Nanton that I learned all the types of playing in Dagbon. And when I came to Tamale, I started learning the dances of the different tribes, because in Tamale here there are many tribes. And I took it and I went to Kintampo, and at Kintampo I knew I had gone to the right place because the tribes that are in Kintampo are not in Tamale here. It was there I learned the beating of the Wangaras and the Gonjas. And I got up and I went to Kumasi, and I fell in it there. In Kumasi every tribe is there. The Zambarimas, the Kotokolis, the Yorubas, the Dandawas, the Gurumas, the Chembas, they all have got their drummers in Kumasi, and I used to go to them to learn and watch them play. I was there for ten years, and I went to Accra and I stayed there for three years. There are a lot of Mossis in Accra, and that was where I learned how to play the Mossi dance. And I went to Takoradi. It was there I learned the dance of the Walas. And when I came back here, I stayed, and Tamale is my town, and all the knowledge that I gained, I have used it in teaching people here. And I am still learning more. Now if we go to someplace and the Hausas or the Konkombas or the Mamprusis or the Basaris or any other tribes are there, when they come out and they are for their town's dance, we know how to play it for them. If it is a wedding house or a funeral house or any place, no one can come out and ask us to play any type of dance and we will not be able to play it. It is only the white man's dance that we cannot play, because we have never seen their drums.

"We Dagombas have a proverb that says, 'If they call you a monkey, you should let your tail be long.' Why do I say that? If you want to learn a type of work, you have to learn it very well. If you are doing some work and you don't know it, you are only wasting your time, and you are spoiling the work too. If you are a drummer, you must try your best, and what you are learning, you must learn it with seriousness or you are always going to be suffering. If a lion is lying down and you come to hold it, as you are holding the lion, you will not like to let it go. You will think that if you let it go, it will catch you. And as you are holding it, too, you are afraid. You don't know that as you are holding it, that is better than leaving it. So drumming is like that.

"If you are a learned person, when you get up, you will search for knowledge, and you will learn to your extent. And it all comes from asking. If you are a wise person, and you go round, you will see people who are also wise. Then you should put down your wisdom and make yourself a fool, and you follow that fellow's wisdom. So the playing of drums, if you want to learn it, you listen to people and you get their way of playing too. Sometimes you can go somewhere and you see someone playing a drum, and you will like to take the way that fellow plays and use it to be drumming. If you know that you cannot leave your way of playing, and his is nice too, you can still hold yours and learn his. You know that your way of playing is good for you, and if you collect his it will be good for you too. You can get it and add to yours. So if you go to someone to teach you, you do as if you don't know and you follow him exactly. If he is playing and you hear it and then you come and change it, have you not lost it? At that time, he will be teaching you, and what you have already learned and he teaches you, he is adding to you, and what you don't know and he teaches you, he is adding to you again. But 'I have already known': that will not give a human being wisdom. Unless you say, 'I don't know.' Drumming is 'I don't know.' The one who knows much, he will teach you, and the one who doesn't know much, he will teach you to the end of his strength. And when you know to the point you want, if there is a drummer somewhere, you can go to him and do as if you don't know, and start again. And that is the way of drumming.

"If you want to learn drumming, you should learn it from someone who respects it and knows much about it. And it is good if you learn it from many people. Or if there is someone who knows much, as he is sitting down, his learning is more than many people, and if you are learning from him, it means you are learning from many. As I am teaching you, I am showing you all the differences in the drumming. Someone can be beating a drum very nicely, and if you give that drum to another person to beat the same type of drumming, there will be differences. And these differences are from the wrist and fingers as he holds the drum and presses it; and again, these differences are from how he turns his hand as he beats. So as I am teaching you, I put my drum under my armpit, and what I play, you also play. It is because the teaching with the hand is more than the teaching with the mouth. As you are watching me and playing, the sound of the drum will let you know. If your heart is there and you are interested, whatever you are learning, you will catch it, and your arm will do the work you want it to do. You will follow the sound of the drum, and you must take your time to learn it well. You can't learn it in a hurry. If I am teaching someone, I will teach the fellow one style today, and tomorrow I will teach him another style, and the following day I will teach him another.

But if I want to teach him three or four styles in one day, he will not know how to play, because to know how to play the different styles in drumming, truly, it is very difficult. So as he is improving, I will be adding styles one by one. At that time, if we are playing, the drumming will seem as if it is a weak thing. We will be playing like that, and what he has learned, he will take it and know where it will go and fall. I will be adding styles like that, and he will be improving. And when he takes it to its end and he knows how it will fall, he will know its sweetness. This is how the elders of drumming have taught me, and this is how I'm teaching you. If you are taught drumming in this way and you learn it, you will learn it with understanding. And the one who has not been taught, he can take his sense and learn it, but even if his styles are many, his playing will not be as nice as yours. Only someone who is very clever can take his sense to learn it well. But the one who has been taught, he can take his sense and add, and what he has added and is playing, there will be understanding in it. Because the understanding was in it from the starting. So the starting is like the foundation of a house. If you are building a house, you should make the foundation strong, and then what you put on the foundation will stand.

"How you are learning now, if you go outside, you should follow those who are matured in drumming, and be watching them and be listening to their playing. I would like to contact Amadu to arrange for you to see a special Takai dance which would be played by old men. Takai is a dance for young men, not for old people, but the younger ones should not be included. Only the old ones would be those to play for you, and you should watch as they dance. And again, they would include women, old women too, for the Tora dance. How they would make their lines and come out to begin the playing, it would be very interesting. If you decide to see it, it will be good. The old men have knowledge and they have experience, so it means their minds are clear. The old drummers know many styles more than the young people, and they don't change fast. And the old dancers have got experience, so they too don't want it fast. They want everything to be following the drums. So the slowness and the experience make the difference between the old men and the young men, and these make every dance to be nice.

"I want you to know that all young people are crazy. In this Dagbon State, if they show you a crazy man and tell you to go and bring a crazy man, and you can't get a crazy man, then you have to get a young man to stand for the crazy man. An old man has got experience to make everything in the right way. But the young people usually play by heart."

I interrupted him. "What do you mean when you say 'by heart'?"

"They are not careful when they are playing. They don't cool their bodies and take their time. The Dagbani word is *yirin,* by heart. If you do something that is not necessary, if you are rude or rough, if you beat a child without reason, if you miss your road and go to the wrong place, if you are supposed to see someone before doing something but you go ahead without seeing him, it's yirin. So another way to say it is that, as they are playing yirin, it has no meaning. Or we say *yoliyoli,* which means 'nothing, nothing': it has no meaning. The young people dance faster and they usually play faster too. When they are playing, before an old man will play this or that, the young man is already on top of it. That causes the yirin of the dancing. The yirin of the dancing is that they don't play at the same speed. For example, if we are playing slowly and you come to dance with a very fast dancing, it can't be nice. You don't follow the drums. The young men too are usually taking big steps and shaking their bodies when they dance. The old men play quietly, and everyone prefers them; they are the right people for the dance. But the young people don't follow the steps of the old people. The young people shake their bodies like that because they don't hear what people say. That is why I call them crazy people."

"But," I asked, "how can the old men be more flexible and dance more smoothly than the young men?"

"That is how they learned it. When the young people grow, the shaking will reduce, but it will still continue. How they play! It's a lazy play. And it is because they are learning it in a lazy way."

"So how do you talk about Takai when it is played in the best way?" I asked.

"We say the music is sweet, *dema nyagsa,* or the music is falling, *dema lura.* Takai is best when it is cool. That is *baalim.* Baalim is not 'cool' in the way that water or the weather is cool, but rather it means 'slow,' or 'gentle.' Baalim can be used in any topic, for everything. You can say that someone is walking baalim, coolly, or even if a fan is running too fast, you can make it baalim, make it turn slowly. The young men play yirin, by heart, but the old men play baalim, coolly."

"But if you are playing like that, how do you make the music powerful or exciting?"

"Powerful drumming needs hard beating. But sometimes if you beat a drum very hard, the sound will reduce. And if your wrist is too fast in beating, your drumming will not sound. 'My wrist is fast': that is not drumming. As you are beating, it is your heart that is talking, and what your heart is going to say, your hand will collect it and play. And unless you cool your heart, your drumming will not stand. When your heart cools, your arm will cool too, and as you are bringing your strength, you will also be leaving it. At that time, the drum will cry well, and you will beat and not become tired. The one who has learned to play well can beat a drum and the sound will spread out and you will hear it vibrating inside the ground. But the one whose heart gets up and he is beating hard, his drum will not sound. You won't hear it well, and again, the sound will not change. It's not nice. And it's all from the learning. Someone can learn drumming with strength, that is, to be using force or strength in beating the drum. Someone too can learn to play without using force. The one who has learned well, he plays with understanding, and he has added his sense and cooled his heart; if he is beating hard, it will be more than the one who is using only force to play. And as he is beating, he will never become tired, because the understanding is not finishing. And again, the one who has learned to play with force can never play baalim. Sometimes when we are playing hard and then come to make everything cool, and the one who knows only force is beating, we just hold his hand and collect his stick so that he won't play again. That is all. Then we can reduce to cool the music. Otherwise he will spoil the whole thing. And as he is beating only with strength, he will not play and know how the music will fall. As he is playing like that all the time, we will always be collecting his stick. Because any time too that we beat the drum very hard, then that time is a serious time. By that time we say that your eyes are red. Everyone who is looking at the dance knows that this time is a time for a strong beating of the drum. Do you understand?"

"Not quite."

"If we are playing somewhere, by the time I am beating the drum very hard, it is the right time for me to beat the drum hard."

"How can someone like me know the correct time to bring the music up?"

"You can change at any time. The time you feel it, you may be excited by the dancers, or maybe the gongon beater is bringing some styles into the drumming. By that time you can change to bring the music up. If you have been playing with the same people for some time, you will all get the same idea of changing, and you will know how to be changing so that dondon and gongon can be following each other. If you pick a style that doesn't give a good sound with the others, you can keep on changing until you find one that fits. Once you have got a good one, you can keep on playing it and moving with the group. As the dancers become interested, those watching will also show it, and you can bring the music up. But any time you decide to bring a style into any of the dances, you have to get a style which can follow the sound of the dance. Whether you want dondon styles or gongon styles, it must be following the beat of the dance. Otherwise you will spoil it.

"That is why it is important to learn the beat very well. You have no fault in your playing; what I am teaching you is what you are doing. But as you have been playing here, sometimes you become confused. Do you know the reason why? Sometimes you need to pick some styles, and by that time you become confused because as you decide to pick a style at the moment you are playing, you don't know the kind of style you are going to pick. By all means you have to become confused. But anytime you can get the one which is following the sound and also which can be sounding the same as the one you are playing, then it can be put inside and there will not be any confusion in it. Then you can even mix the dances and it will be all right because you will be bringing a correct style to be moving straightforward with the beat. Sometimes when we are playing Takai, I used to bring a style which can sound like the Gonja people's Damba. I can play it for Takai while it is not for Takai, and I can also pick styles from the Dagomba side to put inside the Gonja dances, and all will be following correctly. And as for Kondalia and Takai, we can mix them too. Sometimes I used to say that when you yourself are playing gongon in Kondalia, it sounds like Takai. It doesn't matter. When you understand a particular beat and are perfect in it, you will know what styles are suitable inside.

"What you should have in mind if you are going to make a style or change to another topic on the drum is that you should lower your drumming down before you take your style. If you don't make up your mind or cool your drum before you make your style, you will spoil the whole thing. The one you are playing, you will spoil it, and the next style too that you're getting to, you will spoil that one also. If you are playing by heart or very fast, you will spoil everything. You have to make it baalim; you have to be slow before you get to the next style.

"The moment you are to start, you have to start it slowly. You should be thinking of the present style and how it should be. When you get inside a little, you can start beating it hard. By then you will think for yourself and you will remember some styles. According to my experience as I have been watching you all this time, the reason why you sometimes make mistakes is that you are not relying on the style you are beating. Whenever you get into one particular style or dance to beat, don't be thinking to the next one. You are thinking, 'Oh, I am playing this; well, I also know how to play that.' You should stop thinking of that and just rely on the style you are beating to lead you and help you remember. By then all confusion will be out of you when you change. Whenever you are playing and you want to move to another particular style, you have to think about the styles you have made already and compare them to the next style you are getting to. You have to think about the beat you are making. Then compare the styles together and see how you are going to pick an easy way into the next one.

"Here is an example. From the time you are to begin, you begin about three or five seconds and you have got the main style as your first style, which also resembles the next one you have to get to as your second style. So you have the first style and the second style which resembles it. Come to it slowly and then get the second style easily. Your new style is then coming on top of your present one and following it. It is best to be moving from the low ones and then come up, up, up to the new ones, and not be introducing them fast. Then you can bring styles and you can also play backwards without any confusion. If you find a style and you like it, you can continue beating it for some time so that people can hear it well before you bring some changes. You can't just start at this moment and then change to another style again. It's not good. You have to play for some few minutes, and you can compare the styles and the sound of the dance; you can be thinking, 'I want to bring this style inside. Will it be nice for this dance?' By then you can rely on the topic of the drum and pick a style which fits and put it inside. But to bring on the new style by heart is not good. You will spoil the dance. You have to follow my steps and play with respect."

"Play with respect?" I asked.

"Yes. That is how I drum. I am playing with respect. I don't play roughly; I pay attention to what I play. Sometimes when you know something too much, you can do it in a rough way and add something unnecessary inside. I don't do that. If you are beating a drum, you shouldn't beat by heart. You can change styles any time or you can just continue beating a particular style if you want it. It is according to the dance. One who knows the beat very well can keep it moving with the dance. Those playing only the same style have not learned how to drum, and those changing styles are the better ones. You once asked me about the differences in the way they are beating Takai in the villages and in the towns. I told you that in this Dagbon, it is the village people who play one main style of the dance and don't change. And it is the village style that people won't like. It is because those in the towns have had more experience with the beat, and they know it better.

And they have added more styles so that they can play and keep on changing the beat to make the music more interesting."

"How do you talk about all this in Dagbani?"

"*Wadol' yini* is the main-style music, the one they don't change or bring other styles inside. It is steady music. The young people are playing like that. Usually they don't know styles and they play wadol' yini, that is, only the main style. Or else they play by heart, yirin. They are always trying to change it in a rough way because they don't know how to change smoothly. But if an old man is playing, it will be steady and it also changes. We call it *wagolgirli*, that he is curving the dance. It is steady changing play. That is the best. The changes come according to the dance. As he is beating and changing, it is *dol' soli,* that is, he is following the way.

"Steady changing music is the feeling of the drummer, that is, the particular one who is drumming, that's what he feels. As he is drumming, sometimes people are also dancing. He watches their feet and how they take their feet for the dance. He watches the movement of the body and the feet, and as the dancer takes his steps in the dance, he will drum according to it. That is why I told you earlier that I had wanted you to call the Takai drummers and dancers for you alone to study, because there is one particular man who is very good at dancing, and you will see how he will be taking his feet. There is also one particular drummer who really watches that man. When the dancer lifts his feet and moves his body, then that man will play the music according to the movement of the body. Then you will see clearly how it comes together and how it changes according to how he dances. If he starts moving his feet and his body, the drummer will drum according to his movements. Immediately he stops, you will see that the one drumming in tune with him will also stop. Then you will see how it is his dance movements which bring the changes of the drumming.

"There are many different styles of dancing, and you would see all of them and know them. We have individual dancers and they have individual styles of dancing, and we know how to play with each man and he will dance according to our playing. And you will see how we change according to each individual dancer. Also, they dance in a circle, so when a particular dancer comes to the one drumming, the one beating will drum according to that dancer. Another man will come and the one drumming will drum according to his movements, and you will see how individually we play in accordance with their movements. Immediately a dancer comes to us, we give him his beat. Because already we know the type of his dance, we just play in accordance with his feet and the movement of his body, and we get him.

"So it is the particular beat and the movement of the feet and body that tells you how to change your styles. But when we are playing alone and there are no dancers, and I keep on changing the beat, that means that I am talking with the drum. When a dancer comes just to look and not to dance at any particular moment when I am drumming, then he knows what I am doing. That dancer knows what I am saying with my drum.

"The steady changing dance is the best play. Sometimes a new dancer jumps into the dance. You have to keep on changing the beat until you see the type of beat that is good for his dance, and then you play that tune for him and he continues dancing. I will give you an example. Sometimes you can go to find a girl outside. You meet her and talk to her, and you want to have contact with her. You would not think she has some styles within her, but when you take her to your room, immediately you get into her you see that she will give you some movement. By all means you have to give her a reply. Likewise too, if you bring a girl to your room and she is not experienced, if you get into her and she does not give any movement, sometimes you will try to move her to see whether you can get her active. And if she does not become active, that means you have to do it coolly with her just as she is lying. So it is the same thing with drumming. Immediately a dancer runs in, you give him different styles. If it is a new dancer, you change until you give him his type of beat, and then you continue with that beat."[14]

In African music, excellence arises when the combination of rhythms is translated into meaningful action; people participate best when they can "hear" the rhythms, whether through understanding or dance. The most important issues of improvisation, in most African musical idioms, are matters of repetition and change. We have already discussed repetition as a way of emphasizing and clarifying the drum language, and now we must understand repetition as a corollary to the notion of a rhythmic phrase. Within the various ways that African music is repetitive, a drummer takes his time and repeats his styles to allow an interesting beat to continue, or a repeated rhythmic response provides a stable basis to clarify other rhythms which change. Repetition is an integral part of the music. It is necessary to bring out fully the rhythmic tension that characterizes a particular "beat," and in this sense, repetition is the key factor which focuses the organization of the rhythms in

an ensemble. The repetition of a well-chosen rhythm continually reaffirms the power of the music by locking that rhythm, and the people
listening or dancing to it, into a dynamic and open structure. The
rhythms in African music may relate by cutting across each other or by
calling or responding to each other, but in either case, because of the
conflict of African cross-rhythms, the power of the music is not only
captured by repetition, it is magnified.

The forceful and exciting organization of the rhythms in an African
musical composition has often been refined over the years, as in any
classical tradition, by masters of its technique. The power of the music
is already within the dynamic way the rhythms are established in relationship; it does not come from any single rhythmic line. As we have
noted, the main concern of an African drummer is not so much to
create new rhythms as to give form and organization to those already
there. A drummer avoids "rough" beating because *precision* of play is
necessary for maximum definition of form. He demonstrates the potential of rhythms which are in an interesting and familiar relationship,
and he does not seek to demonstrate his technical virtuosity with innovations which cannot fit into the ongoing musical context. New styles are
built from simple modifications of existing patterns, perhaps through
the replacement of a single note. The flashiest or fanciest drumming is
often criticized as secondary, and truly original style consists in the
subtle perfection of strictly respected form.[15] The lead drummer is the
focus and not the basis of the music: the quality of his improvisations
depends on their ability to highlight the other drums; similarly, without
the other rhythms, the improvisations of a great drummer would be
meaningless. In short, a drummer uses repetition to reveal the *depth*
of the musical structure.[16]

It is usually quite difficult for a Westerner to understand this approach to repetition. The connection between repetition and depth is
one of the dominant themes emerging from the study of African music,
and I hope that the significance of this connection will become clearer
as we examine it from different perspectives throughout the rest of the
book. Jones was probably the first scholar to recognize and write about
this dimension of the music. Referring to a song, he defined what he
called the Rule of Repeats: "The first half of the song is repeated and
then followed by the second half which is repeated three times in all.
The complete performance makes one unit."[17] What we perceive as
merely repetition is perceived as a whole unit. In effect, African music
is *both slow and fast.* A participant or a spectator will pay attention to
the movement of the improvisation as well as the intricacies of the beat.

The repetition of a style is important as a way of maintaining the tension of an ensemble's beat, and the duration of the style is important in terms of the crucial decision of when to change to get the maximum effect. In the timing of the change, the drummer demonstrates his own awareness of the rhythmic potential of the music and his personal control of its inherent power, but most important, he *demonstrates his involvement with the social situation* in a dramatic *gesture* that will play upon the minds and bodies of his fellow performers and his audience. Charles Keil has provided a fine illustration of this point:

> When a jazz buff wants to convince you that a particular performer is great, he is likely to point to a single gesture or a portion of the music in which the musician is playing with the pulse in a particularly perverse manner, asking simultaneously, "Isn't that bit a gas?" To exaggerate slightly, a classics fan will wait respectfully until the piece is finished or, better still, put a score in your lap and ask "Do you see how beautifully it all fits together?"[18]

As the music engages people to participate by actively and continuously integrating the various rhythms, a change at just the appropriate moment will pace people's exposure to the deeper relationships of the rhythms, involving an audience for different lengths of time with the various rhythms which have been judged to fit most properly. In the control of his changes, the drummer directs the movement of the whole occasion. People are involved with the rhythms of the scene, and the drummer, through the depth and care of his aesthetic command, organizes and focuses the expression of the power of both social and musical relationships.

The changes in African music, therefore, emphasize the power of the rhythms in several ways. As a gesture, a change in style reaffirms the preceding style by not putting so much pressure on the rhythms that they lose their distinctiveness or clarity, and the change reestablishes the tension in another way. In his changes, a great drummer converses with different drums and paces the audience through a rhythmic commentary which stresses and asserts the complexity of the ensemble. The drummer keeps the music moving forward fluidly, and by continually changing his accents and his beating, he thus relies on the multiplicity of *possible* ways to cut and combine the rhythms. Westerners trying to appreciate African music must always keep in mind the fact that the music is organized to be open to the rhythmic interpretation a drummer, a listener, or a dancer wishes to contribute. *The music is perhaps best considered as an arrangement of gaps where one may add a rhythm, rather than as a dense pattern of sound.* In the conflict of the rhythms, it is the space between the notes from which the dynamic tension comes, and it is the silence which constitutes the musical form as much as does the sound. It is in this sense that the small boys tapping on bottles can make more forceful music than a group of Westerners pounding on drums with all their might. Just as important as his own contribution is the time a drummer allows the other musicians to have their say, and most important, of course, the musicians leave room for a dancer.

A good rhythm, if it is to enhance itself, should both fill a gap in the other rhythms and create an emptiness that may be similarly filled. One note placed at the right point in the music will prove the strength of the drummer more than the execution of a technically difficult phrase. The good drummer has the strength to listen to all the ongoing rhythms and still find a place to add his own beat, balancing his accents on the edge of disorder and confusion, rendering a complementary wholeness out of the separate and conflicting parts. A musician can afford to take his time because of the openness of the arrangements to various rhythmic interpretations. He does not have to change much because he is not trying to monopolize these possibilities. He understands that he is only a part of the ensemble. He knows that he is not responsible for providing all the interest and that he can only suggest some of the potential which is there. It is for these reasons that the old men are recognized to be the best drummers. They can play for hours and not get tired, while young men in their prime will exhaust themselves with strenuous displays of virtuosity. The old men do not become confused: they listen and they have the patience to wait for the right moment. Further on in this chapter we will examine from several perspectives this element of maturity in judgement which characterizes the best music, but for the moment, we can relate good improvisational judgement to a recognition that the rhythmic arrangement, as both a structure and a process, is what effectively organizes the power of the expression. Crucial as the changes are to keep the music dynamic, African music is more dependent on repetition. There is progression in a melody, continuity in a rhythm. It is only after we have become accustomed to African music, therefore, that we can begin to recognize how slowly the music changes. Some rhythms will always remain stable and unchanging, and if there is to be a transition in an ensemble's arrangement, all the rhythms will usually shift together into the new relationship.

In contrast, in Western popular music which has been influenced by or derived from African sources, more supporting instruments in an ensemble will tend to make changes at various times, and what is obscured is the improvisational focus on a beat that emerges from rhythmic relationships. Basically, this observation is another way of saying that the polymetric character of African music has been partially abandoned or lost; a single main beat has taken an increased role in the creative development and appreciation of the music. On the other hand, James Brown is the most popular Afro-American musician in Africa partially because the rhythms in his arrangements are extremely open and stable, and his songs generally involve a bridge in which all the instruments change together and then return to their former relationship. To an African ear, James Brown times these changes extremely well as he and his band move through the transitions of a song, and his arrangements bear close comparison with African arrangements.[19] His music makes sense, particularly, as we shall see, in terms of the relationship of African music and dance. Contemporary African musicians who are creating in the popular genre have probably been influenced by James Brown and other Western, Afro-American, and Latin musicians, yet the African musicians are building their music, usually quite self-consciously, on traditional arrangements and rhythms. They are playing for African audiences whose sensibilities are also shaped both by the continuingly vital older traditions and by the innovative potentials suggested by electric instruments and imported recordings.

There are many great musicians recording popular music in Africa today, and it is fitting here to list some of them from just a selected few of Africa's nations. Their individual styles are distinctive of their countries of origin, where they are celebrities, but most of these musicians can also point to an international following of people who identify with them and who are proud to claim them as "Africans." In a very real sense their names and their music enhance sentiments of African unity. From Nigeria come rhythmically innovative composers like Fela Anikulapo Kuti, Sonny Okosun, and Victor Uwaifo; Juju musicians like Sunny Ade, Ebenezer Obey, Dele Abiodun, I. K. Dairo, Prince Adekunle, and Idowu Animasawun; Apala musicians like Haruna Ishola and Ayinla Omowura; and Highlife musicians like Stephen Osadebe and Paulson Kalu, along with their younger counterparts Oliver de Coque, Nico Mbarga and his Rocafil Jazz, and Ikenga. From Zaïre and Congo comes perhaps the most popular music in Africa, played by Franco, Le Seigneur Rochereau, Verkys, Trio Madjesi, Jean Bokelo,

Dr. Nico, and the great orchestras O. K. Jazz, Lipua-Lipua, Kamale, Bella-Bella, Vèvè, Kiam, Cavacha, Sosoliso, Bantous, Conga-Succès, Minzoto, Mando Nègro Kwala-Kwa, and L'Afrisa International. The prolific Ghanaian Highlife scene features Nana P. S. K. Ampadu and the African Brothers Band, K. Gyasi's Noble Kings, Jerry Hansen's Ramblers International, Wulomei, Sweet Talks, City Boys, Ashanti Brothers, Royal Brothers, Dzadzeloi, Parrots, Nananom, Uhuru, Amaniampongs, and the groups led by Konadu, Yamoah, Akwaboah, K. Frimpong, Oko, F. Kenya, Ebo Taylor, Eddie Donkor, Koo Nimo, Teacher, C. K. Mann, Pat Thomas, E. T. Mensah, Eddie Quansah, Opambuo, Maa Amanua, Oppong, Kakaiku, Bob Pinodo, and the Sannah Brothers. Ivory Coast has François Lougah, Ernest Djedje, Eba Aka Jerome, Amedée Pierre, and Daouda. Kenya has the Western Jazz Band, Victoria Jazz Band, Sakade Band, and DO 7 Band. Benin claims the marvelous Orchestre Polyrythmo de Cotonou. Mali is represented by the Ambassadeurs, Super Biton, and Rail Band. Guinea is represented by its wonderful singer Kouyaté Sory Kandia, the Horoya Band of Kankan, and the Ensemble Instrumental de la Radiodiffusion National; and the country's fantastic musical creativity is being displayed by the more modern orchestras Camayenne Sofa, Bembeya Jazz, 22 Band de Kankan, Super Boiro, Balla's Balladins, Syliauthentique, and many others. The South African Miriam Makeba is now resident in Guinea, and the music of South Africa's Dark City Sisters can be heard throughout the continent. Great stars like Nigeria's Rex Lawson and Celestine Ukwu and Ghana's E. K. Nyame have passed away, and we may expect that the names on such a list will be changing; but many of these musicians have been playing for years, and we may hope that they will remain as prominent in their field as they have been. They and the other fine upcoming talents represent the continuity of the genius we are examining within the classical musical traditions.

When we can perceive the unities within the styles of these diverse musicians, we are beginning to use our growing recognition of the aesthetic sensibility common to African musical expression. As the various elements of this sensibility begin to assume, in the course of our study, a systematic coherence, they begin to form an extremely complicated network. In the verbal exposition of a topic, the various elements of the whole are necessarily isolated and elaborated in individual focus, and to perceive the relationship of these elements requires patience and effort. At this point, before we move into another aspect of our discussion of improvisation and musical excellence, it may be worthwhile to pause in order to remember that the troublesome complexity of the relationships these elements assume is what indicates to us that we are successfully beginning to recognize the integrity and distinctiveness of a different cultural world. Though in some instances we may feel as if we had been able to step easily into a full perception of someone else's way of looking at things, achieving such a perception is generally a very difficult project. On the one hand, we can authentically recognize the integrity and distinctiveness of a different cultural sensibility only if we perceive it as a whole, preferably through personal experience. We might move into an alien sensibility if we had a chance to live with it for a long enough time, but we would not necessarily become aware of the significance of its distinctive elements, and we might not be able to draw in detail the lines which separate two cultural worlds. Thus, on the other hand, if we wish to be able to discuss and to think systematically about the many dimensions of an alien sensibility, we must proceed unhurriedly until a full pattern emerges. The reader may perhaps be encouraged by what we already know about the context of African music, that in one sense the deepest unities may be achieved when people relate through a better awareness of their differences.

Let us review, then, some of the notions presented thus far. We have discussed several ways in which a kind of tension is built into the formal organizational characteristics which we considered in the preceding chapter. The interweaving of diverse and multiple rhythms is coherent only when one actively participates by finding and maintaining a point of reference from which to perceive the conflicting rhythms as an ensemble. Synchrony is incidental and derivative from the cross-rhythms, not deliberate and normal as in Western music.[20] Through the way an African musician accentuates and changes his phrases, he places subtle pressure on the rhythmic relationships of the ensemble and on the dynamic qualities of transitions. By choosing rhythms which will relate clearly to the other rhythms, by controlling the duration of a rhythm, and by timing the introduction of discontinuity to his beating, he creates with a mind to generating and coordinating an expression of maximum power and vitality.

We can continue our discussion of the musician's aesthetic intention by inquiring into the purpose and meaning of such musical expression in the African context. We will begin this discussion through an examination of how variations arise in Ewe drumming. All in all, the Ewe drummer creates with many of the same considerations as a Takai drummer, but certain points may perhaps be more easily understood if presented in the Ewe context because they follow from things we have already learned about Ewe drumming. In many Ewe dances, the drumming is specific to the choreography, and a drummer must change his patterns continuously. Though Ewe master drumming is extremely complicated, a drummer is likely to have a clear order in his mind because many dances are performed by clubs which rehearse extensively before submitting their efforts to criticism. In Agbekor drumming, the recurrence of the turning phrase gives the master drummer a chance to think, and he can of course watch the lead dancer for cues. As we saw in the preceding chapter, a master drummer's patterns leave room for the ensemble, and a master drummer is concerned to time the alternation of his longer and shorter phrases.[21] Jones aptly applies an organic metaphor in his description of Ewe master drumming:

> To play a string of master drum standard patterns even if each is repeated several times is simply not African music. The full flower of the music is in the variations of which the standard pattern is the nucleus. The musical technique is this: the master announces a standard pattern and repeats it several times to establish it. Now each standard pattern consists of several phrases or sentences. Any of these can serve as a nucleus for variations. But the first phrase is all-important. It is the SEED of the pattern. The whole standard pattern grows out of this seed. So also do the variations on that pattern. Thus after establishing a standard pattern, the master drummer, by extension, simile, or any other artifice at his command, using that first phrase as the germinal idea, builds up spontaneously a series of variations which continue as long as the inspiration of that particular phrase lasts.[22]

The full turning step of the slow Agbekor dance is played with two sticks, and I was taught to play it as *Ton rebegeden, ton tegeden, ton tegedegen, gazagezegen, tenten, rebegeden, gazegezegen, kleben tenten, kleben tenten, rebegeden, gazegen, dza dzadza*; the drum language is *Tro godogodo, to trogodo, mitro godogodo, mia dzo, kpamkpam, godogodo, mia dzo, godo kpamkpam, godo kpamkpam, godogodo yigodo, blewu blewu.* ("Turn, and be sure. Stop, and turn around. You turn, and be sure. We are going far away. Be sure. We are going. Be sure. Far away. Be sure. Far away. Be sure. You must go, carefully, carefully.") The rhythmic phrasing of the turning tends to avoid the four beat, though the drummer will keep his time in fours. Looking at the notation, we should remember that *be, ge,* and *ze* do not have quite as strong a stress as *te* and *de,* and that *ga* is here only a marking beat struck by the edge of the fist that holds the stick. Extending through nearly six bell patterns, the full turning lasts more than fifteen seconds, and as the central rhythmic theme of the dance, it can provide dozens of variations. That the variations come from the turning pattern gives the drumming *continuity* and *unity* throughout the changing phrases and accents. As Ibrahim Abdulai might say, it is steady changing music. In the rough notation of the turning and variation illustrated here, note how the breaks give the supporting drums their say. The variation is on the fragment *rebegede* (here standing for *milawoe, meaning* "we will do" or "we are ready"), and the stress shifts from *ge* to *be* to *ge* as the drummer returns to the full turning at the midpoint of the bell pattern. The notation, as usual, is schematic, ignoring some delays and nuances particular drummers introduce into Atsimewu's beating. The purpose here, however, is to show the movement of a typical variation.*

Slow Agbekor (full turning and style)

Bell

Rattle
Atsimewu

Atsimewu

Ton   re-be- ge- den,   ton te-ge-den,   ton te-ge-de-gen,   ga-
Tro   go-do- go- do,   to tro-go-do,   mitro go-do-go-do,

zege-zegen,   ten-ten,   re-be-ge-den,   ga- zege-zegen, (ka)(ka)   kle-ben   ten-ten,
mia dzo,   kpam-kpam, go-do-go-do,   mia dzo,   go-do   kpam-kpam,
Atsimewu

x   x   x   kle-ben   ten-ten,   re- be-ge- den,   ze-gen,
(ka)   (ka)(ka)   go-do   kpam-kpam, go- do-go-do   ga-   dza
                                                          yi-go-do,   blewu
Atsimewu

dza-dza.   x   x   x Rebe- ge-de,   re- be-ge- de,
Atsimewu blewu. (ka) (ka) (ka) Mi- la-woe,   mi- la-woe,

re- be- ge- de,   x   x   x re- be-ge- de,   re- be-ge- de,
mi-   la-woe,   (ka)   (ka)   (ka) mi-   la-woe,   mi-   la-woe,
Atsimewu

re- be-ge- de.   Ton →
mi-   la-woe.

Though the style is uncomplicated, it is particularly lovely in the way it leads back to the turning as the accent shifts, and the best drummers will increase the effect as they pay close attention to timbre and volume. That the variations are derived from the turning phrase hardly limits their potential. Some, like the one given above, are prized for the continuity they contribute, while others, like the two given below, are special because of the accentuation or the dialogues they provide. (The meaning of the first style is *tro godo,* or "turn around," and the meaning of the second style is *mi yi ngogbe, mi yi ngo, mi yi ngo, mi yi ngogbe,* or "advance forward, advance, advance, advance forward.")

Slow Agbekor (Atsimewu styles with Kroboto)

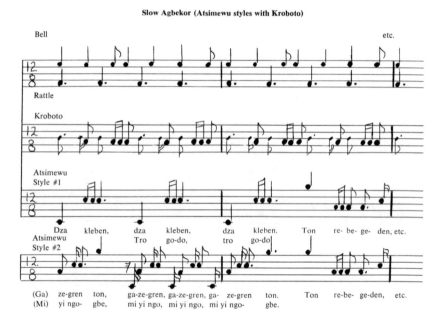

Depending on the variation, the supporting drummers may choose to modify their patterns, much as we have shown for Kidi in the preceding chapter. *

In dances less standardized than Agbekor, the master drummer will use the same techniques. One corollary of the fact that the name of a dance is also the name of a rhythm is that each dance has not only a distinctive "beat" provided by the ensemble but also a characteristic rhythm which serves as a central theme for improvisational elaboration. In Agbekor, the master drummer's variations are based on both the ensemble and the turning phrase, and they work both as accentuation and as a coherent sequence. In many Ewe dances, the generative role of a thematic phrase is paralleled by a focus on various responsive patterns which the master drummer introduces and from which he builds his variations. While the bell, rattle, and Kagan continue with the beat, the major supporting drums change to the appropriate response. Before the master drummer shifts to a new style, he will give a changing signal to alert the other drummers, and then he will play a "mother phrase" for the responsive rhythm he wants to call. Once the supporting drums are established, he can throw in accents or roll in the same way we presented in the notation for Sohu.[23] This format is typical of Ewe drumming, not only in popular dances like Agbadza and Gahu but also in those cults where the drums used are like gongons.*

Everyone thus listens to and depends on the master drummer to keep the ensemble together. If he goes too quickly, he will confuse the drummers and dancers. If his beating is not clear, they will miss their cues. As he displays, he must not play too many beats, for to do so would destroy the relationship of his style to the mother phrase or the response, and he must not overemphasize a particular accent or style by playing it too much. Like the Dagomba lead drummer (who also uses specific rhythms to cue his group), the Ewe master drummer must also take his time even as he keeps the music moving forward. And the way he plays against the responses of his supporting drums parallels the way a Dagomba dondon beater relies on the gongon. Yet again it is important for us to remember that though the master drummer is the one who chooses patterns and puts the most pressure on the beat, the other drums enable him to play his variations. The precision of their responses gives him a chance to hear the counter-rhythms; moreover, should the master drummer forget a pattern or run out of ideas, he can rely on a supporting drummer to suggest something by playing a different response or by improvising on the response he is playing.

Beyond the obvious interdependence of the musicians, we can clearly perceive here for the first time a significant dimension of the African drummer's improvisational attitude. The master drummer derives his variations as much from the specific master rhythms which epitomize the dance as from the responsive instrumental background and the characteristic beat; the forcefulness of the music, therefore, comes not only from the orchestral organization but also from the improvisational organization itself. The best drummers distinguish themselves not through the intensity of their off-beating but through the *complexity and movement of their improvisational organization.* Jones comments nicely on this point:

> While Mr. Tay [Desmund Tay, the distinguished Ewe musician, for
> many years Ghana's cultural attaché in London, who collaborated
> with Jones on *Studies in African Music*] was actually drumming his
> variations they appeared to the European listener to be a fascinat-
> ing and effortless flow of kaleidoscopic patterns in very free rhythm
> which crossed that of *Gankogui* [the bell] with complete abandon
> and yet which were obviously harnessed to it as the periodic reappear-
> ance of the little phrase *gaga gi* ending on the low bell-note bore
> witness. [Jones then transcribes the drumming into the onomatopoeic
> nonsense syllables.] What have we here? it is none other than a
> spontaneous yet closely organized poem in pure sound. This is no
> random collection of rhythmic patterns, loosely based on the stan-
> dard original.[24]

Jones's suggestion that we might listen to African drumming as if we
were listening to poetry is very good advice. Without tight organization,
the improvisations become meaningless, and the ensemble cannot continue because the supporting drummers will lose their precision and
sense of involvement. In the notion that the music is both slow and
fast, therefore, we realize again that a great drummer uses his improvisational organization not so much to extend or expand a rhythm as to
reveal its depth. Beyond a drummer's rhythmic accentuation is the
slower beat of the responsive framework and the even slower movement of the variations on the central rhythmic phrase. Those who have
pressed us to recognize the achievements of extemporaneous improvisation have often underemphasized the importance of organization to
the critical aesthetic sense. Ultimately, precise and impressive control
of improvisational style distinguishes excellence in African musical
idioms, and the worst mistake in such a context is not participatory restraint but random expression.

In African music, expression is subordinated to a respect for formal
relationships, and technique is subordinated to communicative clarity.[25]
On this consideration stands the integrity of the music as a social force.
J. David Sapir has written a marvelous article on the aesthetic standards expounded by a native critic on a form of funeral praise-singing
in Senegal. The greatest improvised verses and the cleverest lyrics mean
nothing unless they work with the chorus to build clarity and not confusion, "the smooth and harmonious interchange between solo and ensemble, between individual and group." Sapir's exposition is this:

> Control of the on-going movement is completely in the hands of the
> soloist who is singing at the time, with the crucial manipulation
> being the *buj*, i.e., "kill" or termination. It is here that the soloist,

by pre-figuring the melodic line, announces that he has completed
his verse. If the *buj* is executed correctly the ensemble will *fon,*
i.e., sing the melody, without pause and in unison; otherwise there
will be confusion. It is exactly here that the inexperienced singer will
fall down, and as far as the singer's judgements are concerned the
buj is the acid test for correct performance: "But when you hear
the song without precision (any old way) and the singer becomes
quiet without killing (then the ensemble is lost). . . . Should you speed
up and forego the killing it will not be good. The singer . . . looks
for the road by which he is to kill so that everyone in the ensemble
will hear the song and remember it.[26]

A good number of Dagomba dances are played in a similar way, with
long speeches by the lead drummer followed by a unified ensemble response.* Likewise, within the complicated off-beat accentuation patterns
of Ewe drumming, the way to stay on time is to play forward to the
beginning of the next phrase or the next point of unity with the bell.
What Sapir describes is the same kind of decision and responsibility
that a Dagomba or an Ewe drummer must face.

As our critical approach to African music becomes more alert, we
should recognize that the aesthetics of the music seem more and more
based on a sensibility which values a particular *balance* of inherent
tendencies. We cannot say simply that repetition intensifies or that off-
beats astound. Examples proliferate of the dialectical manner in which
the aesthetic potential of African music is realized: the specialization
of cross-rhythmic apart-playing should evoke the mediated appreciation
of wholeness; the overlapping of call-and-response yields intriguing
accents; the traditionally established rhythmic organization reinforces
the situational commentary of the songs; the continuing dynamic tension of conflicting rhythms is varied through the appropriate timing of
dramatic gestures which change the tension; the concentration on precision and control stabilizes the expansion of feeling. The balancing of
disparate modalities of musical expression is contrary to what we as
Westerners expect to find in an African musical event.

We are accustomed to think that things work in traditional societies
because people are secure in their knowledge of the symbolic meaning
of what they do, that there is perhaps a symbolic representation of this
feeling of shared meaning which may be attributed to their art and to
all their expressions and activities. It is a simplistic view, one which
our own conceptions of what a "tribe" is sometimes make us prone to
project: that in any social situation, since those involved believe in and
know what they are there for, they can do it wholeheartedly so that

everybody feels satisfied and the occasion becomes a harmonious success. In African contexts, the symbolic, esoteric or moral meanings of songs and dances are certainly significant, but common knowledge of these meanings is not as important as we often imagine it to be for the effective integration of a community in a musical context. With our Western notions of "meaning" as being a special kind of knowledge, we must be cautioned against assuming that African music functions primarily on such a level and that we fail to understand the music because we lack knowledge of the details of the music's symbolic meaning. Dagomba drummers, as Ibrahim Abdulai noted, use their drums to beat languages they do not understand themselves, and many Dagombas, including drummers, do not know the drum language of some of their most important music, like Bangumanga or Zhem.[27] Particularly in African religious cults, where the power of music is very vividly manifested, the language of songs and drums is often obscure. M. J. Field, in her study of Ga religion, observed that "The religious songs [of the *Kple* cults] are in the forgotten *Obutu* dialect, and are often mere gibberish to both singers and hearers."[28] And Alfred Métraux, in his fine book on that most intricately syncretistic African religion, Voodoo (that great symbol of the virtuosity of Western misinterpreters of Africa), has also made note of some data illustrating that our lack of identification with the cultural base of shared feelings and meanings is not always at issue:

> Little attention is paid to what the words [of the ritual songs] mean. Many are incomprehensible, particularly when the song contains passages in 'langage'. *Hungan* and *mambo* [officials in the religion] make no attempt to hide their embarrassment when asked to interpret them. They get out of it by making things up. What is most important in ceremonies is the celebration of the *loa* [the divine spirits] by song and dance and not by phrases, often meaningless, foolish or absurd, which merely serve as vehicle for the vocal music.[29]

In the words of a Macumba priestess in Brazil, "The rhythm is more important than the meaning of the words. Our gods respond to rhythm above all else. When the rhythm changes, their behavior shifts accordingly."[30]

In Tamale I went to great efforts to record the famous singer Yakubu Silmindo, known popularly as The Entertainer. When I asked him what the songs he sang were about, he said that he did not really understand some of them, that he would have to go ask the old men who had given him the proverbs which he had set to music. People from various walks of life told me that The Entertainer's songs were in "deep Dagbani," which they could not "hear." They did not have to understand the songs to be moved, but nevertheless, they valued the songs' expression of their deepest traditional sentiments. What was important to them was that the songs had a depth which they enjoyed trying to interpret even while they acknowledged that the songs were often beyond them. In effect, the music does and does not rely on a specific traditional meaning. In more than one sense, music carries the mark of tradition to an occasion, and at a rudimentary level it thus signifies the traditional solidarity of a community; but aesthetically, the music involves people with their community in a more dynamic way, thus recreating the tradition, and, as we discussed this issue in the first chapter, the nature of this involvement is the key to understanding the integrative power of the music. The music works more by encouraging social interaction and participation at each performance than by affirming a fixed set of sanctioned conceptions or beliefs.

In our examination thus far of what musicians do with rhythms during a performance, we should be beginning to recognize that the integration of an African musical event proceeds in a more complicated way than we might have imagined at first. In a context of multiple rhythms, people distinguish themselves from each other while they remain dynamically related. We fail to understand the music because we have difficulty participating with adequate sophistication within the *rhythmic* framework of a specific event. The aesthetic requirement of participation in such a context is the ability to stand back from the rhythms of the scene and find an additional *rhythm* which complements and mediates those other rhythms. As Robert Thompson has keenly observed, the "notion of balance . . . is an aesthetic acid test: the weak dancer [or drummer] soon loses his metric bearings in the welter of competing countermeters and is, so to speak, knocked off balance. . . . Multiple meter is, in brief, a communal examination of percussive individuality."[31]

We are now in a position to state a number of basic conclusions of our discussion of African music. The styles that a drummer plays and the style that he displays are, we must recognize, essentially a commentary on the quality of the rhythmic relationships which have been or can be established in a situation. The quality of these relationships is the relevant aesthetic issue, and in African music, this issue is addressed at every event when a structure of individual rhythms becomes a process which is both mediated and immediate. In this sense, style is another word for the perception of relationships, a dynamic aesthetic attitude which focuses the music on the occasion. Participation in such a multi-rhythmic context involves, in the maintenance of balance, an act of rhythmic interpretation and critical judgement. The formal and traditional relationships are respected not necessarily because they contain any specific meaning but because it is the musical arrangement which provides the possibility for comprehensible improvisation. The formal relationships are vitalized and enhanced in good music, but the musical form is open rather than rigid, set up so that it affords a focus for the expression of individuality that subtly distinguishes an occasion within the context of tradition. The beauty of an expression comes from the special and distinct way the formal structure of the music becomes a process, the way the tradition remains alive, through a rhythm that moves and a particular movement that sophisticates. People look at a musician's style as an exposition of their continuing involvement, and their criticism in such a context is offered as a gesture of support to help him achieve his purpose. A musician's mastery of his art is evidence of his concern to bring forth a fresh dimension of involvement and excitement to the community in which he creates. The confidence and virtuosity of his improvisations therefore demonstrate the power of his mind in the literal exercise of aesthetic command.

In the cult ceremony as well, a young musician is presented with an elaborate and comparable model of music-making. He begins his career with the understanding that power comes from tradition, that his hands are guided by the hands of the dead drummers who have created in his tradition before him, that he should find confidence and not anxiety in their influence on his efforts to achieve an expression of his own particular talents. The model is a way of describing an individual musician's continuity with a deeper source of inspiration than even his own genius and discipline can provide. Thus the individual musician demonstrates his personality precisely by accepting the support and respecting the limitations and potentials of his many relationships to what was before him and what is around him. Then he uses his understanding to bring a living togetherness to the separate elements of an occasion, to provide the music which is Africa's most celebrated means of recreation. His musical creativity directly dramatizes his mind as it is balanced on the understanding that his individuality, like the rhythms that he plays, can only be seen in relationship. In the distinctive style of the expression which he must bring forward in the fulfillment of his complex social role, the personality of the musician becomes important in the sense that the quality and maturity of his aesthetic contribution either

limits or expands the realization of a general concern, determining
whether the people present constitute a community.[32]

For a most satisfactory illustration of the central themes of this study,
we will examine the music-making process on the day when I finally mas-
tered the playing of Kondalia, one of the Takai dances.* Kondalia has
the most difficult drumming of any of the dances of Takai. Ibrahim Abdulai told me that many drummers "fear" the Takai dances because "it
is difficult to breathe well when beating them." If asked, he said, many
drummers would just say they do not know how to play them. Each
dance has its problems. For example, Nyagboli is extremely fast, and
Ibrahim advised me always to keep on changing quickly "or the styles
will just get missing from your head." Kondalia, he said, is usually the
most confusing to the drummers and dancers. The beating is relatively
fast, and though the supporting dondon pattern is the same as in Takai
proper, the composition of the Kondalia "beat" is very complicated, and
the styles of the lead dondon cross the other rhythms without the benefit
of those clear points of improvisational unity that so helpfully emerge in
the other dances. Kondalia thus presented me with an opportunity to
find my limitations as a Westerner playing African music; with the other
dances I could not be sure if I were "cheating" by inappropriately
stressing convergent notes as cues to my timing and changes. The impli-
cation is that though I was succeeding in duplicating the rhythms, and
even if my tones and accents were correct, I might not be *hearing* the
music as my teachers were hearing it and I would therefore lack the
sensibility to create with authority within the music's form. Proper performance of Kondalia, on the other hand, would offer as close an opportunity as I had to measure a concern which was not very easily objecti-
fiable. In the design of this book, my success with Kondalia can serve as
the third of three events, beginning with my alienation and recognition
of a different cultural world in the cult and continuing with my resolution and commitment on the bus, which I am using as symbols of the
progress of my participation in my first year of learning about African
music.

After all my early efforts, frustrations, drifting, and fun, after all the
extreme and ambiguous personal situations in which I had tested myself,
a long process of learning to see myself as I was seen had brought me
to a point on the bus when I was ready to pursue what I had been looking for. By avoiding well-defined social roles and by refusing to judge
my experiences from any single point of view, I had exercised a kind of
discipline in the hope of opening myself to the potentials of my identity.

The subjective complexity which had originally attracted me to Dagomba drumming had become a part of all my involvements, and I had come to terms with my motivations so that I was willing to be led by my love for the music in a way that freed me from the vanity of thinking that what I might accomplish would have any importance or use should I return to the United States. In one of the first years of the drought which recently destroyed so much life in the Sudan, I left cool Accra to live in Tamale when getting a bucket of water for a bath was often a major difficulty there. The caretaker at the Government Workers' Transit Quarters, where I stayed, was an old man who helped me when I knew no one in town and who entertained me with stories about a time when animals made the night unsafe for people. Another old man, whose tiny restaurant was known simply as the Old Man's, treated me with special kindness when I took my meals, discussing my progress in my learning and encouraging me in my work. Most important, I found in Ibrahim Abdulai a serious man and a great master, who recognized the source of my dedication perhaps more clearly than I, and who, in an act of generosity, was willing to teach me throughout its unfolding.

Tamale is a wonderful place for music.* Almost every evening, I could go walking and find music; I would follow a sound to its source and watch and listen. People from many different tribes live in Tamale, and they are often either practicing or displaying their cultural music. Depending on one's luck, it is possible to meet Akans doing their beautiful Adowa dance, Dagartis practicing their xylophones, or Ewes celebrating a funeral with Agbadza drumming or sometimes playing Borborbor, a prototypical Highlife beat produced on a number of small drums and, occasionally, a trumpet. Near the Old Man's restaurant, that time, I often saw a blind Frafra man accompanied by a small boy who sang. The man used only a gourd rattle slightly smaller than a basketball; indeed, he tossed it around in his hands as if he could be a member, or even the star, of a certain famous barnstorming basketball team. He accented the various rhythms of the seeds inside the gourd by slapping and tapping the outside with his palms and fingers, and seeing made it rather more difficult to believe that only one person was playing.[33] On the other side of town, a Gurunsi man sang every night about how lonely he was, to the accompaniment of a three-stringed *moglo* guitar, homemade in a modern way, the body from a one-gallon can and the neck from a mop handle. The Gurunsis resident in Tamale sometimes gather to play their music, using several gongons and dondons but primarily relying on a number of whistle-like flutes on which they build rapid, driving melodies with each musician contributing a single note in his turn; the dancing, unfortunately, is quite beyond description. The Gonjas too have an interesting style of dancing and some marvelous drummers whose beat I particularly enjoy. Anytime an important chief of any of the tribes comes to Tamale, his people generally meet outside the house where he is lodging to play their music and dance late into the night. If many chiefs are coming to meet each other, then everybody, it seems, turns out. Such occasions, of course, are infrequent, perhaps for the good: a stranger is saved from the problem of deciding whether by staying at one place he is missing something somewhere else.

Tamale is, nonetheless, a Dagomba town, and the Dagombas are the most prolific music-makers there. They love music, and the range of their creativity is astounding. For the past two hundred years or so, Dagombas have had musicians who play fiddles which have strings made from horse tails.[34] Though not as central to the Dagomba tradition as drummers, the fiddlers are very popular, and to dance to their music is a lot of fun. The rhythms of their singing and playing are given an extra punch by a number of rattles in cross-rhythmic accompaniment. One meets fiddlers at weddings, funerals, and festivals, and also at the *pito* houses, where non-Muslim Dagombas and others sit and drink a local beer brewed from sorghum. In the evenings, the Simpa groups, which are like clubs for the young people of various neighborhoods, practice for their competitions, singing songs with flute or harmonica and drum accompaniment to Highlife, Rumba, Cha-cha, Kalakala, Meringue, Soul, and Agbadza rhythms. Simpa began about fifty years ago, originating from Kotokoli musical influences. Different groups use different types of instruments, from dondons to sets of square-frame drums to sets of conga and jazz drums made of metal by local blacksmiths. In an active Simpa club, members come out every evening to sing in the chorus. The dancing is done by twelve- to fifteen-year-old girls, who come out, one or two pairs at a time, to dance matching, studied steps with intense concentration. Simpa styles are diverse and always open to influence and change. In recent years, popular movies from India, musical romantic fantasies, have caused a sensation. People remember the songs and set their own words to them. Along with the singing, the melodies provide inspiration for long improvisations on plastic flutes. To fit the music, a young man called Ali Bela, after the swashbuckling hero of some of the films, created a whole style of drumming by using the fingers of one hand on different parts of the bottom of a five-gallon oil drum while using the other hand to play accents on the rim with an empty, small-sized can of evaporated milk. The music is beautiful, and I was impressed by the notion of walking in the streets of Tamale and coming across a musical group with a name like Bombay, gathered to sing Dagomba homilies fitted to Indian movie tunes, their instruments acquired from Western oil companies and food processors and from Asian toy manufacturers. And the young children, who are always interested in music, also have their own style, called Atikatika. Formerly the children danced traditional Dagomba dances when they gathered to play, and Atikatika is a recent development which has swept through Dagbon. The children are true believers, and only rain—or an Indian film—can make them miss their nightly practices. The drummers are boys eight to ten years of age, usually slightly older than the dancers. The dancers, boys aged from four or five to eight, dress in white singlets with matching colored shorts and beanies; they tie metal shakers to their ankles, and they dance precision acrobatic steps in a circle, using the shakers in various ways to cross the heavy, characteristic 12/8 beat of the drums. Unbelievably, the Atikatika children are known for singing witty political songs; several times they have been in trouble with local authorities and the national government, and their music is periodically banned.[35] The chorus is composed of young girls led in high-spirited singing by an older girl, perhaps in her early teens. A few older people help the Atikatika groups solve organizational problems, like acquiring uniforms or arranging transportation when the group is going someplace to display, but it is the children who sit together and plan the music, songs, and dancing.

Musical activity in Tamale reaches high points during festival months and especially during the several months when Dagombas customarily perform the final funeral celebrations for their departed, generally a few months after the burial. Dagomba funerals are spectacles. The final funeral of an important or well-loved man or woman can draw several thousand people as participants and spectators. Small-scale traders also come to do business, setting up their tables to sell cigarettes, coffee, tea, bread, fruits, and other commodities to the milling crowds.[36] Spread out over a large area, all types of musical groups form their circles. In several large circles, relatives and friends dance to the music of dondons and gongons. The fiddlers are also there. After a session in the late afternoon, people rest and begin reassembling between nine and ten o'clock in the evening. By that time, several Simpa groups have already begun playing. Two or three Atikatika groups also arrive and find their positions, and by eleven o'clock the funeral is in full swing. After midnight more groups come to dance Baamaya or other special dances like Jera or Bila, though the latter are not common. Baamaya dancers dress outlandishly, with bells tied to their feet and waists, wearing headdresses and waving fans. The dance is wonderful, and strenuous: while gongons, flutes, and a dondon play the rhythms of Baamaya, the dancers move around their circle, twisting their waists continuously until the funeral closes—at dawn.

Less frequently seen are the *jenjili* singers; two of Dagbon's finest, Yakubu Silmindo and Fuseini Tia, live in Tamale. A jenjili is a bow with a single wire, plucked like a guitar string; an open gourd attached to the outside of the bow is held against and moved away from the chest, giving the instrument somewhat the sound of a jew's-harp. Most jenjili playing is an evening pastime in the villages, but at certain times of the year, jenjili singers roam through the towns, telling stories and singing songs of proverbial advice. During the month of Ramadan, when Muslims fast through the daylight hours, households awake by four o'clock in the morning for early prayers and meals. At that time, jenjili singers are making their rounds of the houses, and their music cheers people up and helps them observe the obligations of their faith with good feelings. At harvest time, the singers are also busy. At night, families sit in the open compounds of their houses to remove corn and sorghum kernels from the cobs. It is tedious work, but when a jenjili singer enters a house, people do not feel sleepy or bored, and the work moves well. The time I was trying to record Yakubu, he put me through some very funny paces because I did not have as much money as he hoped to get for allowing me to record his singing. He lived in a small compound several miles outside of Tamale, and a friend and I walked out to his house one night after we had made arrangements with him during the day as he worked in Tamale at his trade of repairing bicycles. When we arrived, he informed us that he did not feel like singing and sent us away. Before we left, he called us back to lend us a flashlight since, he said, the road we were taking was filled with snakes. The next night we went back to return the flashlight and to beg him again to sing. He refused again, but the next day, out of the corner of my eye, I saw him sneaking a look at me while I worked with Ibrahim, and that night he gave me a beautiful recording.

I was by then working very hard, in the mornings with Alhassan and another drummer at a secluded spot near the Transit Quarters and in the afternoons with Ibrahim at his house, and I was perhaps exhausting myself. I had made so much progress that many people in the town had begun talking about me and coming to watch my afternoon practices, and I too was even a bit surprised at myself. I was especially popular with the children, who followed me everywhere in great numbers, jumping and skipping, giggling and piping out in their tiny voices as they practiced their first English phrases and saluted, "Hello! How are you? I'm fine, thank you!" They were cute: as soon as they saw me, a big cheer would arise, and the littlest ones would race up to me calling my name, their arms outstretched, trying to carry my dondon as I walked to my lesson. If I stood still, they would come up and hold my legs as if holding a tree trunk.

After a while, when I found myself too preoccupied with my work to enjoy fully these happy processions, it was a sign that I was encountering problems. I was learning a great many dances and pressing to learn more, but the time I would be able to stay in Tamale was beginning to seem too short for the task. Possibly because I was aware of how rapidly I was developing, moreover, I was frustrated because I felt that something was missing when I played: still as shy as I had been in Bawku, I could not bring the necessary concentration to my playing to make the music powerful and exciting. When Ibrahim was not there, Alhassan, who had become clearly bored with teaching after the first few weeks, would fool around, and the other drummer would seem to be dreaming. Finally, one morning when Ibrahim was at his farm, my frustration and fatigue provoked me to lose my temper with Alhassan. That afternoon, Ibrahim demanded a long and serious discussion to straighten me out and to hear my grievances, and he himself called a formal translator. Using the conventions of formal conversation, the praise before each criticism, the quietness of tone, and the absolute attention, we talked for two hours. He talked about confusion and patience. He said that every way of approaching things has its own dangers, and anything can be good or bad. My loss of temper had been bad, a serious indication to him that I was learning too much too quickly. He had been amazed at how quickly I could learn, but he had tried not to teach me everything because he did not want to confuse me. He sincerely believed that our efforts were worthwhile, but he now thought that I was becoming confused and would be unable to manage to play well. He summed up his lecture with a remarkable speech.

"All the old people who are above me and all those who are either below me somewhat or at the same size with me, they all like how you are making practice with the drumming and learning it. Any time that Alhaji comes to me, he says that what I am doing is good, that he wants the friendship between you and me to get better. But some of these very drummers you know, the younger ones, they don't understand why you have come to learn all our secrets and again why we should teach you our drumming and the drumming languages. They have been talking against it."

"Why do they do that?" I asked.

"Some of them are jealous. They can't be able to say it, but they are annoyed because you know more than some of them."

"Oh," I said, "as for that, I don't think so."

"What! I know them. Some of them have children—grown children —and they can't play as you are playing."

"Well, what are they saying?" I asked.

"What they are saying is that this drumming is for us Dagombas and not for anybody else, and that you have come from a far land. They say that it is a shame because I have revealed our secrets and the meaning of our dances to someone who does not belong to our tribe. So it means that I have sold our customs. But I don't mind them."

"What do you think about their reasons?" I asked.

"Their reasons are nothing," he said. "Look at the sort of reasons they are having. They say that I should not be teaching someone who is not a Dagomba to be beating our drums and take them to his home town. But if you learn this drumming and take it somewhere, what can happen? Nothing can happen.

"Some others—some of them too are not Dagombas, and some too are whites—they are coming to me and saying that I should charge you heavily, and sometimes too they will come and say that as I have been teaching you, I must be very rich. I never said anything, but I am just laughing at them. You must know that if I am just sitting here at my house and making these drums, that my profit will be more than whatever you have been able to give me. But as I am teaching you to drum, I have not considered this. This is how we Dagombas are. As you have come here to learn this drumming, we have to be teaching you. And when you go, if you give me sugar or you give me salt, it's all right.

"And how I am teaching you to drum, the Dagomba people are happy. Wherever you go, don't you know that people are following you? They can pick you out easily. Anywhere in this Northern Region where Dagombas are living, they know you. As you are sitting here beating the drum, during market days when they are passing by, they are just look- ing at you, and they can remember you any time. So whatever village you have been to, they know you very well, and they know you are from me. And everything you need, they have to give you. Yes, the Dagom- bas are very happy as you are beating the drum. And they take it that I am a patient person to show you how to drum.

"But you should know that it is not because of anything like that or because of money that I am showing you. I have seen that you have shown great love since the time you came, and I have taken pains to show you. The first time you came, we did not know the character of one another. I saw you as a human being and I liked you. That is what I saw. I saw you as a person coming to learn drumming, coming to seek a general idea of drumming and then go. Sometimes foreigners will come and say, 'Drum and I will tape it.' And I have been charging them, and they tape and go away. Did you watch well on the day when you came to learn drumming and we sat down and we came to an agreement? Did you know that I could have refused to teach you? You might have brought a lot of money and you might have come from a far place, and with all your suffering in coming here, your suffering could have been useless. I could have refused you, and I would not have taught you how to drum. But I considered one thing: respect.

"It was an exchange of respect. If you give respect to people, they will likewise give it back. I will give you an example. Let's say you are an expert in drumming, and because you are an expert, someone comes to you but you start disgracing him: you talk rudely to him and you insult him. All this means that you will not get respect from him. And you should not get the respect. You have to have respect before you get respect.

"You should watch this thing. If you are passing within this lane to this house, you will see something wonderful. I have not seen something like it before. You will see all the small children calling you by your name: 'John, John.' It is because of you that they know you. It is because you have made yourself low to us. That is respect. That is why everyone knows you, and you see that they are all giving back your respect. You know that there are many white people in town here, and no one even cares to know their name. And it is also because of the respect of drumming itself that they know you. This drumming you are doing has carried your name to all parts of Dagbon, to places you don't even know. As you are here, people are saying that a white man has come to sit down with us and learn drumming; no one has ever said, 'A white man has come to work with a machine.' So every day you are getting back your respect. I know that you have respect, and I give you back respect.

"That is why I have been teaching you drumming, and I want to add some further instructions. You must be patient to learn this drumming. You should not ever be unhappy or annoyed. Rather, we are the right people to be unhappy with you. And also, if we are unhappy, then you are the right person to beg us. Not that I am annoyed with you. The reason why I'm saying these things is that we Dagombas have a promise that once we know you, then it is a must that we know you. There is no time we shall say that we don't know you again. If it comes to a time whereby we say we don't know you, then the whole thing is from you. As you are here at present, everyone has come to tell me that as you are living with me here, that I am the only person you know here. How people are saying that you and I are friends, if it should come to a time when they will say you and I are no longer friends, will it be good? If we are not patient to stay with you, then you must be patient to stay with us, and if you are not patient to stay with us, then we must be patient to stay with you. Patience gets everything, but annoyance will let you go mad or get to someplace where you don't want to go. But if you have patience, you will get whatever you want.

"So you should know one great thing, that the heart gives the best and the worst in a person. A person's intention is within the heart, and whatever intentions you have within your heart are going to be your achievement. If you have a bad intention, you are going to achieve the worst; and if you have good intentions, your achievements are going to be good. And if you do something good, you will forever hold that; and if you do something bad, you will forever hold that. The only things you hold in this world to keep you going are your intentions within your heart. You should know that if you open your mouth to speak, whether you are telling the truth or you are telling lies, it is within your heart, and no one can know except you yourself. Your best thoughts are within your heart, and your worst thoughts are within your heart.

"Here is an example for you. If someone asks you to go to a slaughter house and then to get a fine and better meat from the whole meat of a cow, which two most important meats would you pick?"

"Myself?"

"Yes."

"I don't know."

"Whenever they slaughter a cow for you to pick the important meat, you must pick: heart and tongue. These two meats, they are the right meat, they are the important meat, and they are the bad meat. Why is it that I say so? Without the tongue, you can't speak; without the heart, you can't think or make any decision. And this heart and tongue, they can also lead a person to do something bad. So these are the right meat and the bad meat. The heart can let you do something that is good, and at the same time it can let you do something that is bad. And the tongue too can speak what is good, and it can speak what is bad. These instructions are some of the instructions I want to give you. In the past, if you did not know that the heart and the tongue are the human being, then today you know. How I have talked to you about this, how do you find it?"

"As you are telling me this," I said, "I hear it and I understand that it is good for you to give me this kind of advice."

"Today I am going to tell you much about this heart and this tongue. I am showing you wisdom, with thick talk and much advice. And here is a point. You must know that the heart is the eyes at the same time. A person may be just like us, but it may come to a time whereby he has become a blind person. But the heart knows where the person stays. And if the person has gone out, he knows the way to his house, and he knows how he can step inside his room. It is his heart which is showing him. And if a person is sleeping, what happens to him in his sleep?"

"He dreams."

"Is it the eyes which think or the heart which thinks?"

"The heart."

"But have you ever seen this before, that the heart can be sleeping while the eyes are opened?"

"No."

"It can be so. Sometimes somebody can be speaking to you while you just open your eyes to him but you are not listening to him. For instance, I will meet you outside; you are coming forward and I am also coming toward you. Then I can just be looking at you, and you will also be looking at me. My eyes have seen you, but my heart is not on you. My heart is at somewhere. So I can just come and pass you, and you will say, 'Oh, why is it that Ibrahim Abdulai has come and passed and he could not say one thing?' Simply because my heart is not looking at you. Although my eyes are looking at you, my heart is looking at somewhere. It is the heart which sees first before the eyes. This heart, it is the one which is doing everything for human beings. Yes, it is the one which is doing bad and good. It decides let's do this, let's do that. But the eyes cannot decide for a human being.

"Sometimes you may be having a friendship with somebody, but unfortunately something happens between you people. The heart makes you speak roughly or speak something bad to that fellow, and later on you will get back to sit quietly. This very heart will try to tell you that, oh, you have done wrong, get back and apologize to the fellow to whom you have done wrong, that I am sorry for what I have done to you. It is this very heart which is directing you to do all this. Does it not happen? So the heart is doing everything. And it is also the heart which gets annoyed. But if your heart gets annoyed, is it good? If you let your heart get annoyed, you have decreased your respect.

"In this world, sickness and death are the bad things against a person. But when a person has patience, and he is never sick, all that he wants, he will get it. He will get what he wants. Only one with no sense will get something and say he has got nothing. If you have patience and sense, you will get something which you were not expecting to get. The one who is watchful of these two ideas will be observant of all that is happening around him.

"Abdulai the boxer is my brother's son. Not that I don't like him, but he is beating gongon with hard blows. And Alhassan, not because he is my son that I am going to say something good about him, but Alhassan's wrist in beating gongon is much more interesting than Abdulai's. Abdulai's wrist makes more noise, because he is strong. But have you ever seen me playing as Abdulai does, to be moving about, shaking my body, and raising my hand high and then be beating? You have not seen it. But how I play, is it interesting? I have taught Alhassan how to play gongon, and I know how to play gongon very well too. If Alhassan were to have followed my steps, he would have been perfect on gongon. But already I have told you that a child is a crazy person. That is why he does not want to take my steps, to get to my position in beating this gongon. All the time he used to be crazy, playing by heart. If not because of that, no one could play gongon better than Alhassan. I know that what I have taught Alhassan, he will pick it. And if he can't pick all, he can pick a little of it. If you stay with a learned person and you don't know anything, at least you will know the number of people in your house. But Alhassan should have been perfect in beating gongon. But as he is too crazy, he can't follow my steps. As Alhassan has been getting annoyed all the time, if I am going to be the same as Alhassan, is it good? If my heart gets annoyed, then I have to take my experience to cool everything down. If I do just what my heart tells me to do, would it be good? As for Alhassan and some others, if their heart gets up or they get annoyed, they try to do whatever they want, and this is because they have no experience. That is why I am calling them crazy people. But as a crazy person is walking about, is he not a human being? And as he is crazy, don't you have to do something which is better for him?

"A history for you: a future history. As you are here to learn drumming, you will take it back to your country. We are friends at present; all the time we are friends. We are living in the world, too. Probably you will have a wife to be bearing children, and I have also got a wife to be bearing children. And it would come to a time when you are very old and I am very old. And it would come unfortunately to my death. By that time too, your children know that you are a drummer. Maybe you will leave some history down that you have come to Tamale to learn drumming and other things, and this is the sort of person you met in Tamale who taught you drumming. Your children will read through this history about the time you came to Ghana, and they will say, 'Oh, by now our father is old, so let us go to Ghana and find the one who taught our father drumming.' Then they pick a day to come to Ghana. And when they came to Ghana, they came straight to this Tamale and they could not meet me; they came to hear that I have died. And in the meantime they met my children and they explained to my children what they are about, how they have heard about their father from their own father too, that they have come to see their father. Is it nice? Is it increasing the whole friendship or is it decreasing the whole friendship?

"That is the reason why we don't promise and fail people. That is why I am living with you peacefully. I don't want to do something bad to you so that you will be annoyed. As you have come to learn the drumming, whether it will make you rich, it will make you happy, it will take you to someplace or it won't take you to any other place, we don't know—only you know. That is why you have come to learn it. You know what you mean to do with the drumming. If you go to a person to greet him, and you greet this person, then by the time you are leaving to your place, the person could not say good-bye to you, is it good? I want for you and me, when it comes to the time when we are to separate from each other, by the time you are old and I am also old, or by the time I have died, then it must be good-bye and not annoyance. For us Dagombas, that is how our ways are, to be living with others."

The next day, I had stayed a bit with the Old Man after lunch, and Ibrahim was late as well. I took a brief nap on a bench outside Ibrahim's house, until Ibrahim's little son Fatawu woke me, stroking my arm and whispering in my hear, "John, John, get up, get up." As usual, a crowd of spectators was gathering to watch and encourage me. That afternoon, as Ibrahim, Alhassan, and I played through the dances I had learned, the crowd was in high spirits. Several elders passed by to inspect my progress, and some danced to everyone's satisfaction; old market ladies, as usual, took time to come, shaking their heads and smiling in wonder at the notion of a Westerner playing their drums; my fans the children were struggling among themselves for good vantage points. I myself felt very calm, and I decided to begin Kondalia. I was looking at my dondon under my arm as I went through the styles I knew, playing each several times while I tried to remember another to move into. Generally in my practices, when I had finished executing the variations I knew, Ibrahim, on supporting dondon, would play something new for me to follow. I looked at him and continued playing the steady quarter-note waiting pattern on his off-beat. Then he stood up and came next to me playing his pattern, looking me in the eyes and smiling. He began playing gradually louder, beating the dondon in my face. I began to find it difficult to continue with my rhythm, and I stood up to help my playing; though my arm was becoming tired, I held on to my beat. I concentrated on my dondon, trying to think of a style to play. He was calling my name, "John, John." I looked back at him, and I found myself becoming stronger in my beat as I listened to him. I watched his stick strike his dondon until I could barely hear myself. My arm relaxed and the music seemed to slow down. I listened to Alhassan's gongon beating, and as I maintained my rhythm I looked at the crowd and at Alhassan and noticed them smiling. I heard my own beating clearly and then I realized that I was leading the group. I laughed and looked at everybody. At the moment when I saw all their faces clearly, I shifted directly into a complicated style. Ibrahim almost fell over backwards into his chair. A cry of astonished approval came up from the crowd, and people began jumping up and down, congratulating me: "Oh, the way you played! It moved me! It was sweet!"

The incident offers a particularly rich illustration of the music-making process. Ibrahim had let me know what was involved in proper playing, first during our talk about morality the day before, and then, to make his message explicit, by putting me on the spot in a context of aesthetic criticism. That spot was balanced on his off-beats, and the situation could be interpreted as if Ibrahim were testing me, trying to throw me off the beat. His talk had prepared me to accept the gravity of his challenge, to get down to the fundamental issue of whether I could maintain my balance, my composure, and my creativity when I knew that what I did would be understood to be the best I could do. One can pass a test as well as fail it, however, and Ibrahim did not want to knock me off the beat but was rather giving me the *better chance to succeed.* When I stood up to respond to him, I was ready to prove to him, to the crowd, and to myself that I could continue my beating and that even as my concentration became more intense, I would wait until I could "enrich my instrument with other voices."[37] It was only by listening to Ibrahim and Alhassan that I knew what to do. With each of the single beats I threw in, each of us became stronger in himself and in relationship, perfecting the form of Kondalia through precision. As we realized the beauty of Kondalia's beat, the excitement increased; Dagombas might say that we "felt it within ourselves" or that we were "enlightened."[38] And as the beauty became almost too much to endure, the change of styles was wonderful because it carried the beat through smoothly and with assurance, cutting both the old and the ongoing rhythms distinctly and keeping the tension under control. Under pressure, I struggled, but I managed to stay composed, and the crowd stayed with me, making an effort to hold on. When I was able to keep them there, it was an indication to me that they recognized a dramatically important moment in my life and that their support went further than I had ever imagined, that they believed I could make it if I tried. They gave me the confidence to laugh when I was on the line, and I showed my understanding at that moment, giving them an effective demonstration of my involvement with their art.

In short, what was at issue was not technical proficiency or emotional expressiveness but my personal understanding of certain fundamental principles which can best be described as ethical. If I had not finally understood the issue, I would not have been able to listen for, look for, and judge the proper moment. I would have demonstrated, through a random gesture, my lack of concern for the people there. To Ibrahim and the crowd, my education in African music was an education in my awareness of spiritual and ethical principles, the prerequisites of the clear mind and experienced judgement I would need to play really well. As Ibrahim told me, patience and sense are necessary to bring one's power to the service of form and beauty, and balance through dialogue is essential for the avoidance of overstatement and isolation. A Westerner might find rhythmic conflict an overwhelmingly intense experience; in an African musical context, rhythmic conflict brings coolness to communication. Dagombas say that "music cools the heart,"[39] and coolness in a musical situation calls for mediated involvement rather than concentrated attention, collectedness of mind rather than self-abandonment. In Western music that has complex rhythms, one nevertheless follows the rhythmic changes. In African music, the emphasis shifts from rhythm to rhythm or part to part. Without balance and coolness, the African musician loses aesthetic command, and the music abdicates its social authority, becoming hot, intense, limited, pretentious, overly personal, boring, irrelevant, and ultimately alienating.

When Africans focus on specific rhythms in their music, as in certain religious contexts, they do so for specific reasons within situations which are otherwise controlled in every aspect, situations which are organized to lend extra power to the music and in which concentration or loss of balance is not out of context. Those whom the music beats through are usually specialized spiritual mediators who function in the more authoritative spiritual presence of either a priest or priestess or some other individual who is equally specialized at cooling down "hot" people. Our word "ecstatic," which some people like to apply to African music, means literally from its Greek origins, "extended out of the state one was in," and the word could not be more inappropriate to describe African music in general. The feelings the music brings may be exhilarating but not overpowering, intense but not frenzied. Ecstasy as we see it would imply for most Africans a separation from all that is good and beautiful, and generally, in fact, any such loss of control is viewed by them as tasteless, ridiculous, or even sinful. If you ask an African why he goes out to listen and dance to music, he may tell you, "I worked hard all day, and now I want to refresh my mind." In the cult, I assumed that my self-consciousness was a sign of my alienation. Though I did not realize it at the time, the unobtrusive role which I stepped into as an observer actually helped me to participate and play properly: I did not focus my energies or my anxieties so sharply that I would lose my appreciation of the wholeness either of the scene or of the music I was making, for it is necessary to be somewhat abstract in order to play apart.

We can perhaps better understand the meaning of some of the African aesthetic notions we have been discussing by comparing the performances of two magnificent artists, one Western and the other African, each a virtuoso within his tradition. While we cannot compare the relative quality of African and Western music, except of course by preference, we can possibly understand how certain similar artistic concerns —concentration, command, clarity, composure, and technique, among others—are brought to different expressive purposes and different aesthetic effects as each tradition achieves its own kind of greatness. The point of such a comparison is to help us make distinctions about those African concerns which we might feel we recognize within our own traditions as well, that we may appreciate the different implications these concerns have in the African context.

Several years ago I had an opportunity to witness a concerto performance by the great Russian cellist, Mstislav Rostropovich. I have not forgotten how deeply I was moved at the extra dimension of feeling this man managed to give to the music. When he came on the stage, people in the audience were already excited, and he acknowledged their applause with brief bows. Then he sat behind his cello; the hall became absolutely quiet, and people sat a bit forward in their seats. After a nod between Rostropovich and the conductor, the orchestra began, and when Rostropovich entered, it was with a clarity and a precision that made some people near to me involuntarily open their mouths. He did not look up from his instrument, and as he played, his body came forward over it until he seemed to envelop it. As he reached the technically most difficult section of the music, his concentration became so intense and his playing so perfect that the audience was riveted to attention and the slightest note impressed us with his dedication and virtuosity as he communicated the beauty of the music. The intimacy of his involvement with his instrument fascinated me, and when with a few definitive strokes of the bow he brought the concerto to an end, we in the audience joined together in wild applause for his genius.

On another occasion I had the chance to hear Koyaté Djimo play the *kora* when he was on tour with the National Dance Company of Senegal. The kora is a kind of harp; a gourd which serves as a sounding box hangs in front of the musician, and he plucks the twenty-one strings which are attached to a neck on a pillar extending away from his body.[40] M. Koyaté is famous throughout Senegal as a virtuoso on the kora, but when he stepped on stage, few people in the audience, I am sure, were aware either of his prestige among his countrymen or of the potential of the strange looking instrument which he carried. He barely glanced at the audience, and he looked down at his instrument in deep concentration as he began to play a simple melody based on an uncomplicated rhythmic foundation of three against two. As he played this simple music, he watched his fingers, and he seemed to be meditating on the musical theme which he quietly established. As he elaborated on this theme in greater rhythmic and melodic complexity, he began to demonstrate his incredible technical virtuosity. Finally, at the moment when his improvisations were reaching their most difficult and wonderful point, he raised his head and looked out at the audience, smiling slightly as he turned his head and his eyes to survey the scene. His demonstration of coolness and poise gave those in the audience, more clearly than the drummers and dancers they had come to see, their most accurate understanding of the depth and meaning of the tradition he was representing, and as he looked at them and smiled, they acknowledged this insight with a spontaneous gesture of applause which transformed the concert hall from a Western to an African musical context. When he finished his piece, the people in the audience actually looked around to smile at each other while they applauded him again.

Both these artists, each a disciple of a great musical tradition, brought their aesthetic command to effective display, but the meaning of their virtuosity was in each case different. Rostropovich's aesthetic effect was implicitly moral, an inspiration to be appreciated and internalized; Koyaté's aesthetic effect was explicitly moral, a display to evoke participation and respect. In Africa the practice of art is an explicitly moral activity because African art functions dynamically to create a context of values where criticism is translated into social action. The meaning of the music is externalized through an event in which participation parallels the musician's artistic purpose: an artist's coolness lends security to intimacy, and the rhythms of an ensemble become the movement of an event when people dance.

In what is probably the most insightful scholarly article written about African dance,[41] Robert F. Thompson has suggested that all the formal characteristics of African music can also define African dance. Indeed, we might expect that because of the integrity of African art within its social context, all the arts would manifest the same aesthetic concerns, but especially, it is through the dance that the music and its context are brought together. In my own experience, whenever I explained that I was learning to play music, I almost invariably received the reply, "I hope that you are also trying to learn the dancing." One who "hears" the music "understands" it with a dance, and the participation of the dancer is therefore the rhythmic interpretation which we have described as the aesthetic foundation of appreciation, the essential foothold on the music, so to speak. On an elementary level, as we have noted, dancing and keeping time are the same phenomenon, but an accomplished African dancer uses different parts of his body to emphasize different parts of the music; dancing gives the rhythms a visible and physical form. In the eloquent words of a chief of the Banyang people of the Cameroons, "The dancer must listen to the drum. When he is *really* listening he creates within himself an echo of the drum—then he has started really to dance."[42] When Freeman Donkor, for instance, would forget the sequence of the Agbekor drumming patterns he was teaching me, he would dance the steps and then, having remembered the proper rhythm, he would return to the drum. As Thompson says: "Africans unite music and dance but play apart; Europeans separate dance and music but play together. . . . West Africans perform music and dance apart the better to ensure a dialogue between movement and sound."[43]

Western observers of African dance need to recognize this dialogue or they will tend to interpret the dance as it appears to us, as an image.

A Western dancer uses the body for expression: a movement or a posture conveys a feeling or an idea through representation within the vocabulary of dance, as in pantomime. Our little children hop on tip-toes with their arms out if they want to dance like light and happy birds, prance and shake their heads if they want to suggest wild ponies, stomp their feet and slump their shoulders if they want to be sad gorillas. A modern dancer can communicate abstract conceptions like anxiety by putting the parts of the body at disjointed angles, isolation by slowly drawing the body into itself, serenity by gracefulness, doubt by random movements and pauses. Western dance is basically imitative and iconographic, and it is no wonder that many people have suggested that an African dancer, through the certainty of feet placed squarely on the ground, knees slightly bent, weight moving downward, is communicating a sense of rootedness and solidity in the world, the security of an unambiguous tribal life. The sense of rootedness and security is there, of course, but if we understand the music, we know that the rootedness and security are founded in the conversational engagement of the dancer to the drums, and that the confidence of a foot is the placing of communicative certainty into a context of rhythmic ambiguity.[44]

The African dancer may pick up and respond to the rhythms of one or more drums, depending on his skill, but in the best dancing, the dancer, like the drummer, adds another rhythm, one that is not there. He tunes his ear to hidden rhythms, and he dances to the gaps in the music. Thompson has described African religions as "danced faiths,"[45] in which worship becomes a style of movement that manifests one's relatedness for all to see. As the dance gives visible form to the music, so too does the dance give full and visible articulation to the ethical qualities which work through the music, balance in the disciplined expression of power in relationship. The "visible faith" of our saints has traditionally taken a different form, and the notion that one can dance one's faith would tend to lead us in one of two directions, toward an ecstatic freedom of movement that breaks the limitations and boundaries of self and body, or toward a quiet and solemn uniformity of movement that gains power as a community unites to testify a covenant of duty and love. A brief survey of the music which Westerners consider to be religious would make evident why Westerners have had difficulty perceiving the religious and philosophical sentiments in African dance: if you tried to dance to Handel's "Messiah," you would end up marching.[46]

Western observers may be prepared to accept the deep meaning of dances like Agbekor when the dance is wrapped in the elaborate symbolism and language of tribal tradition. Yet the aesthetic meaning of African dance remains the same in the nightclubs of the cities, and the following examination of popular nightclub dancing should indicate that the aesthetic tendencies of African music and dance stem from an indigenous sensibility which is perhaps deeper than the specific articulations to which we sometimes limit our perception of culture. In village or nightclub, the African dancer will dance marked and unmarked beats, striving for a rhythmically appropriate and precise expression to confirm the wholeness and integrity of the occasion.

Once we orient ourselves to the notion that a dancer converses with the music, it is easy to see how a dancer and an orchestra cut across each other's movements, as if the dancer is a part of the ensemble. In many of the Afro-Cuban dances which are popular in Latin American cultures, for example, the basic rhythm of the conga drum emphasizes the fourth beat of the measure while the dancer steps the first, second, and third beats.

Conga basic

Dancer

left   right   left   right   left   right

The two rhythms vitalize each other: as the conga drummer improvises, he accents the dancers' movements, and his basic beat punctuates a movement of hips or shoulders. Latin dancers know that it is a great thrill to be cutting the beat while the drummer on conga or timbales is improvising (when a novice will be thrown off the beat) or to meet the band when it comes out on time after a bridge. In Meringue dancing, popular in Haiti, the steady beat of the bass carries the dancers' hips from side to side, and when the bass player periodically shifts his rhythm in a brief riff with the orchestra, the dancers' hips go with the accent and return to the beat. The Highlife, West Africa's most popular dance, is based on a rhythm which can be variously played:

Highlife

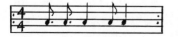   or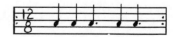

In terms of the dance, the differences in the notation are not significant. The basic footwork is an alternation of double steps on the four beat, but these are subdued, and the most important movement is in the hips, accenting the "open," third beat in the measure. The bass player also figures his rhythm on this beat, and the drum riffs run from just after the third beat to the beginning of the next measure. A dancer will step or do something special to fill the gap, and the movement will be directly followed by the drums.

Just as they listen to the supporting drums in a drum ensemble, African dancers listen to the rhythm section of a band—drums, bass, rhythm guitar, perhaps piano—and put some part of their bodies into a steady and relevant rhythmic pattern so that they can better hear and enjoy the melody or the improvisations. If you ask someone how to dance properly, you will be told to "hear" or to "feel" the beat, but unless you want deliberately to do funny things, you will "hear" the beat as I "heard" the beat when Ibrahim was teaching me Kondalia, and you will dance to a different beat that fits, the one you feel, your own. Throughout a dance, a good dancer will maintain a correspondence between certain rhythms and certain movements, thus building a coherent unity into the dance by using the organization of the music. When there is a significant shift of emphasis or accentuation in a musical arrangement, a good dancer will change his entire style of movement to fit the changing rhythmic motifs. He shows how the beat moves; watching someone dance to a particular beat can help you learn to appreciate it. As Ibrahim Abdulai told me, "When you are watching someone dancing and the dancing does not match the drumming, it's not nice. And the fault is from the one dancing. When you are beating and someone is dancing who doesn't know how to dance, you beat and follow how he is dancing: he will change his leg and leave you, and as you follow him, he will leave you again. Then you too have to leave him. You will beat your beat and he will dance his dance. When he finishes, the one who knows how to dance will come in. Whether you know how to play or you don't know how to play, he will dance the dance the way you are playing it, and it will match. And at that time the music will be nice, and our eyes will lie on it."

Above all, then, a good dancer dances in a steady relationship to the beat, and it is such a dancer who establishes the mutuality of which Ibrahim spoke when he conversely linked drumming styles and dancing styles in his lecture on improvisation. If you are playing for dancers, you can follow those who stay close to the beat: their movements are clear, and it is indeed easier to improvise on a drum when someone is dancing well. Without dancers, many drummers cannot bring forth a wide range of variations, and in this regard we can suggest that dance probably played one of the important inspirational roles in the early development of jazz. In Highlife music, because some people like to dance to different instruments in an orchestra, many musicians, to help their creativity, like to pick someone who is dancing to their beat and play styles according to the dance. In traditional contexts, a drummer may explicitly call and "challenge" a particular dancer to come forward in the same way Ibrahim challenged me, in order to inspire a display of precision and improvisational skill, of balance at the boundary of force and form. Spectators watch dancing style with the same concerns they bring to music, hoping to see the drummer and the dancer demonstrate their reciprocal involvement in a dialogue on the relationship of time and presence.[47]

If we know enough about the techniques of drumming to recognize the same sensibility at work in dance, we can understand that dancers relate rhythmically to each other as well as to the music. As Thompson says, "To dance with arms enlaced around the partner, in the manner of pre-jazz Western ballrooms, lessens the opportunity to converse,"[48] certainly in terms of dance movements. Just as a second rhythm can make a single rhythm more interesting, so is it more interesting to dance to African popular music with a partner. The movements of hips, feet, shoulders, and hands can be placed in relationship to a partner's or a group's movements. In the nightclubs of Accra, you can see the bar girls laughing as they dance with European businessmen, who shake in different directions, their eyes looking blankly somewhere in space. The girls are not so much laughing at their partners' ineptness; they are laughing at themselves trying to dance in such a confusing way, at such variance to the music. What is significant is that they do not question their own tendency to converse. If you want to communicate with your partner, you must dance *with* him or her. What matters is the relationship of movement, and your partner will be more easily charmed when you are subtle, perhaps even hardly moving, than when you are showing off or doing tricky or posed steps. He or she will know that you are trying to communicate personally and not with an imaginary audience.

In contrast, many Western commentators, popular and professional, have described the African-derived dancing of white American teenagers as a kind of unbridled movement, a general locomotor response, like calisthenics, with everyone more or less dancing by himself.[49] As a part of the continuing American dialogue regarding African culture patterns, such a perspective imparts, and often projects into the continental African context, a notion of a Dionysian and regressive loss of personal boundaries and the consequent disappearance of social communication.[50] Maybe the reporters and social analysts were observing accurately, but in such a context they were watching the untutored or inexperienced attempt to find the beat, because a good dancer in an African context does indeed give the beat and does not go off in all directions. Among the better dancers, there will be more control of movement. It is particularly difficult to dance to white rock music, however, because the main-beat emphasis is retained and the use of off-beat accentuation and multiple rhythms is restricted. There is no room inside the music for movement. What is missing is exactly the African sensibility to rhythm, for the teenagers have adopted and subordinated the music to their own expressive purposes.[51]

In African dance as in African music, personal coolness and communicative purpose are the essential elements of good style. Thompson describes the conversational relationship of dancers

> in the world of Spanish Harlem ballrooms, where Puerto Ricans improvise constantly varying steps—dancing apart while their partners maintain a recurrent movement. These men "interrupt" the movement of their women in a call-and-response manner, for they begin a new step or flourish considerably before their partners have finished the execution of their basic movements.[52]

In Accra one night I witnessed a very lovely display of Highlife dancing. A huge woman was dancing the slow step most gracefully, and every ounce of fat on her rolled smoothly in easy rhythm. Her partner was a very thin man, a foot shorter than she. To the slow rocking of her massive hips, he darted in and out with steps sometimes quick and sometimes slow, with highly stylized and dynamic movements. The pair caused quite a stir, and a few people left the dance floor to watch them more attentively. Unmatched in size, they nonetheless seemed a beautiful couple, and their dance became to several commentators on the scene a metaphor of complementary principles in harmonious relationship, each asserting itself with clarity. Everything the man did emphasized the woman's mass and gracefulness as well as his own energy and skill. In all this dancing, they carried on their faces the same trace of a smile. After their dance, everyone applauded their fine and tasteful efforts.

Like a drummer, a dancer should not try to do too much or he will lose clarity or become pretentious. A dancer's subtle refinement and good taste will enliven the music by enriching the occasion, pulling the whole scene into a movement rather than attempting to project the strength of one performer. Good dancers get into the grooves provided by the rhythms and add their bodies to the elaboration of rhythmic sophistication and power. The Banyang chief we have quoted says of a good dancer, "Once he is seeing the echo [of the drums], he is dancing with pride."[53] I remember a conversation I once had with several Ghanaian army officers who had spent time in Zaïre in the early 1960s as part of the United Nations Emergency Forces. According to these soldiers, who knew very well how to enjoy themselves, the people of Congo and Zaïre are "really good-timers," and "very cool in their ways." Several months later I was with Gideon in a bar in Togo on the border with Ghana, and I was amazed when I saw some Congolese dancing to one of their popular Rumba tunes; in spite of their reputation for lively dancing, it seemed that they were not even moving. One dancer raised his knee as if he intended to take his foot off the ground, but he never lifted it. He stayed poised to move. Gideon said, "Wow! Look at him dance!" and had a beer sent to the man's table. The beauty of the dance was in the expression of calm on the man's face as he heard the music. The collectedness of mind which distinguishes the great drummers can be seen in the head of a dancer. When Africans dance, the head seems to float apart from the body, becoming the center of balance and control. Even when the shoulders and feet are violently active, the head is stable. If the head is cool, the body is cool. The first evening I went dancing in Accra, I had sweated through my shirt before the first number was over. Later I could dance every dance and keep a dry forehead.

Thompson epitomizes his discussion of dance in most evocative terms.

> Multiple meter essentially uses dancers as further voices in a polymetric choir. The conversation is additive, cool in its expressions of community. The balance struck between the meters and the bodily orchestration seems to communicate a soothing wholeness rather than a "hot" specialization. . . . Dialogue in apart performing . . . [and in] call-and-response . . . [is] a means of putting innovation and tradition, invention and imitation, into amicable relationships with one another.[54]

In the African context, performance in music and dance responds ultimately to a single aesthetic concern, the realization of community, and "moral edification and entertainment, excitement and decorum"[55] can coexist as united aspects of an aesthetic display which thus has profound implications to the people for whom music and dance are essen-

tial to the proper observance of any important event. To perceive and
mediate the many relationships of the music and the occasion requires
a special style of involvement, a dynamic attitude with which an individual may distinguish himself as he places his own rhythmic insight.
One does not dance to go into a trance but to come out of a trance, to
join a diversified assembly with a separate contribution, for dancing is
a reminder that one is only part of the whole.

African music and dance are not performed as an unrestrained emotional expression; fundamentally, African music and dance are ways of
posing structures and restrictions for ethical actualization, and the
spiritual element present is one of wisdom. Only thus can we really
understand why the old men are not only the best drummers but also
the finest dancers. Expert art makes for effortlessness even in the most
fantastic displays. The younger people do not respect their elders' skill
merely out of deference to a traditional African social formality; the
proper sensibility does indeed reside with the expression of dignity and
balance that the older people bring, and not with virtuosity. Symbolically, the drum is the "voice" of the ancestors, those who watch over the
moral life of a community, and proper drumming and dance are founded
on a sense of respect and gratitude to the ancestors for the continuity
of the community which uses music and dance to restructure and re-
focus its integrity as a source of strength in the lives of its members.
The elders, to put it most simply, participate best because they know
more dead people, and their drumming and dancing will communicate
and contribute their greater awareness of the deepest moral forces
which can serve to bind the living community. African music and dance
are art forms which permit them to demonstrate and express this wisdom for all to see.

In almost any account of an African festival or dance, the witness
will note that the occasion is not complete without spectators.[56] The
children are present, the young people mingle, the strangers watch. One
not only dances with the community, one always dances before others.
Someone is always watching you, says African folk wisdom. In many
festivals and celebrations in many African cultures, a chief is *required*
to dance before his people. We have discussed the implicit meaning of
"style" as a sense of relationships, and when the meaning of "style" is
made explicit, to us as well as to many African peoples, there is a suggestion of "display" or "showing off." What is there for the chief to
show off, and what do people wish to see displayed? It is not the vanity
of self-expression that some observers have taken to be the source of
the dancer's pleasure, nor is the chief merely proving that he is still

healthy. In his dance, the chief combines aesthetic command and moral command, and the satisfying beauty of his dance is a visible display of his closeness to the ancestors and his fitness for authority. The chief asserts the community through a dance in which gracefulness implies the tranquility of mature strength, elegance implies the bounty of life, precision implies dedication of purpose, happiness implies the accessibility of compassion, composure implies the discretion of power, and dignity implies destiny. Even among the common people in the nightclubs, this attitude remains. In the collectivity of the moment, it is the pretentious or unsociable dancer who is mocked or shamed. The most profane songs and dances can be vehicles of indigenous ethics, for what is important is not the specific activity so much as its style, the degree to which behavior is measured against its social value, to which coolness enhances the appreciation and enjoyment of the many people with whom one finds oneself. At an African musical event, whether listening to the comments of the spectators, or observing good and bad dancing, or understanding the improvisational principles and decisions of a great drummer, we should be conscious of the fact that music-making in Africa is above all an occasion for the demonstration of character.

4

Values in Africa

The essential criteria for distinguishing excellence in African music are, as we have seen, as much ethical as aesthetic. Yet African music does not become the subject of abstract and systematic discussions about morality and ethics, and people do not become analytical about the fundamental social themes displayed in their music: the point is to participate in the appropriate way. If the music is good, people listen, dance, and enjoy themselves. If it is bad, they will try to correct it in whatever way they can, perhaps by making fun of a vain dancer or anyone present with a bad attitude, perhaps by offering suggestions or encouragement to the musicians, perhaps by buying some beer, or perhaps, if their mood is hopeless, by being sensible enough to leave the place. One of the central assumptions of this book, therefore, has been that since an African musical performance is so much a part of its social setting, we can recognize African critical standards by what happens in the situation itself. In such a context, everything one does becomes an act of "criticism": people express their opinions by participating. They make a contribution to the success of the occasion, and they behave with the understanding that what they do is an act of artistic participation as well.[1]

It is in this sense that African music can offer us an especially valuable approach to African culture. Other kinds of activity and other kinds of institutions may give us complementary perspectives on life in Africa, but in their arts, Africans are directly involved in bringing quality to a social situation. A typical musical event, with its distinctive patterns of interaction and communication, presents us with a basis for an interpretation of African social life, an interpretation modeled on Africans' own standards of order. The depth of music's integration into almost all the various aspects of African social life is an indication that music helps to provide an appropriate framework through which people may relate to each other when they pursue activities they judge to be important—or commonplace. Music is essential to life in Africa because Africans use music to mediate their involvement within a community, and a good musical performance reveals their orientation toward this crucial concern. As a style of human conduct, participation in an African musical event characterizes a sensibility with which Africans relate to the world and commit themselves to its affairs.

As a cultural expression, music is a product of this sensibility, but more significantly, as a social force, music helps shape this sensibility. The development of musical awareness in Africa constitutes a process of education:[2] music's explicit purpose, in the various ways it might be defined by Africans, is, essentially, socialization. An individual learns the potentials and limitations of participation in a communal context dramatically arranged for the engagement, display, and critical examination of fundamental cultural values. These values form part of an elaborate set of generative themes which pattern the experience of everyday life and the institutionalization of customs. In the midst of change, they characterize a culture's continuity from generation to generation, suggesting the underlying strengths which vitalize the efforts of individuals and communities as they meet the realities of new situations. In depth and complexity, the values which inform the African musical sensibility embody the philosophical and ethical traditions of African cultures. And they are located in a particularly viable institution. At a musical event, as we are aware, the values of African traditional wisdom are integrated into a style of communication which is both musical and social. In such a context, they do not have to be made explicit; they are there to be understood in action, and their validity is measured by their social effectiveness.

In this chapter, we will rely on our knowledge of African music to portray a few of the ways in which the concerns we have recognized in musical contexts are woven into the fabric of African social life. The "values" we will discuss, however, are not quite comparable to the abstract beliefs, conceptions, or rules with which we as Westerners often "define" our values. Rather, we will be discussing the implicit expectations—what a social scientist might call "norms"—with which people orient themselves to situations, what they take for granted about the nature of social life and what they respect as reasonable when they make judgements about appropriate behavior. Not surprisingly, because African music is a part of so many different kinds of activity, our awareness of music will help us understand the meaning of much of what an ordinary traveler might observe about the personal, social, and cultural characteristics of African life. Our sensitivity to aesthetic concerns can enable us to perceive several fundamental unities of style amid the diversity of African peoples. Basically, if we can appreciate their music, we are in a better position to appreciate their world.

We can recall our discussion of music with renewed meaning. At an African musical event, we are concerned with sound and movement, space and time, the deepest modalities of perception. Foremost is the dynamic tension of the multiple rhythms and the cohesive power of their relationship. Founded on a sense of time and presence, the art of improvisation involves the subtle perfection of this rhythmic form through precision of performance, complexity of organization, and control of gestural timing. The act of creation is above all purposeful, never random, and the goal is balance and a fulfilling interdependence. As they display style and involvement, people make their music socially effective, transforming the dynamic power of the rhythms into a focus for character and community. We are even quite close to a metaphysics of rhythm if we remember that sensing the whole in a system of multiple rhythms depends on comprehending, or "hearing," as Africans say, the beat that is never sounded. At the convergence of essence and form stands the master drummer, not creating new rhythms but giving order and organization to those already there. Every place, a drummer once told me, has its own rhythms which give it character; going there, one must find a rhythm that fits, and improvise on it.[3] On the man's drum was painted the popular slogan, "God's Time is the Best." In applying a musical metaphor to social situations, this drummer asserted that his musical sensibility could serve him well as a basis for participation in African social life, and in the following discussion, we will briefly explore some of the dimensions of his orientation.

African affinity for polymetric musical forms indicates that, in the most fundamental sense, the African sensibility is profoundly pluralistic. One of the most patronizing Western biases regarding people in societies we call "traditional" is the notion that the events of their lives are nestled in and determined by the ready-made patterns of a culture they uncritically accept. Indeed, the idea of a traditional "sensibility" sometimes arouses in us a kind of romantic nostalgia, as if people in traditional societies live in a world of continuously meaningful experiences. Actually, life in African societies seems, possibly even more than in our own, to be marked by a discontinuity of experience in the encounters and status dramas of daily life. Just as a participant at an African musical event is unlikely to stay within one rhythmic perspective, so do Africans maintain a flexible and complicated orientation toward themselves and their lives. Relying on their sense of appropriateness, they may participate equally in what we might think of as exclusive kinds of identities, perhaps being both nationalistic and tribalistic, Animist and Christian or Muslim, traditional and Westernized. The sensibility we have found in musical expression more accurately appears to represent a method of actively tolerating, interpreting, and even using the multiple and fragmented aspects of everyday events to build a richer and more diversified personal experience.[4] In African cities, one can find magnified almost all the factors which various social analysts have said are the source of our contemporary anxiety: rapid change, congestion and noise, unemployment and poverty, uprootedness and family dispersion. Without suggesting that the situation is good, one at least notices that it does not seem as debilitating on the human level as it could be. In this disorganized and potentially alienating world, the adaptability and strength of an African's sense of community and personal identity reside in the aesthetic and ethical sensibility which we have seen both expressed and cultivated in one of its aspects, music. As such, the values in an African musical event represent not an integrity from which we are moving away but rather an integrity which, with understanding, we might approach. It is a felicitous orientation in a world of many forms.

There is a clear parallel, certainly, between the aesthetic conception of multiple rhythms in music and the religious conception of multiple forces in the world. Discussing traditional African religions, Robin Horton writes:

> It is typical of such systems that they include, on the one hand, ideas about a multiplicity of spirits, and on the other hand, ideas about a single supreme being. Though the spirits are thought of as independent beings, they are also considered as so many manifestations or dependents of the supreme being. . . . They are the basis of a theoretical scheme which typically covers the thinker's own community and immediate environment. The supreme being, on the other hand, provides a means of setting an event within the widest possible context.[5]

A comparison of the world posited by religion and the context defined by music is at least intriguing. The power and dynamic potential of the music is in the silence, the gaps between the notes, and it is into this openness that a creative participant will place his contribution, trying even to open up the music further.[6] Theologically speaking, it is God's drum (Drum Himself) which beats the note that is never sounded; it is God's drum which affirms the possibility of continuing vitality within the music. In Africa the passenger cars and trucks which bear the motto "Except God" express this basis of faith: all that we can say, all that we can do, all that we can know, all truth may be applied to all things, except God.[7] From an African religious perspective, anything in the world, no matter how powerful or effective, is limited, and in Africa the individual and the Creator God seem to have very few direct dealings beyond the basic humility and personal confidence that distinguish faith and inform action. When Paul Bohannan writes about the Tiv that "in their religion, they are far more interested in the Creation than in the Creator,"[8] he is in effect saying, as other anthropologists have said about other African peoples, that Africans try to be more realistic than idealistic as they relate to the world. The music, of course, is a way of getting down to more significant concerns: its context is a context of action, of social life; its reality is that of the community. The continuing music consists of many rhythms, and the "beat" emerges from the way these rhythms engage and communicate with each other. While various rhythms may be more important, no single rhythm can provide a complete focus, and in this sense there is no central point of unity, except God.

Yet where Absolute reality stands removed, people must acknowledge the complexity of a plural world. Equanimity with multiple rhythms and the silent beat can and does serve to inform social relations with a cosmopolitan attitude of toleration, rationality, and pragmatism. And every time people in Africa relate to music, among other aspects of their social world, they get practice in standing back from a complicated scene in order to play a part with style and confidence. To a Westerner, the way people get things done in Africa may seem, at first glance, to be as confusing as their music, particularly because a Westerner is likely to assume that ethnic life is limited or simple. But in a busy village market or on a busy city street at midday, the constant activity and noise can disorient a Westerner. The diversity of individual personality types is amazing. Each event is a seemingly disjointed and chaotic enterprise. If a Westerner is adaptable, however, his eventual orientation does not reduce the hurly-burly: he learns, like the Africans, to make music out of the fragmentation and discontinuity of events, to respect pluralism as a source of vitality, and to bring to any situation the social presence and poise which is the counterpart of the African's religious faith.

To maintain their poise in their social encounters, Africans bring the same flexibility which characterizes their participation in musical contexts: they expect dialogue, they anticipate movement, and most significantly, they stay very much open to influence. The many ways one can change a rhythm by cutting it with different rhythms is parallel to the many ways one can approach or interpret a situation or a conversation. And there is always an in-between, always a place to add another beat. A musical occasion, like any other social occasion, is therefore beyond any one perspective a person can bring to it, and people in Africa are usually realistic enough not to try to impose a single point of view on the larger context in which they are playing a part. It is not only that one rhythm cannot monopolize all the notes; one rhythm means nothing without another.[9] In a musical context, separation of parts heightens rhythmic dialogue, and in a musical ensemble, singlemindedness of purpose would be equivalent to poverty of expression.[10] And, of course, if a rhythm must be cut by another to be meaningful or interesting, its meaning can be influenced, altered, or defined by another. There are those of us who would feel insecure in a context where who we are is more dependent on other people's perspectives than on our personal self-image, but in Africa a person will generally be prepared to connect his self-image with what others see him doing, and he may hope and expect that people will be steady enough to make sense of him in a complementary way. If you wish to sit alone in a bar, and you politely refuse an African's invitation to join his table, you may be cautioned in a friendly way that someone who sits alone may have crazy and meaningless thoughts, staying too long inside his isolated imagination and misperceiving things: it is better to develop one's thoughts with the open-mindedness ensured by the presence of other people. Their potential to reciprocate or to differ helps provide balance.

On a pluralistic continent, communication is founded on an acknowledgment of diversity. People are interested in and hospitable toward strangers, and in many African languages, the word for "stranger" is the same as the word for "guest." People are also interested to learn about different places and different ways of life, partly because they themselves often move from place to place as they pass through life

—and they expect to greet and be greeted by the people they meet on the road. Even in small towns, you can hear many languages being spoken, and I have met illiterate villagers who said they knew as many as a dozen languages. When I doubted one man, he admitted that he was not perfect in several of the languages, but that if he were among people who spoke one of those languages, at least no one could sell him. And within individual societies where people, for lack of privilege, opportunity, or desire, cannot easily isolate themselves from each other, where children find themselves within a hierarchy of status responsibilities as soon as they have younger brothers and sisters, and where it is an essential practicality of life to know when and how to use one's many relationships within one's kin group, people learn that their differences from each other provide the significant or interesting focal points of their involvement.

A pervading sense of formality and civility is thus usually very evident in their interpersonal conduct. In more than one way, though, both the openness and the sophistication of African social worlds indicate that people actually try to build complexity and complications into their relationships. In African music, as we know, respect for an established rhythmic framework provides the possibility for comprehensible improvisation, and in daily life as well, people adopt a highly mannered approach in their relationships so that they may act with clarity and relevance. Ibrahim Abdulai could not think of what to do without a second dondon; a master drummer, minding his own improvisations, listens to a "hidden" rhythm, in effect creating another rhythm for his own to engage. In a musical context, the diverse rhythms help people distinguish themselves from each other while they remain profoundly involved; in the discrete encounters of social life, people maintain their boundaries, even in their closest friendships, and a Westerner in Africa may have trouble deciding whether the people he meets are being friendly or circumspect in their approach to him. Though it may seem paradoxical to a Westerner, Africans use stylized social forms and conventions to achieve interpersonal intimacy, but, as at a musical event, Africans impose a formal institutional or social framework on their affairs in order to personalize their behavior and expressions against a specifically limited context of meaning. From an African perspective, once you have brought a structure to bear on your involvements, and made your peace with it, the distinctive gestures and deviant idiosyncrasies of personality can stand out with clarity. You are free to introduce subtle refinements in a dramatic way to focus on the quality or status of your relationship at any moment. Thus, Africans do not so much observe rituals in their lives as they ritualize their lives.

In the model of community presented in an African musical event, integrity is ideally a combination of diverse rhythms which must remain distinct, and the power of the music comes from the conflicts and conversations of the rhythms, from vivid contrasts and complementary movements. The music is judged in terms of the success of each performance, that is, by how well the formally established relationships of the rhythms are continuingly open to fresh and vital participation. Good style, as understanding and as display, links the force of personal creativity to the arrangement of on-going action, always working within the possibilities of the beat. No matter how familiar the participants are to each other, in every musical performance, in every economic transaction, in every chance meeting, and in every seduction, they will observe and repeat appropriate formalities to allow an explicit recognition of their specific involvement. Once Gideon and I were invited to Vodza, a small town near Keta, to display at a funeral. Gideon was to play his three drums, and I was to play Agbekor while Gideon danced. The one who had invited us to come, paid our expenses, and made our sleeping arrangements was the deceased man's best friend. When we arrived at his house, we sat down, and after everyone had greeted one another, the man asked Gideon why he had come. Gideon gave a detailed reply, introducing himself and telling who we were and that we had come to drum at the funeral of the deceased man. Our host then welcomed us again and showed us where we were to stay. If my friend Sartana had been there, he would have commented, "Yes, the man is making the correct beat."[11]

Westerners, who tend to internalize the personal meaning of their lives, often have difficulty understanding the crucial role that ritualization plays in fostering individuality. Western ideals of freedom in relationships seem characterized by a search for newness, naturalness, or a utopian openness, and we often tend to see social conventions as limiting to our freedom.[12] In an African context, interpersonal intimacy is achieved not through the elimination of social conventions but through the effective integration of as many social formalities as possible. Another mundane example may serve best to illustrate how Africans ritualize a situation, getting down to basics in order to elaborate and clarify personal expressions. One of my friends in Accra, Jimmy, an Ibo who had come to Ghana during the Nigerian civil war, was preparing to return to his country, and a few of his best friends organized a final get-together for him. Such a situation is quite common for friends everywhere, but it can be very problematic for people who view social conventions and etiquette as artificial forms which inhibit the expression of authentic personal feelings. We started the evening by going to a restaurant and ordering chicken and beer, and then each of us in turn stood up and gave a short formal speech praising Jimmy and recalling how our friendship had come about and grown. Jimmy then stood up and thanked us in turn for our friendship, and we drank and ate to our good wishes for his good luck and our eventual reunion. In an informal situation which could have had a completely different character, this little ritual, with its subtle touches of formality, isolated our most significant communication and gave us as individuals a simple framework to express easily and directly our love and hopes for Jimmy. We were freed from the awkwardness which might have resulted if we had tried to build and sustain our feelings as a group into the general interaction of the whole evening. The ritual was a gesture of Jimmy's community of friends in Accra, but it was arranged with a sense of dramatic focus so that Jimmy would see himself as a person with friends rather than as a member of a group.

Africans pay a great deal of attention to social formalities, to etiquette, to status differences, and to institutional procedures and roles because these conventions stand as the foundation of their community life, providing a framework to help them know what is happening and to get into it. If someone is demonstrating lack of etiquette, people will say, "The man comes from bush," for not to be civil is not to be civilized. We may perhaps further understand this point with reference to our discussion of time and rhythms in musical communication by understanding that a ritual is basically a way of explicitly establishing the rhythm of a relationship. Africans use ritualized social arrangements to externalize and "objectify" their sense of a relationship because, if a relationship is to be meaningful to them, the recognition one person gives another must be visible outside their own private involvement. For example, in many African societies, a gift is obligatory as just such a visible token of recognition that people have become involved or have done something together, a display that acknowledges one person's participation in another's life and often initiates reciprocal responsibilities. Formalities provide a means of setting people's involvements into patterns of communication which have precedents and continuity and which thus extend meaning.

Like a ritual or a musical event, a community too is basically an ordered way of being involved through time. Africans rely on music to build a context for community action, and analogously, many aspects of their community life reflect their musical sensibility. Knowing what we do about artistic realization in African musical events, we should be better able to appreciate the way that, in Africa, the power of community comes from the dramatic coordination and even ritualized opposition of distinct personalities. On a simple level, in a conversation, someone listening will punctuate a speaker's phrases with what a Westerner might consider to be meaningless noises, but without these utterances at the right time, the speaker will stop to wait for encouragement or for an indication of involvement. A speaker may even stop on purpose to elicit such a response, indicating his own need for dialogue. On the broadest level, the African musical sensibility offers a highly sophisticated example of a tendency frequently seen in traditional African political and economic institutions, a tendency toward situating multiple conflicting and opposing forces into a process of mediated and balanced communication.[13] Relying on this sensibility, Africans are perhaps better prepared than Westerners to manage the status dramas of their daily lives without anxiety or depersonalization because the way they orient themselves to their social arrangements permits the addition of a personal touch. If they use the variety of their community forms to provide discrete contexts for intimacy, so too do they build ethnic solidarity and cohesion from individuation rather than conformity.[14]

Within the complex balances of community activities, Africans manage to retain a focus on the individual. Just as they encourage a musician's confidence in order to enhance creativity, so too do they encourage participation in order to enhance possibilities for personal happiness and community realization.[15] They regard participation as an effort to contribute because they believe that involvement will lead to caring and that a participant will find a way to complement a situation. One of my friends in Accra used to greet me always laughing, saying, "O.K. What *really* happened?" Sometimes, of course, he was merely teasing me about the events of the previous night, but he knew I was doing research, and he was also alluding to what we both knew could not be easily seen by an "observer," that my perspective on what had happened somewhere would reflect what I had done there, a summarized gesture of my involvement. To have been unmoved, critical, or negative would have been "bad-minded"; it would have meant, to him, that I had wasted my time because I had not made an effort to be involved in a better way. Whenever a situation was not up to expectations, my friend would point out the uselessness of bad-minded or discouraging attitudes by saying, "After all, we are here in it."[16] A situation is what

people make of it, and Africans who are concerned about the appropriateness of their participation are concerned about how they carry
themselves and present themselves to others. They show their readiness
to participate by "giving good face," and they describe a person with
bad mind as someone who "gives bad face"; the idealized expression on
the face of a dancer or a carving is in aesthetic contrast to the ugliness
or lack of composure of someone who "squeezes" his face. In their
public life and in public view, Africans express themselves according to
their sense of the appropriate, demonstrating generosity, respect, de-
light—and foolishness. Like the bar girl dancing with the European
businessman, people in Africa spend a lot of time laughing at the irony
of misguided efforts and the distortions of participation. Yet in its way
too, their sense of humor continues to show their concern for community: they have a preference for satire, and even the most satirical
imitation is displayed to encourage better participation. In art, satire
usually seems to be an exaggeration of the opposite of the aesthetically
fine, and thus satire accentuates and points to those features of art or
behavior which limit or fall short of aesthetic or social possibilities.

If people are concerned that the possibilities of life should be realized,
they are also aware that the limitations of life must be acknowledged.
Continually and in many ways, in funerals, in libations, in proverbs,
songs, and advice, they remind themselves of a human being's mortality,
the fundamental basis of respect between people, whether strangers or
friends. When participation is not a joke, when the situation passes
from the comic to the serious, people try to be tolerant and sympathetic
because they admit the complexity of circumstances and the need for
open-mindedness and support. In a world of individuals, it is easy to
be disappointed or surprised, difficult to be earnest or dogmatic. When
participation becomes a problem, people can count on others for encouragement. Even on a city street, in a bad moment, faced with be-
trayal, disappointment, inadequacy, or failure, they might look up and
see the motto that the driver of a passing truck or taxi has painted on
his vehicle: "No Condition is Permanent" or "Patience" or "God Will
Provide" or "People are Bad" or "Keep Cool" or "Still Smiling" or "I
Cry" or "Remember Death" or "Think Twice" or "Don't Mind Them"
or "Late But Serious" or "Experience!" or "Psalm 23" or "John
Wayne" or "Suffer to Gain" or "All That Glitters" or "They Act as
Lovers" or "Don't Forget Your Six Feet" or "Mysterious" or "Such
Is Life" or "Observers are Worried; Believers are Enjoying" or "All
Days Are Not Equal." Alhassan used to console me during practices by

saying, "Every mistake is a new style." The Ewe people who allowed me to play their sacred music on sacred occasions responded to what I felt was my inadequacy by saying, "Fine. You're trying."

In Africa the notion of participation as a significant gesture of active effort, as a contribution which gives life and meaning, has provided a central theme of religious intuition and practice. In French-speaking countries, if you are invited to observe a certain event, perhaps a ceremony or a musical performance, the people who expect you merely to watch in relative ignorance will nonetheless use the verb "assister"; in English-speaking countries you will be invited to "witness." Even when spectators are not openly involved in the proceedings, their presence is never passive. While other peoples have focused the main force of their philosophical and religious energies on such issues as love, suffering, or fate,[17] Africans have devoted their greatest attention to the relationship of time and presence. Perhaps the most significant characteristic of their religious heritage, of which music is such an important part, is that it brings into their lives a fundamental sense for the appropriate as it concerns other people. In both village and urban settings, people are constantly alert and ready to recognize each other, and they become extremely sensitive to the way they participate. Their presence at an event, in faith and gesture, implies an engagement of minds and bodies to endow their social forms with life. Dynamic power is present in the cosmos, but as at a musical event, it is shaped and given form, incorporated into effective communication, and made willfully present where there was only potential by the power of human understanding, and it is not revealed but directed.

In this sense, the African ritualization of community forms represents a coordinated effort to encounter, to mediate, and to control the power of life. Africans bring conflict and opposition into their social relationships because order and stability are matters of human responsibility and not Divine invention.[18] For Africans, ideas of community serve as the foundation for conceptions of the order of the world and for evaluations of the meaning of life. They refer to their community traditions as "ways of living," and their communities have meaning for them as multifaceted and open arrangements designed, it seems, to allow them to participate and thus to be involved to their extent with power as they live their lives. Religiously considered, participation adds the value and strength of a person to the continuity of commitment that creates a heritage.[19]

We should be cautious, therefore, of trying to understand their community life through our own models: they do not seem to think of their communities as defined primarily or necessarily by territoriality, by a kind of total mystical involvement, by a fixed collection of ideas, symbols, or beliefs, by a civil consensus required to restrain "human nature," or by an economic agreement to provide the necessities of life. These aspects of community solidarity are honored, of course, but people are pragmatic about the customs and institutions of their societies. A specific convention is important because of the meaning with which it has been and may be invested by others, dead and alive, but people respect the intention as the essential element of reality in the procedure, the wisdom of the heart which has flowed through their finest cultural achievements. Concerned with appropriate effect, they set their standards of success and richness in life with an awareness that the conventions they observe are functional, and people expect and are prepared to modify them according to circumstances.[20] As one African student phrased it, "We are traditionally socially adaptable."

In broader terms, then, individual destiny is inseparable from family, community, and history. In African religious belief, the departed continue to watch over the community, and the departed themselves are judged and their lives are expanded by those who remember them and continue to live in the world of meaning. A person truly dies when his influence on the living ends, when he is forgotten, and in this sense we can perhaps understand the gravity of the offense for a drummer to make a mistake when drumming the names of the chief's lineage. One's relationship to the ancestors is, like music, a vehicle for character and an indication of purity of heart, but it is not often that an African will refer to the ancestors in a discussion of morality or character. Instead, a person who truly dies only when he is forgotten will speak of children in order to affirm and testify to the importance of personal virtue because he understands their survival as the meaning and strength of his place in community. God has set the stage of the world, but it is to one's children that one must turn for judgement. The ancestors are the guardians of morality because they represent the generational continuity of concern and respect.[21]

When an African thanks his ancestors with libations before he eats or drinks, or when he asks you whether you have "learned to like" something rather than whether you simply "like" it, he is indicating that, to him, his chance for pleasure and happiness is only possible within society, through the efforts of those who have taught him to appreciate life. The importance of the parent-child relationship is extended to a ritualized attitude of respect and obedience to all one's elders, and a child learns the etiquette of this relationship as the fundamental basis of all formalities. Most people in Africa do not romanticize or idealize

childhood as a period of unsocialized innocence and spontaneity: creativity, expressive beauty, purity, and freedom are respected as attributes
of maturity and experience. But in musical situations, where the elders
excel at demonstrating character, we can also see the family situation of
the child who must master his egotism to develop character. In our
discussion of drumming techniques, we found that each performance
demands a special attitude, combining both discipline and freedom. Specifically, the organization of the many rhythms imposes restrictions on
expression. The old men demonstrate the best musical style because they
are able to let the other parts speak, to build and control a more forceful and organized expression. They know how to be free without domi-
nating or ignoring the other rhythms, and they use their insight to open
the rhythmic relationships to participation and communication. They
demonstrate character by knowing the boundaries of participation; they
have learned to mediate conflict and to control their expressions in reference to the limitations of an organized structure of relationships. The
elders' depth of character is evident in the subtle complexity of their
coordination and in the fullness of their integration of multiple rhythmic relationships.[22] They are masters of responsible involvement and
communicative clarity. Their individuality is developed on a community
foundation, and informed audiences find beauty in their maturity. In
contrast, we Westerners often tend to think of character as the uniqueness we assert, as a special or essential quality which distinguishes a
person, the mark of individuality which sets a person apart. According
to our conception, too, character is something which can be acquired or
lost or sometimes proven at a single, concentrated point of crisis or confrontation.[23] But in an African context, such as a musical event, individuality is related to participation, and in the complex relationships of
an African community context, character is understood as a sense of
one's relationships with others, as a continuing style of involvement and
making do, and hence as a focus for moral judgements.

As the music makes clear, presence of mind is the essential attribute
of mature creative authority, the ability to act with initiative and to command with insight under the pressure of conflict and change. Not just in
Tamale but in all of Ghana, one of the worst things you can say about
someone is that he is "by heart." Such an individual acts "at random";
his expressions are rough and "without purpose." "Purpose" in this
sense is not the resolute motivation toward a goal by which we define
the term but rather is a concern for the meaningfulness of one's actions,
a sense of proportion in self-awareness, and an attitude of thoughtful-
ness in self-expression. Random behavior is the exact antithesis of the

ritualizing orientation. In music, random improvisation and imprecision spoil the delicate structure of the rhythms, and in society, random expressions spoil the delicate structure of communication. In effect, someone who is "by heart" is neither reasonable nor sensible; he does not act with well-tempered consideration of the world around him; he cannot act with appropriate responsibility or effective concern or even genuine feeling; and he will abuse life. In short, in Africa someone with bad character is essentially someone who lacks respect, someone who has withdrawn from participation in society and whose intentions have become inaccessible. A person with good character demonstrates it by binding his feelings and his imagination to the service of his mind, by finding the road to comprehend his situation and execute his actions with balance and control. In the broadest terms, evil may be equated with a lack of "purpose" and good with an effort to care.

It is not easy, however, to be evil when music is playing. It is possible to be in bad taste, of course, but if somebody makes trouble, music stops. Africans rely on music to maintain the happiness and vitality of their social worlds. As we know, in its varied institutional roles, music provides a focus for participation in social activities, helping people orient themselves to what they are doing together. In Africa, music helps people to work, to enjoy themselves, to control a bad person or to praise a good one, to recite history, poetry, and proverbs, to celebrate a funeral or a festival, to compete with each other, to encounter their gods, to grow up, and, fundamentally, to be sociable in everything they do. We may readily understand the reciprocity inherent in rhythmic call-and-response or the goal of connectedness in apart-playing and dancing. But from our discussion of the artistic dimensions of African music, we also know that music teaches people to recognize and judge what is valuable in social and personal life.

A musical occasion is an occasion to see people, usually at their best. Music puts people on display, and in Africa it is possible to criticize or appreciate both music and behavior through the same concerns. To Ibrahim Abdulai, Alhassan's character often prevented him from playing tastefully, and my own anger at Alhassan cast serious doubts about my ability to progress to full competence; in the cult as well, the quality of my performance was entrusted to the ancestors to ensure that I would play with strength and with a clear mind and a pure heart. Proper performance of African music requires the respect and enjoyment of the organization of power. To balance the exciting conflict of the rhythms, to incorporate change into an ordered social expression, and to give power a personal form, all these issues of aesthetic command are the concerns of good character; and we cannot be surprised that in any situation, people whose purpose is to exercise power are concerned with beauty. In some African societies, a physically deformed person is not qualified to become a chief. Robert F. Thompson, in another of his fine essays, comments nicely on the relationship of beauty and character:

> I once complimented the elders of Tinto-Mbu in the Banyang portion of the United Republic of Cameroon on the fine appearance of their chief. Whereupon they immediately corrected me: "We say people are not judged by physical beauty but by the quality of their heart and soul; the survival of our chief is a matter of his character, not his looks." However, no matter how ordinary his face, it is important for the chief to dress as beautifully as possible in order to attest his fineness of position in appropriate visual impact. He must consequently prove that he knows and controls the forces of beauty as much as the forces of polity and social pressure. Beauty, the full embodiment of manly power, or the power of women, in feminine contexts, is mandatory where it is necessary to clarify social relations. It would not make sense . . . to strike balances between opposing factions without aesthetic elaboration.[24]

Thompson's writings on African sculpture have elaborated on his description of the shining image of maturity and creative authority. Within its own form, sculpture articulates the same ethical themes as music, showing the presence and continuity of the sensibility which influences so many African social expressions. We have been able to discuss the aesthetic dimensions of an African musical event by analyzing its role as an institution, observing how rhythms work, and examining human relationships and behavior within an ongoing context of social action; but sculpture does not lend itself so easily to such an approach. As an art historian, Thompson has utilized language, myth, religion, and the knowledge of indigenous artists and critics in order to study the meaning of traditional Yoruba sculpture. In several passages, Thompson discusses the values embodied in sculpture, values we have learned to recognize in a musical performance.

> The nine million Yoruba of southwestern Nigeria and Dahomey value power and command (*ashe*), composure (*itutu*), and character (*iwa*). Composure is essential to grant focus and restraint to power, and character assures that power accrues to the benefit of mankind.

The ideal of composure (coolness) is one essence of man in an
idealized state. But anger and heat are qualities which are somehow
to be accepted and controlled. Myth says that the hot and the
cool occur together. . . . Balance is achieved by recognition of the
elements of bad which complement the elements of good. The
wisdom of the elders time and time again strikes through to the
hidden complementarity within the strife and divisions of life.
The care and precision of art, the total involvement of the self
which its proper execution demands, is a kind of generosity which
lessens the distance between the sacred and the profane. To be
generous in a beautiful way seems the essence of morality and the
assurance of continuity.

Images show a concentrated expression of vitality tempered by
balance and a sense of moral depth. . . . The sharply rendered
features within the accented dimension of the head make visible the
importance of mind as a source of character and luck even as
the physicality of the frame is strongly shaped. Vividness is cast
into equilibrium; again and again bodily force disappears into
controlling aspects of stability and mind. Force returns in the
intensity of the dance and lends power, by contrast, to the frozen
visages of the masks and statuary, riding the energy like emblems
of the intellect.[25]

In music, the contrasting, tightly organized rhythms are powerful—
powerful because there is vitality in rhythmic conflict, powerful precisely
because people are affected and moved. As people participate in a musical situation, they mediate the conflict, and their immediate presence
gives power a personal form so that they may relate to it. Thus while
people participate with power as a way of relating effectively to each
other at a musical or social event, they also participate with power as a
religious force. In limiting and focusing Absolute power to specific
forms, they encounter power as a reality which is not overwhelming and
devastating but strengthening and upbuilding. In a pluralistic world,
their conscious sense of boundaries enables them to bring power into
their lives as a positive force. When Africans allow a person to become
possessed or identified with power, as when they celebrate or praise a
particular cult god whose rhythm "rides" or "comes up" to a dancer,
they are using music and dance as a technique of religious experience,
and as we noted, they do so most often under strictly controlled circumstances in the presence of a religious figure, a specialist at cooling down
"hot" people. In Africa, power is not something inherent in an individu-

al, nor is it identified solely with physical strength: a man of strong, muscular physique will be described merely as "a tough fellow." Power is always and only known in its effects: it is the full potential of what a person can do or be, and from an African perspective, someone who "has" power is someone who is capable of directing his energies with a sense of purpose.

The possibility of engagement and meaning which personality lends to power stands idealized as the person who keeps a calm head in order to maintain communication, to meet another's expressions with a different and balancing presence. In their community life, people respect collectedness of mind as the foundation of understanding and definitive action. Their ability to be effective, socially or aesthetically, requires that both heart and mind work together to guide power into their relationships. People respect a man like Ibrahim Abdulai because his command of music is evidence not only of his ability to influence them but also of the broad scope and disciplined effectiveness of his mind. Such a man can bring both pressure and insight to bear on his activities, and people recognize, respect, and admire the maturity of his judgements whether he is beating the drum, whether he is meeting his obligations to his family and his community, or whether he is teaching a young stranger how to use power with care.

In its own way, the approach that I took developed from a fortunate coincidence of temperament and circumstances. Probably because I enjoyed music more than scholarship, I was interested in finding a place for myself within a musical context rather than finding a place for my involvement with music within a scholarly context. Just a few weeks after I had arrived in Ghana, I was dimly aware that in the cult I was accepting other standards of judgement, that African values would define the meaning of my actions. I was deferential and self-conscious because I assumed that I did not know what to do in most situations. I accepted what people told me about myself and what I should be doing, perhaps because I felt that I could trust them, or perhaps because it seemed that I had no other choice. I was patient with the limitations I imposed on myself, and while I waited to see what people would make of me, I tried to be friendly and I did not mind if they found me amusing. They taught me, I believe, because they knew that I was trying to be receptive and responsible. By staying cool I learned the meaning of character. I learned that a person is what others see him to be and that he finds himself insofar as he is accessible to their influence. I thus learned to participate in African social life before I tried seriously to make music, yet all the time I was having fun with people, I was learning about music. As Ibrahim said, the heart sees before the eyes.

After more than seven months came the first time when I actually told somebody to do something. Not incidentally, this first use of "power" was to protect from abuse the people on that very bus which was carrying me from Bawku to Tamale to begin my lessons on Dagomba drums, the bus on which I had accepted some of the implications of my involvement in their lives. The other passengers told me that when I spoke to the abuser, he was afraid of me. Surprised, I asked why. They tried to explain a certain confidence I had expressed that forced him to respect me. When Ibrahim called my name as we played Kondalia, he was calling me to show what I could do, that I might know that the time had come when I could assert my presence and not fall down. He was also telling me, as many others had as well, that if I were going to be involved with their lives and study their music, I would have to tell my own story too. And probably, in their eyes, to be able to fulfill this personal obligation was my purpose for being there, that I might understand the meaning and etiquette of the relationships of life and bring forth my own strength in the service of beauty and goodness. From their perspective, while strength is communal, faith must be personal. A Highlife song asks, "When shall I raise my head? I have kept it low; now when will I lift it up?"[26] I doubt that I could have learned to play the drums without their interest first in the growth of my character so that I might have the proper sensibility to know what I was doing.

In raising certain cultural themes to the level of institutional processes, music informs character and provides continuity with traditional values. Under the pressure of conflict and change, Africans achieve the composure and confidence of purpose which ties the expressions of their lives to the expressions of composure and confidence on the faces of their ancestors, whose statues affirm the presence and power of moral judgement in a dynamic world. The values of their art thus speak of continuity, of a sense of creativity and strength that must have effect on the forms that a changing world takes. Under the impact of industry, bureaucracy, and urbanism, the loyalties and social forms of the past are being radically transformed, but Africans will bring their sensibility to the challenges of change. As Africa industrializes and as its bureaucracies and its cities grow, the profound humanism of the African sensibility will give a particular shape to institutions and processes which we Westerners have to this point been able to judge only from our own experience and history. As they remake Western institutions in their own way, they will display for us fresh alternatives and possibilities for effective participation in a world of human responsibility. Their history will be a complicated history, perhaps one in which our participation will begin to show the generosity of spirit that has elevated their community expressions to the realm of art. In the way that their approach to life can show us new things about ourselves, they will help us, and we can seek moral guidance in their sensitivity and adaptability. In my study of their music, I learned to recognize the meaning of their wisdom in my personal life, but I have hoped that a scholarly approach to the themes of African music will enable readers to participate in my experience from their own points of view, to testify that the focus of this book developed from an attempt to see Africa.

Alhaji Ibrahim Abdulai

Gideon Folie Alorwoyie

Dagomba drum-maker preparing the grass
to bind the ring on a dondon head

Ewe drum-makers sewing a head for Kroboto

Sewing a head for a dondon

Fixing a Kroboto head onto the pegs.
The excess skin will be trimmed last.

Akan dondon beaters

Takai ensemble: dondons and gongons

Holding a Dagomba dondon

Atumpan drums, used for both talking and dance, have
a wide distribution beyond the Akan area

Ewe supporting drums. *Left to right*, Sogo, Kidi, Sogo

A young Dagomba dancer

Atikatika

Tora, a Dagomba dance for young girls

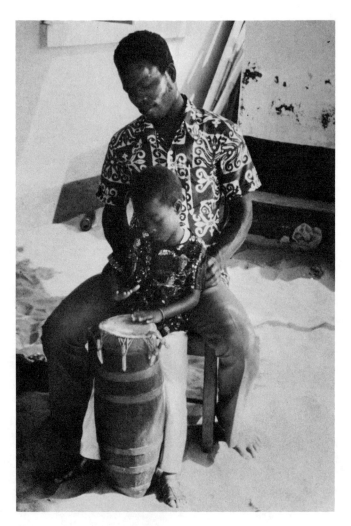

Ewe child learning on Kagan

Takai dance

Dagomba child playing a toy drum

Young Ewe Borborbor dancers sing as they come out
to dance

Akan Adowa dancer. The atumpan drummer watches her, while the spectators show approval

Akan executioner's dance: a dance of agility

Possession in an Ewe cult: cooling the medium

Konkomba dancers. Stringed cowrie shells add extra movement

The wife of a Dagomba chief coming out at a festival

Dagomba dancer

Dagomba drummers playing for Gurunsi dancer

Appendix

In 1965 Charles Keil was doing research in Nigeria, where he collected the following data. He has kindly allowed me to include it as an appendix to this work so that other readers may appreciate it. Professor Keil sponsored a contest in *Spear* magazine, which was somewhat the equivalent of *Life* or *Look* and which had a wide circulation on various levels of Nigerian society, from the most prosperous and educated to those who used the magazine to help them in their early studies of the English language. Readers were asked to respond in thirty words or less to the question "Who is your favorite musician—and why?" Some of the responses, including several essays in which inspiration and concern overcame the word limit, are here reproduced more or less intact, though with the contestants' names omitted. Although somewhat dated, the entries offer an extremely interesting glimpse of how a contemporary and discerning Nigerian audience might talk about music.

Rex Lawson is a simple nontribalistic musician whose compositions are moderate, melodious, original, meaningful and either laudatory or advisory. His understanding of the modern social problems incorporated in his music beautifies them.

He's the gentle, meek, original and responsible OSADEBE. His music reflects the ages' aspirations, cool, admonishing, consoling, encouraging and prayerful. He suits the sounds to the meanings in variable tunes.

My favorite musician (REX LAWSON). Highly original in his frequent but variedly presented productions, Lawson's entreating sonorous voice and appropriate gesticulations entice even non-Kalabaris. Stage fun plus accuracy, manifesting ease and expertness, enliven his music.

My favorite musician is Doctor Victor Olaiya. He is because he is a good composer, a man of policy, a good hypnotist and a good subject for hypnotism himself.

My favorite musician is I. K. Dairo. He begins moderately, sings moderately, ends moderately. No mixing of language. No mumble. Different tones, tunes, and beating in each music. His tunation, tone, and beating molded together keep music unfaded.

My favorite musician is Dairo. In music he appeals to all classes of people: politicians, lovers, and common men. He does not blame in his music. He uses indigenous dialect.

Please, Mr. Editor, my favorite musician is Mr. Cardinal Jim Rex Lawson because his music can make the unhappy to be happy and a divorced couple to be reengaged and an angry lion to be calmed.

My favorite musician is "Cardinal Jim Rex Lawson," because he seems to have discovered his formula for success in the field of popular high-life music. Right now, his records are hot favorites. From Potiskum in Northern Nigeria to Port Harcourt in the South, anywhere Rex Lawson blows his trumpet, he is quickly followed by thousands of wildly cheering and dancing, enthusiastic admirers. His records sell like hot cakes. Moreover, if you go to most night clubs in the cities, as like as not, the band will dish out some numbers—tunes originally composed and recorded by Jim Lawson to the fans. Candidly speaking, Rex Lawson has become a sort of local "pied piper" who does not fail to draw out his high-life fans from wherever they may be.

Rex Jim Lawson is an unassuming young man of medium height with a neat goatee beard. He's a Christian of the Protestant denomination. It is because of his righteous music that some hotel proprietors named him "Pastor," "Archbishop," "Cardinal," and also "Pope," but Rex Lawson, a non-Catholic, refused this title because he felt there should be only one pope throughout the world.

Finally Jim Rex Lawson is riding high on the wave of his popularity. He is in demand all over the country and for each night-stand he takes such handsome fees as would make the mouths of less popular dance bandleaders water.

Rex Lawson is my favorite musician. He is clairvoyant and an illustrious vocalist with originality and varied patterns of rhythm. His instruments syncopate to produce music fabulously rich and exhilarating.

My favorite musician is Victor Olaiya. His music is up-to-date and always adapted to his audience. Decency, morality, originality and efficiency are the attributes of Olaiya the King of highlife.

My favorite musician is Stephen Osita Osadebe. This is because most of his musics always advise people how to live peacefully and successfully in this world.

Jim Lawson is my favorite. His records are adviserly, prayerly, and melodiously composited. The underground sound of instruments thrills even a mad person to dance and escape madness meanwhile.

My favorite musician is Haruna Ishola. He is an artist who renders Yoruba homilies in rich and melodious songs to the tune of classical Apala music that makes one remember the Poetic and artful past.

I am a regular reader of your *Spear* magazine. I became one since 1962 because your articles are so helpful to me in my study of the English. In your *Spear* magazine issued this month you asked who is my favorite musician. With my practical ability my answer follows below.

(1) My favorite musician is I.K. Dairo—M.B.E. Juju Musician.

(2) Because Juju Music was permissible at wedding ceremonies, funeral processions, naming ceremonies, and at the moment high-life and Juju music have evolved as national musical forms and also good for personal enjoyments.

I am a schooler and not very frequent in musical rooms but I have taken up Cardinal Jim Rex Lawson as my favorite musician. He is popular and well-known for his melodious and well-translated music. He has a strong backbone in musical influence and may I call him the Author of modern records.

Cardinal Jim Rex Lawson, though well-known for music and richness, is filled up with the milk of human kindness, sincere, sympathetic and courageous. His players are well-trained and are matured in music, in short they are men of great intellectual ability. So hearty and well built up is his music that all old fathers and mothers like to attend his stage to enjoy their last living. Even young men of youth find it very impossible to sleep when he is in town.

The supremacy of his music has suppressed the interest of others to going to other musical temples. He is the all and all of the Nation's musicians (Primus inter Pares), Master of the masters. His music is so cool and straight forwarded that only Heavens can say. Minus him there will be no exhaltation in Nigeria.

The guitarist is a father of music, the drummer a mother of music, and the sax man is the Alpha and Omega. They should be praised for their good name to the country of Nigeria. I therefore pray to almighty God to let Cardinal Jim Rex Lawson be in peace so that he continues to give us his heavenly music which I may call maker of happiness. I beg to close hoping You and Lawson Good Luck.

My favorite musician is Dr. Victor Olaiya PH.D. Music. He has a complete set of instruments which he uses in producing his melodious records. Every instrument can be clearly distinguished in his every release of records. Also his band has a matched uniform.

MY FAVORITE MUSICIAN IS I.K. Dairo, THE UNBEATABLE SPECIALIST on juju music. His music is the most unrivalled, distinct, melodious, rhythmical and intoxicating. Its slow diffusion into my body makes me dance to the tune while jujus shake heads to the beats.

My favorite musician is Haruna Ishola. As far as the Native Music ("APALA") is concerned in Nigeria today, Haruna Ishola is the best of all. Firstly, the starting of his play is very attractive and pleasing. Secondly, all the beatings are clearly sound and understanding. Thirdly, the whole song's pronunciations are very explanatory that: if someone is far away, and a plate of Haruna Ishola is put on the amplifier at a bit louder, if at all the man does not know how to dance it, he or she will admire very greatly, and will try to move the legs at once.

In fact, I like Haruna Ishola the most. Even Haruna Ishola has cultivated to the progress in Nigeria. All the songs of Haruna are "directory, and full of Advice." Most especially when his fingers are dancing all about on the "AGIDIGBO" together with the maracas, any music lover nearby will forget himself to the very sport. When again, the bass drum is touched together with the small talking drum, I don't think someone will be able again to do anything else rather than dancing. Haruna has taught many people both men and women of Nigeria how to enjoy their lives modernly. Haruna Ishola's music is just like a boy meets with his girlfriend, how joyful they are.

Haruna Ishola, in fact, is a good and popular musician in Nigeria. For one who knows the value of the Native Music ("APALA") will recommend Haruna Ishola as the best Musician. And as such, this is a suggestion to the public, to elect and announce Haruna Ishola as "GRADE A" in APALA music in Nigeria as a whole.

My favorite musician is Jim Reeves because in his songs which are very touching to the heart he always tries to remind us that the world is a temporal place.

Rex Lawson my choice is.
Trading on cop-work not his.
Every composition original,
Melodious meaningful rhythmical.
Though traditionally sounds it,
Nothing modern lacks it.

Roy Chicago is my favorite musician and has been since February 1962. There is yet to appear a musician to equal his exhilarating brand of music which is peculiarly African. The absence of such music in Europe, psychologists claim, is responsible for so many Psychic cases over there. With Roy's music about the place, even the most reserved of persons forgets being shy and really does let go.

To the best of my experience I am of the opinion that King Kennytone (Nigeria's King of Twist) is not my favorite musician alone, but also every young Nigerian Citizen's. I selected him because, whenever I hear him zoom into any of his records—Helen Twist, Suzy Twist, Twist to Happiness, Twist Festival—hey, I go jolly, nutty and excited and forget all my miseries. Above all, I can't do without his records.

Sensible hedonist I.K. Dairo is my favorite musician. Dairo's consistent drumming, sedulousity, impartiality and unservitudeness make him the Shakespeare of Music. An earthly god of music!

Mystical Musicians! Otherwise Ezigbo Obiligbo's rhythm-deep rolling Egwu-egbili' music, marvelously interwoven in wise proverbial Ibo language with the simplest native, harmonious orchestration stays without description and comment.

My choice is Lawson. He makes me happy.

The late Jim Reeves is my music idol. His cool sentimentality, his heart-awakening compositions, the voice and the instruments which make you feel the angels around, surely win your heart.

My favorite musician is Bobby Benson because of his introduction of high-life music into Nigeria whose geographical, linguistic and cultural value today gradually links the different tribes of Nigeria together.

I am hereby to state in as following. My most favorite musician is I.K. DAIRO. Why he is so favorite to me is that the moment of my hearing his music, i will be confused of what I am doing and also having much interest in his music always especially Angelina oltilo yoju. In fact, I take I.K. DAIRO to be one of Nigeria's best juju musicians because his music always shocks everybody when ever one hears it. And his songs always have a meaning. In fact the moment I am annoyed with my girlfriend or feel unhappy with everything on earth and fed up with life, but as soon as I put on my radio and hear I.K. DAIRO's music, I will be just very happy and forget all sorts of bad thinking and start kissing my girlfriend. So please ladies and gentlemen I wish you all to have an interest in I.K. DAIRO's music as I do myself. Because he is so great. Thanks in Advance.

Stephen Osita Osadebe is my favorite musician. His originality in selecting words singles him out as a musical psychologist. The shaking voice added with melodious "Bongos" put man to sleep.

Choice—Stephen Osadebe. Why? Variety of language in his recordings. Notably calm, full of meaning, always composed and not noisy. His natural melodious voice and beat coupled with originality make his music supreme.

He is E.T. Mensah, whose pieces, melodiously repetitive and often duple-timed, are characteristic of Africa. His often sentimental compositions are philosophically tinged with harmonic improvisations and syncopated phraseologies.

He is handsome, has a natural enticing appealing lovely voice which suits the exceptionally particular, peculiar, indigenous rhythm of real historical compositions. A determined preserver of culture. Everybody's favorite—Osadebe.

He is Rex Lawson. He believes in originality, traditionalism, and orderly arrangement. His compositions are educative, classical, charming, and lauded by the majority. He has raised Nigeria's reputation in cultural arts.

Dr. Victor Olaiya plays foreign and indigenous tunes in all Nigerian dialects and English to audience's tastes and doesn't ridicule any sex. He is a non-tribalistic mobile music dramatist. Olaiya means music.

Although I appreciate the efforts of our musicians, I am most indebted to our dear Jim Reeves. Jim Reeves, this dead but living musician, furnishes his music with qualities natural, but rarely employed by his comrades. By subduing his deep voice to the natural laws of sounds and motion he effects a peculiar melody which portrays his ingenuity and geniality.

The rhythm, wordings and choice of material for his compositions infuse into the minds of his listeners an Imaginary State of Inspiration which represents the godfather of works. Reeves, by covering a wide range of topics, entertains the world with unfailing harmonies to meet satisfaction for individual choice. His listeners and admirers are equipped with music suitable for different occasions. His special compositions such as (i) This world is not my home, (ii) I'd rather have Jesus, (iii) Bottle take effect, (iv) We thank thee Lord, etc., are not only living testimonies to his experience in life and music but worthy memoranda.

Thanks to our Gentleman Jim Reeves for his contributions to the world's pleasure in the composition of his entertaining, endearing, and truly sentimental music.

Oh what a choice to have Dairo as one's favorite musician, the man whose music will move the laziest feet to action and will pour undying relief into sorrowful hearts.

I.K. Dairo is my favorite musician whose music has a captivating melody which brings enjoyment to the listener through his proverbial and witty style which arrests audience's attention marvelously.

My favorite musician if I am allowed to say is "I.K. Dairo." My choosing him is based on three different reasons, thus—performances, vocal mentality, and lastly style of songs and beats.

I open this paragraph giving and explaining the first reason, performances. By performances I mean his actions whenever he stages a play. Just imagine a man to be jumping from one instrument to the other one and at times doing or combining two at a time when he plays and at the same time singing on the microphone. In fact his performances alone should be able to convince any person who witnesses his plays.

My second reason is his vocal mentality. I am sure everyone has been listening to various vocalists and can differentiate their voices and most especially that voice of I.K. Dairo from other vocalists. This difference of voice from other vocalists is due to the fact that his voice is smooth and can change from high to medium and to low tunes and vice-versa. This comprises my second reason for having selected him as my favorite musician.

My third reason lies on the styles of songs and beats. Although other vocalists do sing songs of praise, his are more sensational, and inclusive

are his songs of advice. Now the beats which are also easily differen-
tiated from other vocalists by listeners, I am sure they always observe
that Dairo's beats seem to be alternate to people singing although both
the beating and the singers come to end at the same time. The booming
of the band which cracks someone's brain and which forces dumb legs
to move even if unwilling to move and the use of drum in talking should
also be taken into consideration. There ends the three main convincing
reasons for my taking I.K. Dairo as my favorite musician.

DELE OJO. He is a genius who has injected the breath of life into
the traditional JUJU music. Conscious and appealing in his selection
of words. His guitar in particular is alert.

My favorite, your favorite, everybody's favorite is undoubtedly the
only modern musician in the person of Cardinal Rex Jim Lawson.
Cardinal who started music some years back has proved himself the
best musician as high-life is concerned in our present day Nigeria.
Why? Today, apart from being Nigeria's most expensive band leader,
Lawson has succeeded to remain the country's most adored, most talked
about musician. Cardinal has become such a man in town that the
smallest child knows his records when they are being played. Personally,
I presume that Cardinal has given Nigerian high-life a new interpretation. His ways of playing the guitar, blowing of trumpet, the way he
sings, the way he dances are all different from the way other Nigerian
musicians do which has mostly contributed to his being your favorite,
my favorite, everybody's favorite musician.
As a musician with countless fans, he is never disappointful. By this
I mean that Cardinal is always out to impress his fans. Even the most
oldest man or woman, when she hears Cardinal's records she moves,
she dances and rejoices to God for having created such a musician.
Some musicians disappoint their fans, Cardinal is never to be listed
amongst such musicians. If you make a close research, you will surely
discover that youngsters when they go to picnics and Cardinal's records
are nowhere to be found, I am sure that such a party will never hold.
In conclusion I must not fail to assure you that Cardinal will undoubtedly continue to be everybody's favorite. He has no rivals, no
obstacles in his way. As a small boy, this is what I am able to produce
just to show that Cardinal is and will continue to be the best musician
of our country. I am sure more educated and older people will contribute more to make Cardinal never to be forgotten.

Unique Rex Lawson is my musical hero. His songs are original, prayerful, solemn, soothing, lively, rousing, absorbing, superb, masterly, rhythmical, and mellow.

The extra special, expensive, Nigerian celebrated, fabulous Rex Lawson features as my favorite because his musical symphony is unique, touching and jujulike. He produces records according to seasons and happenings.

Dele Ojo. He plays to Impress people.

Cardinal Lawson whose music is indigenous, original and alluring has revolutionized Highlife. His linguistic ingenuity, superb instrumentation, captivating voice have made his beat irresistible. Rex and good highlife are synonymous.

My favorite Musician is Cardinal Jim Rex Lawson. Why: The originality and serenity of his compositions. The wordings interpreted for general consumption remind listeners of original home stories with modern touch and endearing message. Talent and Industry for Production.

Kehinde Dairo uses melodious traditional pleasing tunes, thought-provoking words, proverbs and with observations of the ordinary country folk songs and refines, revives, recognizes, and elevates our traditional Nigerian music.

I. K. Dairo M. B. E. with his originality in composition, spontaneous presentation of his juju folk songs, rhythmical in nature that could move body and soul. His is music without tears.

Dr. Victor Olaiya is My favorite Musician. He uses almost every tribal language in Nigeria in his highlife beats with his uniformed stars. Compendious Composition tunefully reproduced follows the drums under the vivid rhythms of the guitarist.

My favorite musician in Nigeria is Mr. I. K. Dairo, and others like him. He is because his brand of music inspires the youths and takes the old back to his youthful past, which he remembers with awe and admiration. In short, both old and young find in this brand of music melody and rhythm, the magic ingredient with which the music enlightens the hearts and keeps every listener happy and delighted.

By and large, this type of music is very good: it can be used both in sorrows and in joy, it fits in in funeral wakings and it is generally enjoyed during the festivals; at all occasions, it is not out-of-place.

This folk singer entertains persons, whoever comes in contact with him, in the theater of play. In addition, even one who does not understand the language and/or dialect which the folk song used enjoys the melody and joins to sing the folk song with awe and admiration. With further points in support of this juju type of music or musician, it is generally known that all forms of music are enjoyable, yet, such powerful juju cum idiom cum folk song singers will have impact on someone who is in far away countries with the depression of home-sickness, the person will revive quicker if all of a sudden this type of music is played for him.

In conclusion, I am bold to say that such musicians like Nwaoye Awaka Tunde King of Lagos, I. K. Dairo of recent years, and many others cannot be left out if the history of musicians is to be written, their records and names will be distinct and clearly labeled in our archives and museums.

He who is not proud of his color is not fit to live, says the learned Dr. Aggrey. We as Nigerians should be very proud of our Juju music and be very proud of our dear son Dairo for raising the standard of our juju music. It is true that Juju music has taken its origin from the 1930's and this is our national music. The highlife, pop, jazz, etc., are overseas music introduced to our Land but the Juju takes its origin in our own Land.

The old order changeth yielding place to the new. Dairo's new style in Juju is a modernization of the old art of Juju that our forefathers played in this our country Nigeria. With this Dairo's styles, he has kept us of the present Nigeria abreast of the reserved history of Nigeria in his music. His music contains lots of the up and down of his world. It teaches us knowledge, moral spirits and other things.

This has won him the great honor of representing the country, Nigeria, in overseas countries to present some of the records to those overseas. This is a commendable and notable effort on his part and this earned him the honor of M.B.E. References can be made to his records. If I am permitted, I can even write a whole book on him, that Dairo is the musician who has contributed most to Nigerian music over the many years, and I wish my readers could take to my side.

Long life, I.K. Dairo, and may God bless you to put into light in your music more of this country's preservation. Amen.

Notes

Introduction

Scholarship and Participation

1. *The Birth of Tragedy out of the Spirit of Music,* trans. Francis Golffing (Garden City, N.Y.: Doubleday, Anchor Books, 1956), p. 5.
2. Ibid., p. 90.
3. Ibid., pp. 93, 95. A further irony, and certainly a good one on Nietzsche himself, lies in the fact that his book comes very close to offering a practical and substantive approach to an understanding of African music. Social scientists who investigate the meaning of art in traditional societies should be especially stimulated by Nietzsche's approach to the meaning of art and ritual in classical Greek culture. Though I am aware that Ruth Benedict was severely taken to task for utilizing this same book in her *Patterns of Culture* (Boston: Houghton Mifflin, 1934), my reference here to *The Birth of Tragedy* is neither formally nor descriptively parallel to her use of it for model-building, for there are no direct parallels to be drawn, as for example identifying African musical expressions with either the Apollonian or Dionysian modes as Nietzsche portrays them. At the same time, I hope, my reference within a philosophical context is somewhat more appropriate to the content of Nietzsche's books, particularly in terms of his philosophical attitudes toward art and scholarship and the comprehensiveness of his critical orientation toward another culture.
4. *The Birth of Tragedy,* p. 90.
5. *The Use and Abuse of History,* trans. Adrian Collins (New York: Liberal Arts Press, 1957).
6. I hope to rely on notes to accomplish some of this task. I will use notes first in the conventional academic way of indicating the sources, where I am aware of them, of data or reports which I am presenting as facts or excerpting verbatim or which corroborate notions I developed in the context of my own research. Since much of the lore of African music came to me through conversations with unpublished African friends, I will not make, except at some points in the text, citations of informants such as "Issa Yatassaye, wedding celebration, Bamako,

Mali, January 1971; also pointed out by Billy 'Onassis' Atos, table conversation, Accra, Ghana, February 1971." Such references would be difficult for scholars to follow up, and I would prefer that my examples be understood not as data but as illustrative aspects of my interpretation. I feel that in this regard, I have generally been in the position of choosing the most appropriate from the many facts or details which support various themes and issues. Second, in the notes I will carry through certain discussions of specialized academic relevance so that they do not burden the flow of the argument with too many scholastic red herrings. Third, on my intellectual journey through Western "nonfictional" literature, I have found that several academic conceptions, not necessarily specifically related to African music, were relevant or intriguing to me within my specialized concerns. I cannot pretend to comment with authority on these conceptions, but I would like to indicate nonetheless my feeling that scholars who have a deeper grasp of these issues than I do might be interested in some of the points where I think there may be a relevant interdisciplinary connection. Finally, I will use the notes as a place for comments, examples, or sentiments to which I am partial but which I feel are neither firmly enough established nor quite necessary to link or to illustrate the development of my argument. I hope that some notes will be useful for students and that others will be at least entertaining.

7. Lytton Strachey, *Elizabeth and Essex: A Tragic History* (Harmondsworth, Middlesex, England: Penguin Books, 1971), p. 35. Strachey was, it is not encouraging to note, referring to the historical career of another famous prose stylist, Francis Bacon. According to Strachey, Bacon's political ambitions as advisor to Essex were compromised through a lack of simple human sensitivity and insight. The failure of Bacon's intellectual erudition and style resulted, one might say, in the disembodiment of the object of his analysis. Bacon, that great apostle of the inductive method, wrote in *The Advancement of Learning* (London: Oxford University Press, 1926), pp. 101–2:

". . . Poesy is a part of learning in measure of words for the most part restrained, but in all other parts extremely licensed, and doth truly refer to the imagination; which, not being tied to the laws of matter, may at pleasure join that which nature hath severed, and sever that which nature hath joined; and so make unlawful matches and divorces of things. . . .

"Because true history representeth actions and events more ordinary and less interchanged, therefore poesy endueth them with more rareness, and more unexpected and alternative variations. So as it appeareth that poesy serveth and conferreth to magnanimity, morality, and to delectation. And therefore it was ever thought to have some participation of divineness, because it doth raise and erect the mind, by submitting the shows of things to the desires of the mind; whereas reason doth buckle and bow the mind unto the nature of things. And we see that by these insinuations and congruities with man's nature and pleasure, joined also with the agreement and consort it hath with music, it hath had access and estimation in rude times and barbarous regions, where other learning stood excluded."

8. I am using the word *aesthetic* in its original etymological and philosophical meaning of the sense of perception and judgement. During the course of my learning, I thus met aesthetic problems and concerns on a pragmatic level. My use of *sensibility* is conventional and is implied in the text as referring to modes and standards of judgement. See Bergen Evans and Cornelia Evans, *A Dictionary of*

Contemporary American Usage (New York: Random House, 1957), p. 441: "*Sensibility* does not refer to being sensible but to being sensitive, in a special way. It now means the capacity to respond to aesthetic or emotional stimuli, delicacy of emotional or intellectual perception."

9. Arthur J. Vidich's "Participant-Observation and the Collection and Interpretation of Data," *American Journal of Sociology* 60 (1955): 354–60, remains, to my mind, the most thoroughly considered brief discussion of this complex and ambiguous technique. Among the other standard articles, two of value are Benjamin D. Paul, "Interview Techniques and Field Relationships," in *Anthropology Today: An Encyclopedic Inventory*, ed. A. L. Kroeber (Chicago: University of Chicago Press, 1953), pp. 430–51; and Florence Kluckhohn, "The Participant-Observer Technique in Small Communities," *American Journal of Sociology* 46 (1940): 331–43. Useful and current discussions from an interactionist perspective can be found in Norman K. Denzin, *The Research Act: A Theoretical Introduction to Sociological Methods* (Chicago: Aldine, 1970); Herbert Blumer, *Symbolic Interactionism: Perspective and Method* (Englewood Cliffs, N.J.: Prentice-Hall, 1969); George J. McCall and J. L. Simmons, eds., *Issues in Participant-Observation: A Text and Reader* (Reading, Mass.: Addison-Wesley, 1969); and Howard S. Becker, *Sociological Work: Method and Substance* (Chicago: Aldine, 1970). Important and informative statements relating to the genesis of completed studies can be found in William Foote Whyte, *Street Corner Society: The Social Structure of an Italian Slum* (Chicago: University of Chicago Press, 1955), pp. 279–358; and Herbert J. Gans, *The Urban Villagers: Group and Class in the Life of Italian-Americans* (New York: Free Press, 1962), pp. 336–50. An interesting collection of such statements can be found in Arthur J. Vidich, Joseph Bensman, and Maurice R. Stein, eds., *Reflections on Community Studies* (New York: Harper & Row, Harper Torchbooks, 1971). "On Intellectual Craftsmanship," the appendix to C. Wright Mills' *The Sociological Imagination* (New York: Oxford University Press, 1959) is also interesting in this regard.

In the anthropological literature, both Joseph B. Casagrande, ed., *In the Company of Man: Twenty Portraits of Anthropological Informants* (New York: Harper & Row, Harper Torchbooks, 1964) and Morris Freilich, ed., *Marginal Natives: Anthropologists at Work* (New York: Harper & Row, 1970) provide some extremely revealing glimpses of anthropologists' working relationships. Among the many ethnographies which retain an element of personal focus, several studies which might interest general readers are Colin M. Turnbull, *The Forest People: A Study of the Pygmies of the Congo* (Garden City, N.Y.: Natural History Library and Doubleday, Anchor Books, 1962); also by Colin M. Turnbull, *The Mountain People* (New York: Simon and Schuster, 1972); Claude Lévi-Strauss, *Tristes Tropiques*, trans. John Russell (New York: Atheneum, 1972); Kenneth E. Read, *The High Valley* (New York: Charles Scribner's Sons, 1965); and of course almost any of Margaret Mead's writings.

Reading about Read's emotional problems or looking at Turnbull's photographs of people who died while he was among them, one realizes that there could hardly be a field with as much variety in research situations as anthropology. I know an anthropologist who was going into an area so well researched that she knew in advance the names and life histories of almost all the people where she would live. I know of another who is reported to have walked into a place where he

was the first European to visit, snapping pictures of the men who were standing
in trees watching him with their spears raised. In view of the methodological
implications of such diversity, it is unfortunate that the issues of a researcher's
involvement with the community he studies have not received more explicit attention. In many fine monographs, brilliant in theoretical extension or empirical
depth, the intricacies of such relationships are generally seen as difficulties the
researcher has managed to overcome; neophyte field-workers are so cautioned
against the temptations and dangers of what is pejoratively referred to as "going
native" that it is a wonder so few of them actually do so. Current trends in
ethnography, however, suggest that the renewed emphasis on interpretive techniques and the proliferation of theoretical alternatives with the consequent erosion
of an accepted empirical and terminological base will combine to influence the
style of many future monographs toward more detailed presentations on this
matter of humanistic and scientific concern. Whereas a few years ago ethnogra-
phers might have felt that they were compromising their "objectivity" through such
discussions, they will now perhaps be encouraged in the interest of scientific
fidelity to describe the personal genesis and rationale of their selection of an
interpretive metaphor.

10. The importance of this notion of interpretation is currently very evident in
many disciplines, but though theoretical discussions abound, there is very little
literature which can guide a researcher in day-to-day experience. I am most indebted to psychoanalytic and existential writings. The openness of social researchers with regard to the timing of significant interpretations bears close resemblance to what psychoanalysts call "evenly-hovering attention" when they are
listening to someone free-associate or tell about a dream. They have a theoretical
model available, and they also have an idea of what certain symbols or gestures
might mean, but they wait because they have to know about the specific person
who is talking to them, who is, at least in one sense of the term *neurotic*, beyond
norms of symbolization. Therapists must understand the specific meaning of a
patient's communication, based on its particular patterns of relationship, if any
kind of cure is to be effected. Later they can write about it theoretically. In this
regard, Freud's case histories are very enlightening: *Collected Papers*, vol. 3, trans.
Alix and James Strachey (New York: Basic Books, 1959).

Psychoanalytic attention to this problem, of course, began with Sigmund Freud,
The Interpretation of Dreams, trans. James Strachey (New York: Basic Books,
Avon Books, 1965). Leighton McCutchen, "Psychology of the Dream: Dream
without Myth," in *The Dialogue between Theology and Psychology*, ed. Peter
Homans (Chicago: University of Chicago Press, 1968) and Jacques Lacan, "The
Insistence of the Letter in the Unconscious," trans. Jan Miel, *Yale French
Studies* 36–37 (1966): 112–47, are two interesting essays, the first straightforward
and the second involuted. See also Erik H. Erikson, "The Nature of Clinical Evidence," in *Insight and Responsibility: Lectures on the Ethical Implications of
Psychoanalytic Insight* (New York: W. W. Norton, 1964). Freud's papers on
therapy are also to the point, particularly "The Dynamics of the Transference,"
"Recollection, Repetition, and Working Through," and "Observations on Trans-
ference-love," in *Collected Papers*, vol. 2, trans. Joan Riviere, and "Construction
in Analysis," in *Collected Papers*, vol. 5, trans. James Strachey. The multiple tensions and dialogues of transference phenomena as described in the psychoanalytic

literature can add another dimension to the perception of methodological issues in field research, and on a practical level, comprehension of such notions as counter-transference, evenly hovering attention, and the overdetermination of symbols is surely a restraint against premature and ethnocentric interpretation. For a detailed study of counter-transference in anthropological research, see George Devereux, *From Anxiety to Method in the Behavioral Sciences* (The Hague: Mouten, 1967).

In the context of field research, the attitude I am discussing is also an approach to what philosophers of interpretation like Martin Heidegger call "dwelling" or "releasement" or "non-objectifying thinking," in which they regard a text or a work of art as an "event" with its own "world" or "universe of discourse." Heidegger's ideas about historicality and interpretation are becoming increasingly influential among social scientists, and they may be well-met second-hand in Richard E. Palmer, *Hermeneutics: Interpretation Theory in Schleiermacher, Dilthey, Heidegger, and Gadamer* (Evanston, Ill.: Northwestern University Press, 1969). Also useful is Hans Jaeger, "Heidegger and the Work of Art," in *Aesthetics Today*, ed. Morris Philipson (New York: World, Meridian Books, 1961). Useful writings by Heidegger himself are *Discourse on Thinking: A Translation of "Gelassenheit,"* trans. John M. Anderson and E. Hans Freund (New York: Harper & Row, 1966), and *Poetry, Language, Thought*, trans. and introduction Albert Hofstadter (New York: Harper & Row, 1971).

In the same vein, literary critics speak of "putting oneself under the governing claims of the text" in an effort to reconstitute "practical" criticism, that is to say, criticism which helps us to "read" by opening ways of access into the "world" of the text. Geoffrey H. Hartman's essays are eminently readable for social scientists, particularly "Structuralism: The Anglo-American Adventure," "Ghostlier Demarcations: The Sweet Science of Northrop Frye," and "Toward Literary History," all in *Beyond Formalism: Literary Essays, 1958–1970* (New Haven: Yale University Press, 1970).

The parallel notion in sociology is "grounded" theory; see Barney S. Glaser and Anselm L. Strauss, *The Discovery of Grounded Theory: Strategies for Qualitative Research* (Chicago: Aldine, 1967).

Without attempting to pose any exact equation of these various terms (and I might mention as well phenomenological "suspension of judgment" and Bultmannian "demythologizing"), I do think that at least a common theme of significance is the attitude that a researcher's knowledge is inseparable from his existential participation in his work and that what meaning he finds emerges as part of the process by which this relationship changes through time. I also find it ironic that anthropologists (see below, n. 16) should be turning to notions from hermeneutics, which originally developed as a branch of theology uniting the issues of translation and interpretation regarding the problems of translating sacred books. An interesting article tracing the ways in which contemporary social theory is heir to the concerns of medieval theology is Leszek Kolakowski, "The Priest and the Jester," in Maria Kuncewicz, ed., *The Modern Polish Mind: An Anthology* (New York: Grosset & Dunlap and Little, Brown, 1962). Seen from Kolakowski's perspective, ideas about hidden communal structures tying together disparate aspects of reality at a deeper level or about "latent" functions and organizational "imperatives" begin to find a different location within our literary traditions.

11. For an exceptionally lucid demonstration of precisely this point, see the well-regarded study of industrial conflict by Alvin W. Gouldner, *Wildcat Strike* (Yellow Springs, Ohio: Antioch Press, 1954), with the companion volume by the same author, *Patterns of Industrial Bureaucracy* (Glencoe, Ill.: Free Press, 1954). For a succinct statement by a leading sociologist, see Kai T. Erikson, "Sociology: That Awkward Age," *Social Problems* 19 (1972): 431–36.

12. *Design for Living*, directed by Ernst Lubitsch, screenplay by Ben Hecht based on a play by Noël Coward, Paramount Pictures, 1933.

13. My perspective here is very much influenced by psychoanalytic ego psychology, especially by many passages in the writings of Erik H. Erikson. See the following sections: "Allness or Nothingness," in *Young Man Luther: A Study in Psychoanalysis and History* (New York: W. W. Norton, 1962); "Psychological Reality and Historical Actuality" and "Identity and Uprootedness in Our Time," in *Insight and Responsibility*; and "Foundations in Observation," in *Youth: Identity and Crisis* (New York: W. W. Norton, 1968). I agree with most anthropologists that psychoanalytic insight is best integrated into cross-cultural research within the field-worker's self-awareness rather than in a substantive way. Erikson's notions of overlapping and discontinuous sequences of "growth" and learning are certainly quite applicable to my research experience, and his writings are considerably more adaptable to sociological and anthropological research situations than the writings of many other leading psychoanalysts.

14. Several philosophizing friends have suggested a parallel between my research experience and an ideal phenomenological *epochē*. Specifically, the phenomenological literature raises a distinct and competitively viable alternative to standard social scientific methods, particularly in cross-cultural research. On an empirical level, this approach seems most fully developed in the phenomenology of religion. Among the perspectives which I consulted with interest were Gerardus van der Leeuw, *Religion in Essence and Manifestation*, trans. J. E. Turner, 2 vols. (Gloucester, Mass.: Peter Smith, 1967), especially 2: 671–95; Wilfred Cantwell Smith, "Comparative Religion: Whither—and Why?" in *The History of Religions: Essays in Methodology*, ed. Mircea Eliade and Joseph M. Kitagawa (Chicago: University of Chicago Press, 1959), pp. 31–58; and Charles H. Long, "Archaism and Hermeneutics," in *The History of Religions: Essays on the Problem of Understanding*, ed. Joseph M. Kitagawa with the collaboration of Mircea Eliade and Charles H. Long (Chicago: University of Chicago Press, 1967), pp. 67–87.

The orientation of the phenomenology of religion differs from that of the sociology of religion mainly in the attempt to describe a particular religion from the point of view of an "adherent," that is, without utilizing "external" analytic or explanatory standards. To a phenomenologist of religion most of the sociological or anthropological analyses of the lives of traditional peoples might be classified as a literary genre under the heading "Sermons against Animism." Methodologically, however, the phenomenological approach addresses many of the same issues as participant-observation. Whereas many participant-observers assume a dichotomy between involved immersion and objective detachment, the attitude of phenomenologists of religion is more aligned with humanistic disciplines, particularly hermeneutic criticism, and parallels many literary critics' discussions of "putting oneself under the governing claims of the text": the researcher in phenomenology of religion is advised to wait until he is tempted to become a full participant in the alien faith. Willem A. Bijlefeld, in *De Islam als na-Christelijke Religie* (The Hague: van Keulen N.V., 1959), p. 30, cites Walter Freytag's statement, "You have not really understood another religion unless you have been tempted by the insights of this other religion," as one of the earliest expressions of this sensibility toward impartiality in investigation, a sensibility which Bijlefeld also finds evidenced and discussed as "an act of love and self-abandonment for the sake of truth" within certain conceptions of the training of missionaries, who were advised not to begin proselytizing until they themselves were on the verge of converting to the faith of the people among whom they were going to work. At this point, of course, the missionary pulls back whereas the researcher either carries on or attempts to maintain a balance of sympathies, and it is significant to note that a number of the examples of "going native" mentioned by Paul in "Interview Techniques" involved religion. Though much of the literature about phenomenology is philosophical and quite difficult, most readers have probably encountered phenomenological writings: many of the "new journalists," like Tom Wolfe and Jane Kramer, write in a phenomenological vein.

15. An exact translation of the classical Greek elements of the word would be "making the soul visible or manifest."

16. The feeling that the questions of ethnocentrism and relativism are related to the question of abstraction has recently undergone a kind of revival in anthropology, representing a possible rapprochement with various humanistic disciplines. Clifford Geertz, an anthropologist with impeccable credentials, has recently recommended looking at culture as "an assemblage of texts," "imaginative works built from social materials," but notes that the idea "has yet to be systematically exploited." See "Deep Play: Notes on the Balinese Cockfight," in Clifford Geertz, *The Interpretation of Cultures* (New York: Basic Books, 1973), originally appearing in *Daedalus* 101 (1972): 1–38.

Cognitive anthropology is a branch of anthropology also directed toward this problem, though from a different point of view than mine. See Stephen A. Tyler, ed., *Cognitive Anthropology* (New York: Holt, Rinehart and Winston, 1969). For a representative study in an African context, see Michael Cole, John Gay, Joseph A. Glick, Donald W. Sharp, et al., *The Cultural Context of Learning and Thinking: An Exploration in Experimental Anthropology* (New York: Basic Books, 1971).

In a recent issue of the *Times Literary Supplement* (July 6, 1973), E. E. Evans-Pritchard, Mary Douglas, Edmund Leach, and Rodney Needham joined forces in a public-relations job on "The State of Anthropology." British social anthropology, we learn from Mr. Evans-Pritchard, has avoided the illusory scientific self-consciousness of American anthropology and has grown up from the grand theoretical approaches which formerly characterized the discipline. What anthropology is all about, according to Mr. Leach, is "translation," one which should make the "others" human and still "other." The researcher's exacting standards often get in the way; very few good translations have been done, nor has any clearcut method been advanced. Mr. Evans-Pritchard trusts the importance of field-work, good description, and closer ties with other disciplines. Mr. Needham is also liberal, and feels that "what will count most is simply the degree of intelligence, erudition, and imagination of the individual anthropologist." If the standards seem fuzzy, we must remember that these are scholars who have given us some of our best monographs, and of course, when one holds a chair at Cambridge or Chicago, one speaks with a certain authority. The editors of *TLS* were skeptical: "Once the practising field-worker feels his subject to be fully the equal of himself, then it could well be that he will start questioning his discipline somewhat differently, to decide whether what he is engaged on is not the organized reification of human affairs. He may not want in the end to turn his tribe into a monograph, merely because of the irresistable fetish of publication and professional advancement." He could review books for *TLS*, perhaps.

17. 2 vols. (London: Oxford University Press, 1959), 1:160.

18. A social scientist, of course, could no more produce a manifestation of an effective causal agent or a latent function than the priest could make one of the ancestors materialize.

19. As a child, I studied classical piano for eight years, and later I studied drumming for four years with a percussionist from a major symphony orchestra, but I am not qualified enough to call myself a musician. I am sure, of course, that there are Westerners who have reached a high level of proficiency in African traditional musical performance, and I know one, Paul Berliner, who became exceptionally competent on the Shona *mbira*, or thumb piano. In conversations, we have compared several ways in which our learning experiences were similar, particularly regarding the length of time we spent finding a dedicated teacher, time ostensibly wasted, but of crucial importance in extending the preresearch acculturation experience until we had the proper aesthetic attitudes and interpersonal skill to keep our teachers committed to us and to understand their most serious instructions.

20. The same thing, incidentally, happened in Haiti in Voodoo ceremonies, after I was blessed by M. Joseph Thèlus, priest. People there looked at an amulet on my arm and nodded.

21. Putting the discussion into esoteric terms like "kinaesthetics" would obscure the issue, since such branches of study are not developed to any degree of reliability. I once asked an eminent philosopher and psychologist, the author of several books, how I might describe this phenomenon, and she suggested that I contact an eminent neurophysiologist friend of hers who might want to run a series of EEGs on me. At the moment, plain language is deeper for my purposes.

22. This opportunity, for whatever reason, was not available to me in the cult. Ethnomethodology, at least in some respects, is a method of investigating social realities by deliberately introducing mistakes into a social situation, thus to engage participants in corrective definition of the implicit "moral order" of norms and values. See Harold Garfinkel, *Studies in Ethnomethodology* (Englewood Cliffs, N.J.: Prentice-Hall, 1967). For a brilliant application of ethnomethodological techniques, see Carlos Castenada, *Journey to Ixtlan: The Lessons of Don Juan* (New York: Simon and Schuster, Touchstone Books, 1972).

23. The long period of my acculturation was obviously of great importance when I finally began to study music. The facility I had in communicating this way was probably equally important in holding the commitment of my teachers by demonstrating my progress, keeping them interested, and of course, simply being comprehensible to them as a person.

There is some literature on body language, most of it somewhat equivocal in practical situations. Those interested might look at Ray L. Birdwhistell, *Kinesics and Context: Essays on Body Motion Communication* (Philadelphia: University of Pennsylvania Press, 1970); R. A. Hinde, ed., *Non-Verbal Communication* (Cambridge: Cambridge University Press, 1972); Edward T. Hall, *The Silent Language* (Greenwich, Conn.: Fawcett Publications, Fawcett Premier Books, 1959). Much valuable work in this area has been done by Erving Goffman, *Behavior in Public Places: Notes on the Social Organization of Gatherings* (New York: Free Press, 1966, London: Collier-Macmillan, 1963); *Encounters: Two Studies in the Sociology of Interaction* (Indianapolis: Bobbs-Merrill, 1961); *Interaction Ritual: Essays on Face-to-Face Behavior* (Garden City, N.Y.: Doubleday, Anchor Books, 1967); *Relations in Public: Microstudies of the Public Order* (New York: Basic Books, 1971).

24. André Malraux, *The Voices of Silence*, trans. Stuart Gilbert (Garden City, N.Y.: Doubleday, 1953), p. 20.

25. Hartman, "Structuralism," in *Beyond Formalism*, p. 8.

26. "Standards critiques de l'art Africain," *African Arts/Arts d'Afrique* 1, no. 1 (autumn 1967): 6.

Chapter 1   The Study of Music in Africa

1. Alan P. Merriam, "The African Idiom in Music," *Journal of American Folklore* 75 (1962): 121.

2. There is a considerable amount of literature on the history of this attitude in America from the days of slavery into the jazz era. The topic is potentially very rich for moral philosophers. Two of the better known discussions are Morroe Berger, "Jazz: Resistance to the Diffusion of a Culture Pattern," *Journal of Negro History* 32 (1947): 461–94, and LeRoi Jones [Imamu Amiri Baraka], *Blues People: Negro Music in White America* (New York: William Morrow, 1963).

3. Alan P. Merriam, *The Anthropology of Music* (Evanston, Ill.: Northwestern University Press, 1964), pp. 14–18, 38–39.

4. The great philosophers and poets of Négritude have accomplished much toward making us aware of the genius of African civilizations, to the point that many others have called Négritude an ideology. Many people consider Africa's great contribution to the world to be its arts, and a foreign dignitary who arrives in an African state will almost certainly be met by some of the artists who are the pride of the country. I find it most interesting, however, that Western students of African societies seem to find a distinctive African genius in whatever area of inquiry they pursue. The historian Basil Davidson, in fact, has written a book entitled *The African Genius: An Introduction to African Social and Cultural History* (Boston: Atlantic Monthly Press of Little, Brown, 1969). Thomas Hodgkin refers to "the African genius for sociability" in his *Nationalism in Colonial Africa* (New York: New York University Press, 1959), p. 85. In the latter part of my discussion of music, we shall certainly have cause to reflect on a statement made by Lloyd Fallers in his article "Social Stratification and Economic Processes in Africa," in *Class, Status, and Power: Social Stratification in Comparative Perspective*, ed. Reinhard Bendix and Seymour Martin Lipset, 2d ed. (New York: Free Press, 1966), p. 142: "This is not to say that Africans have not made the organization of production and exchange a central concern. Except perhaps in those areas of Western Africa where trade has become a highly developed calling, this is clearly not the case. It will be argued below that, much more typically,

production and exchange have been undertaken as an adjunct—a means—to the organization of power, the field in which, it appears, the African genius has really concentrated its efforts."

5. The broadest anthropological discussion of cultural continuities is presented by Melville J. Herskovits in *The Myth of the Negro Past* (Boston: Beacon Press, 1958), and the standard ethnomusicological discussion is by Richard Alan Waterman, "African Influence on the Music of the Americas," in *Acculturation in the Americas*, ed. Sol Tax, Proceedings and Selected Papers of the 29th International Congress of Americanists, vol. 2 (Chicago: University of Chicago Press, 1952).

6. See for example Robert F. Thompson's fine discussion of Eddie Palmieri's brilliant use of different stylistic traditions in the song "Si Hecho Pa'lante" (Tico LP1113 and SLP 1113), in "New Voice from the Barrios," *Saturday Review*, October 28, 1967, pp. 53–55, 68.

7. They identified, specifically, Edahu (Fast Yeve) as Yanvalou and Sohu as Banda.

8. In scholarship, the context of its use determines the value of a generalization, and I hope that my continued use of the adjective *African* does not bother too much those readers who are accustomed to sharp discrimination.

9. For a useful source on the flexibility of the concept of culture, see A. L. Kroeber, Clyde Kluckhohn, et al., *Culture: A Critical Review of Concepts and Definitions*, Papers of the Peabody Museum of American Archaeology and Ethnology, Harvard University, vol. 47, no. 1 (Cambridge, Mass.: Peabody Museum of American Archaeology and Ethnology, 1952). In general, anthropologists use the concept of culture in a special technical sense derived from older notions of folkways and ethos. The African *culture-area* is most generally understood to encompass continental Africa with the exception of the Mediterranean coast, the Horn area, and some parts of East and South Africa, but also to include those areas in the Americas and West Indies populated by people of West and Central African origin.

Discussions of the related concept of style are not common in social scientific literature and are heavily influenced by the conception of style developed by art historians. Interested readers may examine the direction of the discussions of style by Meyer Schapiro in his article "Style," in Philipson, ed., *Aesthetics Today*, also in Kroeber, ed., *Anthropology Today*; or by A. L. Kroeber, *Style and Civilizations* (Ithaca, N.Y.: Cornell University Press, 1957). A significantly different approach is taken by psychoanalytic ego psychologists and is well presented in David Shapiro, *Neurotic Styles*, Austin Riggs Center Monograph Series, no. 5 (New York: Basic Books, 1965). My discussion of style as a dynamic attribute is, I think, the most important distinction between my interpretive approach and the approaches which emphasize formal traits and relationships as symbolic representations. In this broader context, a conception of style must be achieved first to form a basis for and to balance the direction of other analyses.

10. In discussing what many people would call *style* as an ideal type, I am, I hope, consistent with Max Weber's use of the concept of ideal types as a means of access to the setting of social interaction and not as a descriptive referent. The evaluative norms by which I will distinguish aesthetic style will thus be based on *discontinuity* within the musical model, and my thesis will hinge on the way various kinds of discontinuity from structural norms are introduced into and consti-

tute part of the very continuity of music and culture we are discussing in this chapter. See Max Weber, *The Methodology of the Social Sciences*, trans. and ed. Edward A. Shils and Henry A. Finch (Glencoe, Ill.: Free Press, 1949), pp. 89–99. Among Weber's interpreters, I am most indebted to Raymond Aron, *Main Currents of Sociological Thought*, vol. 2, *Durkheim, Pareto, Weber*, trans. Richard Howard and Helen Weaver (Garden City, N.Y.: Doubleday, Anchor Books, 1970).

11. There is an old story about the young man who arrived at prison and went to the yard for exercise period. He was surprised when a convict in one corner called out "87!" and everybody laughed, and then another inmate yelled out "16!" at which many inmates nearly doubled up with laughter. The man walked over to an older con and asked what was happening. "Well, you see," the old man replied, "they're telling jokes. Most of us have been here so long we know all the jokes by heart, so we numbered them and we simply call out the numbers." "That's amazing," said the new arrival, "may I try?" "Sure," said the old con, "go ahead." The young man stepped forward a bit and yelled "24!" To his great embarrassment, the other prisoners just stopped talking and stared blankly at him. Puzzled, he walked back to the seasoned con and asked what happened. "Well, I don't know," the old man replied. "I guess some people just don't know how to tell a joke."

12. Within the discipline of ethnomusicology, this approach has been associated with the work of Alan P. Merriam and J. H. Kwabena Nketia. Each has outlined his notions of the scope and purpose of research for a contextual approach: Alan P. Merriam, "Ethnomusicology: Discussion and Definition of the Field," *Ethnomusicology* 4 (1960): 107–14; J. H. Kwabena Nketia, "The Problem of Meaning in African Music," *Ethnomusicology* 6 (1962): 1–7. Basically, Merriam is interested in the *role* of music as an element of culture, and Nketia, with whom I have greater sympathy, wants to study the culture *through* the music. Nketia's emphasis on understanding the performance is particularly well-founded because it shifts the hermeneutic question of origins and meaning from the tradition to the event. Merriam's and Nketia's observations on method can be augmented by some of the theoretical statements of John Blacking. In his article, "Man and Music," *Times Literary Supplement*, November 19, 1971, pp. 1443–44, Blacking outlined his position based on his work among the Venda of the Transvaal: "Every performance of Venda communal music . . . demands a re-creation of a special social situation as much as a repetition of learned skills. If there is any important difference between Venda music and European written, or 'art,' music, it is that the 'art' composer freezes a particular improvisation and its corresponding social situation, or produces a composite statistical model of several performances of the same song. . . . [Music's] effectiveness is basically situational, and what is ultimately of most importance in music cannot be learned like some technical skills."

13. This point, of course, has been one of the central principles and demonstrations of ethnomusicology.

14. Compare the perception of the phenomenologist of religion, Gerardus van der Leeuw, in his *Sacred and Profane Beauty: The Holy in Art*, trans. David E. Green (New York: Holt, Rinehart and Winston, 1963), p. 268: "Music is a world to itself, with its own space and its own time . . . . 'Concert of religious music' is an announcement that always disturbs me. . . . It is an expression preferred by those who think that art fulfills its function . . . only when it stands

in the service of religion." And pp. 274–75: "Style is a form of life. The style
of a work of art is like the character of a man, taken in the broadest sense: the
way he presents himself, his speech, his feelings, his thoughts, etc. . . . But style
is also what binds artists together, what makes an organic whole out of a group of
men who belong to the same age, the same nationality, and the same school of
thought. . . . The artist, no matter how great and independent he may be, creates
within the forms of the structure which was given to him. . . . Therein lies distance and an approach to the holy, or at least for the possibility."

15. One theme of the chapter on musical form (chap. 2) will be that in African
music it is almost impossible to see structure independent of social context.

16. Only a very few people, however, would be prepared to evaluate the interpretation of the performing artist. Toscanini might have conducted a certain
symphony very fast, and Bernstein might do it slowly. If connoisseurs make a distinction, they do so to suggest that one way or the other is better, that is, the
way the symphony was meant to be played. Only a very, very few might consider
the quality of the symphony as its potential to be played in different ways.

17. We thus prefer to define music formally, that is, in terms of *sounds*. The
great lexicographer Dr. Samuel Johnson originally defined music as a "succession
of sounds so modulated as to please the ear; melody; accordant or harmonious
combination of diverse sounds simultaneously produced; harmony" (*A Dictionary
of the English Language,* ed. and abridged by Robert Gordon Latham [London:
Longmans, Green, 1876], p. 879), and the same sensibility is demonstrated in *The
Oxford English Dictionary* (Oxford: Clarendon Press, 1933), 6: 782: "That one
of the fine arts which is concerned with the combination of sounds with a view
to beauty of form and expression of emotion; also, the science of the laws or principles (of melody, harmony, rhythm, etc.) by which this art is regulated." See
Appendix, pp. 173–82.

18. I am here paraphrasing an insight from Maurice R. Stein, *The Eclipse of
Community: An Interpretation of American Studies* (New York: Harper & Row,
Harper Torchbooks, 1964), p. 64. The full depth of my sociological indebtedness
to this outstanding book will become apparent, I am sure, by the end of my
analysis.

19. Merriam, "The African Idiom," p. 121; A. M. Jones, "African Rhythm,"
Africa 24 (1954): 27–39.

20. See for example the discussions by Paul Bohannan, "Artist and Critic in
an African Society," in *The Many Faces of Primitive Art,* ed. Douglas Fraser
(Englewood Cliffs, N. J.: Prentice-Hall, 1966), pp. 246–54, and by Alan Merriam,
Anthropology of Music, pp. 259–76. A notion like this, however, if taken too
literally, has the potential to be extended into several highly questionable attitudes
about African art, attitudes perhaps derived from the biases of our literary culture
and our more contemporary narrowing of the idea of aesthetics into concerns of
"beauty" and "distance." Taking a superficial view of the integration of art and
culture, some people assume that there is an essential unity which is reflected in
all aspects of a situation. Academically, this unity is understood as "structural,"
that is to say, the inherent organizing patterns and relationships are formally
similar. Engaging or reaffirming people in this unity is the "function" of art. Almost needless to say, this simplification of the role of art implies an image of
traditional societies wherein everything is cut from the same mold. From this

point of view, it is not far from thinking that we can correlate the formal structures of their art, on the one hand, with the beliefs or the mind or the emotional make-up of the person who makes it and the people who enjoy it. While some people are looking at art as a kind of "cultural cognitive map," others are trying to correlate the formal structures of art with the social structures in the artist's culture, down to the way people lay out their villages and build their houses. Contrasted with the ambiguity of our relationship to our own art, such perspectives imply, in a privative way, that questions of aesthetics are not relevant, that the artist is either ritualistically following the dictates of tradition or unselfconsciously responding to the feelings he shares so easily with his fellow tribesmen. This reductive view of structural and expressive continuity often appears under the guise of a sophisticated cultural relativism, but it works, of course, by abstracting the artwork from its context for the purpose of the "structural" analysis.

The irony of this situation is terrific. Out of reluctance to run the risks of "humanistic" interpretation, many scholars have tried to eschew ethnocentric aesthetic biases by studying music "scientifically," as if the modalities of science do not have their own aesthetic dimensions. Even those, like John Blacking and some others, who regard music as a situational phenomenon, persist in seeing music as an "expression" of human experience in social life, its communicative purpose the expansion of collective feeling. (See John Blacking, "Tonal Organization in the Music of Two Venda Initiation Schools," *Ethnomusicology* 14 (1970): 11ff, and "Man and Music," p. 1443.) Some of the assumptions are reasonable: music and culture *are* related, and *people* make music. But art is not merely an expression of something else. When we treat it that way, the resulting analyses, in attempting to demonstrate what the expressions reflect, rather express and reflect the scholar's assumptions about the nature of data. The romantic sayings about music and Life and Vitality, capitalized, are hung as emblems above the doors of so-called scientific inquiry, to paraphrase Nietzsche, while inside, the music is limited to a reflection of "basic" structures and infrastructures. The way and manner in which music emerges within cultures, of course, is intimately related to the types of institutions and other environmental factors which are typical of the place, and the detailed description of these relationships is sometimes interesting. But in its extreme theoretical formulations, taken as guidelines of inquiry, the notion that music must, in the end, refer us to such "hard" realities as the socioeconomic base and the division of labor can become limiting. It is limiting because music goes beyond these realities even while its expression reflects them in some ways, and the problem is that if we are going to claim that these are the fundamental realities against which we measure the validity of our scientific perception of music as a "phenomenon," we have denied its validity as art. Perhaps such is the proper level of study for social scientists, but we will have to wait a long time before all the data is in and we can demonstrate how free Africans who became slaves in Brazil, Haiti, and Cuba managed to continue beating the same rhythms for four centuries; how the patrilineal, Muslim Dagombas and the matrilineal, pagan Ashantis established such a deep history of mutual musical influence; how the daughters of Ga fishermen and Krobo farmers dance to the same Otofu drumming; how freedom-loving Ghanaians can listen to recordings of South Africa's Dark City Sisters; how Cuban Rumba beats did not change after the revolution; and so on. The point, once again, is that we can discuss these matters to an extent, but only to an extent. In the meantime, in the scholarship on the art of different cultures, we have discussions of the aesthetics of Hindu sculpture, Zen brush painting, or even Greek temples, and to my mind it is not excusable, especially for a social scientist working in Africa, to avoid the interpretive difficulties in the search for artistic meaning.

21. J. H. Kwabena Nketia, "Music in African Cultures: A Review of the Meaning and Significance of Traditional African Music," mimeographed (Legon, Accra, Ghana: Institute of African Studies, University of Ghana, 1966), p. 33. Melville J. Herskovits, *Dahomey: An Ancient West African Kingdom*, 2 vols. (New York: J. J. Augustin, 1938), 1: 273; Herskovits also describes a song for the loss of a first tooth (1: 275). David W. Ames, Edgar A. Gregersen, and Thomas Neugebauer, "Taaken Sàmàarii: A Drum Language of Hausa Youth," *Africa* 41 (1971): 12–31. Alan P. Merriam, "African Music," in *Continuity and Change in African Cultures*, ed. William R. Bascom and Melville J. Herskovits (Chicago: University of Chicago Press, 1959), p. 50.

22. Some interesting comments on voluntary associations can be found in Hodgkin, *Nationalism in Colonial Africa*; in Clifford Geertz, "The Integrative Revolution: Primordial Sentiments and Civil Politics in the New States," in *The Interpretation of Cultures*; and in Kenneth Little, *West African Urbanization: A Study of Voluntary Associations in Social Change* (Cambridge: Cambridge University Press, 1965). Specifically, see S. Kobla Ladzekpo, "The Social Mechanics of Good Music: A Description of Dance Clubs among the Anlo Ewe-Speaking People of Ghana," *African Music* 5, no. 1 (1971): 6–22. An interesting historical study of community dance associations is T. O. Ranger, *Dance and Society in Eastern Africa, 1890–1970: The Beni "Ngoma"* (London: Heinemann Educational Books, 1975).

23. A nice article on such musicians is Charles Cutter, "The Politics of Music in Mali," *African Arts/Arts d'Afrique* 1, no. 3 (spring 1968): 38–39, 74–77.

24. J. H. Kwabena Nketia, "Sources of Historical Data on the Musical Cultures of Africa," mimeographed (Legon, Accra, Ghana: Institute of African Studies, University of Ghana, 1972), p. 3; Herskovits makes a covert reference in *Dahomey*, 2: 321.

25. A fine example of the symbolic use of drums is offered in a story told to me by a Dagomba schoolboy. I did not check his information because the simple fact that he told such a story is the relevant point. We were visiting Yo-Naa Abdulai II in his palace in Savelugu, and my friend showed me a set of *atumpan* drums. Atumpan drums, originally acquired from the Ashantis, are used by major Dagomba chiefs. My friend said that in a recent fight between the Dagombas and their Gonja neighbors, the Dagombas had managed to "capture" the Gonja state drums—a set of two atumpan—and had carried them off to Kumbungu, where the chief who traditionally heads the Dagomba army sits. He told me that any time his Gonja classmates would try to assert themselves over his Dagomba classmates, the Dagombas would taunt them by saying, "If you feel so strong, go and collect your drums."

26. "Music in African Cultures," p. 20.

27. *Musique Dan: La musique dans la pensée et la vie sociale d'une société africaine* (Paris: Mouton and École Practique des Hautes Études, 1971), p. 7. The

translation is mine from "Le village où il n'y a pas musicien n'est pas endroit où l'homme puisse rester."

28. See above, Introduction, p. 23.

29. The study of improvisation is the key to intentionality and aesthetic judgement in the music and will be the major focus of chapter 3. The meaning and purpose of the music is not so much the structure itself as what people do within it. Hartman's discussion in "Structuralism," in *Beyond Formalism*, is rewarding on this point. Though I have not found the structuralist method useful in the context of this particular book, Claude Lévi-Strauss's general observation—that in Western art, technique is internalized and expression is externalized, while in "primitive" art, technique is externalized and expression is internalized—seems to be fairly accurate in indicating where a researcher can find data. To my experience, technique is accessible as data. Lévi-Strauss's discussion is in *The Savage Mind* (Chicago: University of Chicago Press, 1966), p. 29. One other way, however, to make Lévi-Strauss's work seem useful for the study of music is to reverse the distinctions he makes in his definitions of art and myth (*The Savage Mind*, p. 26: "In the case of works of art, the starting point is a set of one or more objects and one or more events which aesthetic creation unifies by revealing a common structure. Myths . . . use a structure to produce what is itself an object consisting of a set of events"), and then, as in this study, regard music as being what Lévi-Strauss considers a myth. Thus, instead of a picture of processes of interpretation, we will get a picture of processes of community.

30. In Professor Geertz's words, it is "a story they tell themselves about themselves" (*The Interpretation of Cultures*, p. 448). Also of particular interest in this regard is Meyer Fortes's discussion, "Mind," in E. E. Evans-Pritchard, et al., *The Institutions of Primitive Society: A Series of Broadcast Talks* (Glencoe, Ill.: Free Press, 1954), pp. 81–94. These concerns will be the focus of chapter 4.

Chapter 2   Music in Africa

1. There are other considerations as well. Ewe music has been discussed in a number of publications, and I would therefore hope to provide a bit of continuity to my illustrations so that the reader will not have to meet too many new terms; readers already familiar with the ethnomusicological literature on Ewe music will find themselves in a better position to appreciate many issues in the discussion. I have tried to provide as much of the Dagomba material as literary considerations would permit because the Dagombas are an important group in terms of the richness of their musical heritage. My practical experience, I might add, extends beyond Ewe and Dagomba cultures, and with the variety of written and recorded sources available, it would have been easy to change my examples at each point by citing many different specific dance beats from diverse cultures or various forms of generic rhythms like Rumba or Highlife; alternatively I could have taken any one of those individual beats and utilized it throughout, as I invite readers to do with their favorite styles. I have felt, however, that such an approach to the problems of generalization can be confusing or even misleading. Though I have tried to use some examples from different cultures and from generic styles, I have felt that a depth presentation of two cultural styles is reasonable and adequate.

Beyond these literary and formal considerations, the Ewe and Dagomba musics, like their cultures, are very different: they provide a broad range of musical insights while they are also quite comparable. The very fact that these two musics can be encompassed by the type of discussion which follows is, I think, significant. As discussed in chapter 1, it is as a result of understanding the similarities in the way these different musical styles mediate participation that we can begin to make limited generalizations about African societies.

In the text, though not in the notes, I have italicized major points for readers to keep in mind when listening to African music; quotation marks are used to indicate words which are used ironically or in a restricted context. My terminology has been determined by my effort to present the general discussion in a straightforward way, and the meaning of most key concepts will emerge from the context of the discussion. In the case of a word like *beat*, which has several meanings (as the act of striking a drum, as our notion of the meter or tempo of a piece of music, and as the African notion of the particular relationship of cross-rhythms which characterizes a piece of music), I have used quotation marks to distinguish the African meaning. Of particular note too, the word *style* is used both in our sense of characterizing a tradition or a performance and in the African sense of a particular rhythmic variation or phrase.

I have allowed Ibrahim Abdulai to emerge as a character of major proportions partially for the sake of the presentation, which I feel is enhanced by the intimacy and vividness his presence and lectures bring to the topics I discuss. Most readers will no doubt appreciate meeting such an individual and gaining a feeling of the African musical context from the counterbalance a master African musician provides to my role in the narrative and anecdotal aspects of this book. I hope that those with a predominantly scholarly commitment to the subject will not feel that my perspectives on the points Ibrahim Abdulai comments about are too culturally localized. In addition to the reasons I have already given concerning continuity and literary impact, I regard Ibrahim Abdulai himself as a scholar of high standing who shares many role values with Western professors. He is a master of musical styles from many cultures of the sub-Saharan area, and he can play dances from Basari, Mossi, Kotokoli, Hausa, Gonja, Gurunsi, Mamprusi, Konkomba, Yoruba, and many other cultures. Such proficiency is one aspect of his profession, and he often entertains members of these cultural groups with their own music should they be present at a social function. Furthermore, he does extensive research, observing and studying other styles of music during his life's travels, and even recording many pieces on a tape recorder which he acquired to help him pursue and enjoy his interest. Gideon is the same way, and most people who have been involved with African musicians will recognize and remember the thoroughness of their commitment to their art, the openness of their critical thinking, and their readiness to learn more about new styles. In writing a discussion of the bonds which unify African music and culture, I was fortunate to find in Ibrahim Abdulai a way of presenting readers with a portrait of one person who has united his life with his art.

In reference to the fidelity of the verbatim quotations from Ibrahim Abdulai's speeches, I can add that the quotations are transcribed from tape recordings made in 1975. The conversation on pp. 132–38, which occurred in 1971, was recollected and reconstructed by him, and it conformed, though in greater detail, to my own recollection. Because of the depth of our friendship, we both had reason to remember that conversation, but such acuity of memory is not surprising among Dagomba drummers, who generally know the genealogies of people's families better than the people themselves, and who may ordinarily know the names of chiefs of important towns along with their predecessors back for hundreds of years. Although Ibrahim Abdulai is fluent in Dagbani, Hausa, and Twi, his English is not perfect, and I conducted all interviews in Dagbani with a translator whose English Ibrahim Abdulai was able to follow and sometimes correct, though it would have been a burden for him to attempt to express all his thoughts in English. A second translator took notes on the translations of the first, and my two translators and I all later retranslated from the transcriptions word-for-word in order to reconstruct certain Dagbani idioms. Apart from this slight reworking of the first English translation, I have only had to edit my transcripts to include what I thought relevant or well-stated, much in the same way I would choose a quotation from a book or article written by a Western scholar.

2. Jones, "African Rhythm," p. 26.

3. Willi Apel and Ralph T. Daniel, *The Harvard Brief Dictionary of Music* (New York: Pocket Books, 1961), p. 176.

4. Ludwig van Beethoven, *Piano Sonatina in G major.*

5. Jones, *Studies in African Music,* 1: 193. Still, in William Steinberg's well-known comment, "Great conductors do not dance."

6. Hal Neely, former president of King Records, the most important label in Afro-American music for more than twenty years, told me that Stravinsky, in response to an interviewer's question concerning his favorite composers, once replied, "The three Bs." "The three Bs," Stravinsky is said to have explained, are Bach, Beethoven, and Brown—James Brown. According to Neely, Stravinsky went on to say that James Brown should be considered one of the greatest composers of all time, that he was writing truly American music and portraying the American heritage.

7. Sad but true: Apel and Daniel, *The Harvard Brief Dictionary of Music,* p. 320.

8. Detailed descriptions of the Ewe drums, complete with pictures, may be found in either Jones, *Studies in African Music,* or S. Kobla Ladzekpo and Hewitt Pantaleoni, "Takada Drumming," *African Music* 4, no. 4 (1970): 6–31.

9. The Dagomba way of playing the dondon, which they call *lunga,* is not universal. The Yorubas hold it slung against the hip and use the free hand on the drumhead or the strings. For pictures, see Anthony King, *Yoruba Sacred Music from Ekiti* (Ibadan, Nigeria: Ibadan University Press, 1961). The Ashantis do not sling the drum over the shoulder but clasp it and work the strings with the elbow and arm. For pictures, see J. H. Kwabena Nketia, *Drumming in Akan Communities of Ghana* (London: University of Ghana and Thomas Nelson and Sons, 1963), especially plates 6 and 23. There are many fine pictures of dondons and gongons in various cultures in Francis Bebey, *African Music: A People's Art,* trans. Josephine Bennet (New York: Lawrence Hill, 1975), on pp. 3, 5, 23, 77, 87, 94, 99, 107, 109, 121, and 133. The Dagomba dondons are very well made of heavy wood, and when I was in Tamale, people came from as far away as Ada on the

coast to buy drums from Ibrahim Abdulai who, in addition to his occupations as a farmer and as a drummer, earned extra money preparing the drums which were sent to him from the village where they had been carved.

10. Exact notation, for example using changing time signatures, as Jones does, can even make the music seem more complicated than it is. See p. 57. See also Gerhard Kubik, "The Phenomenon of Inherent Rhythms in East and Central African Instrumental Music," *African Music* 3, no. 1 (1962): 33–42. My notations are schematic, and they should serve only to clarify the text.

11. S. D. Cudjoe, "The Techniques of Ewe Drumming and the Social Importance of Music in Africa," *Phylon* 14 (1953): 286.

12. Herskovits, *Dahomey*, 2: 317.

13. Jones, "African Rhythm," p. 41.

14. "An Aesthetic of the Cool: West African Dance," *African Forum* 2, no. 2 (fall 1966): 93–94.

15. "African Rhythm," p. 27.

16. The question of the off-beat has occupied scholars since E. M. von Hornbostel wrote the first comprehensive article on African music in 1928. Hornbostel, maintaining most logically that the act of beating is the single most important factor of drumming, felt that the beating movement should be considered as two-phased: strain and release; lift and drop. "Only the second phase is stressed acoustically, but the first inaudible one has the motor accent, as it were, which consists in the straining of the muscles. This implies an essential contrast between our rhythmic conception and the Africans'; we proceed from hearing, they from motion; we separate the two phases by a bar-line, and commence the metrical unity, the bar, with the acoustically-stressed time-unit; to them, the beginning of the movement, the arsis [Hornbostel is here referring to the unaccented or weak beat of a rhythmic measure, as opposed to the thesis or main beat] is at the same time the beginning of the figure; up-beats are unknown to them." ("African Negro Music," *Africa* 1 [1928]: 53.) In this passage and its theory of off-beat accents, Hornbostel raised a number of issues which have appeared in various guises in African musicological research, and if we know some of the ideas to be very sound and very deep, others are rather odd. He was in effect saying that Africans keep the main beat with movement, and the point is well taken, as we shall see. But as far as drumming goes, it is evident that Hornbostel, if he ever beat drums, used twenty-pound sledgehammers instead of wooden sticks. A drum is classified as a membranophone because the sound comes from a membrane that is stretched across an opening and that vibrates, and it is also evident that Hornbostel probably never saw a trampoline. Furthermore, the most common additional device a drummer has is to mute or stop his beat by pressing his stick onto the drumhead so that it will not bounce, and he plays this kind of beat by tightening his grip and wrist instead of by relaxing.

Nonetheless, the issues Hornbostel raised are evident in many of the scholarly discussions of such topics as notation, performance modes, and perception modes. For several reasons, we can say that Hornbostel may have been right about rhythm by movement but that he was confused about the beating. Though I have stressed the importance of experiencing the music in its context, I do not want to discount Hornbostel's work because he probably worked mainly from recordings: someone can be right on top of the music and still not come up with something as incisive as that excerpt from Hornbostel's article. Yet one lesson to be learned is that it is very difficult to know how people conceive of the *sound* of their music and that efforts to interpret their performance orientations must be accompanied by a thorough reflection on the levels of abstraction involved in the steps of the interpretation to ensure that the mangoes do not turn into papayas. (See, for example, John Blacking, "Some Notes on a Theory of Rhythm Advanced by Erich von Hornbostel," *African Music* 1, no. 2 [1955]: 12–20.) Such is the fruit of abstract thinking based on ostensibly descriptive notions like up and down, strain and release, lift and drop. To my experience, the act of beating drums is better described by words akin to *turning*; other drummers might complicate the discussion by describing how they rotate their elbows when hand drumming or how they wave their fingers when using sticks. All in all, it seems that Hornbostel and, to a great extent, Waterman picked up many of their frames of reference from psychological discussions of rhythm dominated by the conflict between the motor-behavioral approach and the Gestalt approach. See for example, R. H. Stetson, "A Motor Theory of Rhythm and Discrete Association" (2 parts), *Psychological Review* 12 (1905): 250–70, 293–350, and also Charles S. Myers, "A Study of Rhythm in Primitive Music," *British Journal of Psychology* 1 (1905): 397–406.

17. "African Influence," p. 211.

18. Ibid., pp. 211–12.

19. "African Rhythm," p. 32. The fact that African musicians play with reference to additional rhythms to the ones they actually beat is one of the most important reasons why notations, which of course do not represent unsounded or implied beats, offer an inaccurate representation of African music.

20. Cudjoe, "The Techniques of Ewe Drumming," p. 288. See Amos Tutuola, *The Palm-Wine Drinkard and His Dead Palm-Wine Tapster in the Dead's Town* (New York: Grove Press, 1953), pp. 84–85: "And when 'Drum' started to beat himself, all the people who had been dead for hundreds of years, rose up and came to witness 'Drum' when beating. . . . So when these three fellows (Drum, Song and Dance) disappeared, the people of the new town went back to their houses. Since that day nobody could see the three fellows personally, but we are only hearing their names about in the world and nobody could do in these days what they did."

21. I have heard musicians from different African cultures discuss rhythms as "weaving" in and out. Freeman Donkor, for example, was fond of using a "weaving" metaphor to describe rhythms. The metaphors frequently employed by Westerners—of a rhythmic "fabric" or "texture"—are thus often surprisingly apt. Conversely, some kinds of musical description may be useful for helping us appreciate the repetition of design motifs and colors in African cloth weavings and prints.

22. "A Possible Notation for African Dance Drumming," *African Music* 4, no. 2 (1968): 52.

23. The supporting dondon part could also be thought of as a quarter note followed by a sixteenth rest and then a dotted eighth note and the quarter note again. The difference is very slight, and either feeling for the beat can emerge because both gongon and lead dondon can play with a feeling of either a three-beat or a four-beat, and they change throughout their beating, sometimes following each other and sometimes staying apart. A second gongon crosses them both

in a 4/4 meter. Pitch patterns and intervals can also vary in the beating of the supporting dondons.

24. *Studies in African Music,* 1: 85.

25. Jones has suggested that an extremely fast pulse unites all the rhythms, but this suggestion does not always hold. The issue is an academic one, indicative of ways Westerners may be able to think themselves into the music and certainly useful in that context, but as long as a rhythmic relationship is there, it should not be necessary to break the music down beyond phrases. As we shall see, the music can be thought of as being both slow and fast, but only in terms of the organization of rhythmic phrases.

26. A. M. Jones, "African Music," *African Affairs* 48 (1949): 293.

27. Sohu offers a good illustration of call-and-response, but often, perhaps generally, the responsive patterns overlap on the last note of the solo and the first note of the response.

28. Marius Schneider, "Tone and Tune in West African Music," *Ethnomusicology* 5 (1962): 207.

29. See notation, p. 45.

30. See notation, p. 49.

31. There is also considerable variation among tribes on this point of the freedom of the supporting drums. The suitability of rhythmic changes in different types of orchestras will generally be determined by the contextual use and significance of the music tempered by the specific quality of the tribe's musical sensibility.

32. Peggy Harper, who has written much about West African dance, briefly discusses a dance called Takai which she saw danced by Batonubu people in northern Nigeria, and she reports that it is a dance for Hausas which is danced as far away from northern Nigeria as Benin and Ghana. Her description of Takai as being a young men's dance composed of several distinct rhythms and dance steps ("A Festival of Nigerian Dances," *African Arts/Arts d'Afrique* 3, no. 2 [winter 1970]: 53) certainly suggests a relationship to the Dagomba Takai dance. Such a relationship would not be surprising because many Dagomba customs resemble Hausa customs; significant institutional influences reach back nearly three hundred years to the introduction of Islam into Dagbon by the celebrated Dagomba chief Naa Zanjina, and musical influences could easily go back further. Indeed, the Dagombas say that they as a people came from beyond the Hausa land. It is reasonable to assume that the Takai in Nigeria and the Takai in Ghana are the same dance. On the other hand, I never heard anyone in Ghana trace Takai to the Hausas, nor did I ever see Hausas in Ghana dance anything resembling Takai. It is also interesting to note that Dagomba drummers, as historians, are conscientious about knowing the origins of their dances. The story of Bangumanga (see below, n. 61) is part of the drum history's account of Naa Luro's time, more than three hundred years ago. On one occasion when I heard the Dagomba drum history, the focus was on Naa Zanjina's visit to the chief of the Mamprusis. Describing how the Mamprusi chief came out to greet Naa Zanjina, the lead drummer narrated, "And this is the dance the Mamprusis were beating for their chief," and the drummers beat that music for a while until the story continued. To go back even further, knowledgeable drummers relate that

Zhem, the most important Dagomba dance, was being danced by the people whom the Dagombas conquered when they came to Ghana more than five hundred years ago. Thinking about how ancient some of Africa's beats are can lead us from historical inquiry to metaphysical sentiments, as it has in many African societies.

At any rate, whatever one can say about Takai, Ibrahim Abdulai's perspective seems the most relevant critically. Today Dagombas typically dance to many beats acquired from other peoples, to the extent that, as Ibrahim Abdulai told me, "it has come to look as if they are Dagomba dances." Agbekor, I was told by many people who know about Ewe music, is danced in Togo and Benin. I did not see it, but I did not travel to look for it. Agbadza and Gahu are among other Ewe dances which are intercultural. To the Ewes, Agbekor is an Ewe dance; to the Dagombas, Takai is a Dagomba dance. Our types of historical considerations would seem somewhat absurd, and nearly useless aesthetically, if brought out during a Takai or Agbekor dance. My experience is that few people in Africa are concerned with such questions. Educated people sometimes distinguish generic rhythms like Highlife from what they call "cultural" or "traditional" dances, but both they and the "traditional" people in the villages dance Highlife without problems, and it would be difficult to find a Ghanaian culture whose musical repertoire does not contain a beat that could be considered prototypical Highlife. In the middle are dances which are "cultural" and about which a limited number of indigenous people would be able to point to comparable dances in other cultural groups, such as Ibrahim Abdulai does regarding Zamandunia (p. 102).

The whole matter of the history of specific beats is very interesting, but there has been very little written about it. On a broad perspective, we can note that in spite of the amazing diversity of African music, there is an equally amazing facility with which musical styles spread out and are adopted. Inside individual traditions, we can note the degree to which dances that remain basically the same are transformed from generation to generation. All in all, however, in Africa as in this book, the artistic focus is on the situation.

33. Sometimes Kondalia is beaten for people to dance at weddings or funerals, though the dancing is different. On one occasion I asked Ibrahim Abdulai why they were playing Kondalia for a dancer who had requested it. He nodded his head toward the pile of money the drummers were accumulating and said, "Ah, you see. Life is hard."

34. J. H. Kwabena Nketia, "Drums, Dance, and Song," *Atlantic Monthly*, April 1959, p. 69.

35. "The Techniques of Ewe Drumming," p. 288.

36. One afternoon in Haiti, I was taken by a Haitian friend to a very posh beach which was frequented mainly, it seemed, by personnel of foreign companies. In the adjoining restaurant, a local band was providing some sleepy Meringue music. The singer, an old man, improvised what he sang in Creole, which I translated with the help of my friend and which ran something like this: "Well, here I am singing. But it doesn't matter what I say because no one here understands me; I just say nonsense and the people go on eating. They don't look at me. If they look at me, I look back at them. And they look back at me. Then they look at the little fish on their plates. And I look back at them." And so on.

When I looked at him, he noticed and looked back at me. I burst out laughing, and then everybody turned to look at me! The atmosphere, needless to say, had its flaws, but the singer stayed with it.

37. *Drumming in Akan Communities*, p. 135.

38. Many of the popular Dagomba dance beats are based on the praise-names of former Ya-Naas, the Paramount Chiefs, and people who trace their lines to a particular chief will often prefer to dance the dance which recalls that chief. Sometimes musicians with a wide repertoire of dance beats will find themselves beating only a few types of dances during a family celebration. Among the dances, for example, Nanto Nimdi is for Naa Yakubu (c. 1850). The current chieftaincy dispute in Dagbon is between the lines of two of Naa Yakubu's sons who became Ya-Naas, Naa Abdulai and Naa Andani (II). A popular dance re-calling one of Naa Abdulai's names is Nagbiegu, and similarly, Naanigo is a dance and a name for Naa Andani. Needless to say, if drummers are playing for a wedding or a funeral at a certain house, most of the people from that house will likely be of one particular sentiment on the chieftaincy dispute, and though there is not any strict adherence to the tendency, the types of dances which are called will sometimes reflect their political views. Once when I came out to dance at a wedding, I wanted to dance Naanigo, and several people immediately began teasing me that I was an Andani supporter.

39. "Takada Drumming," p. 20. An extremely interesting comparison may be made between this description of an Ewe drummer and Charles Keil's description of Bobby Bland on stage in *Urban Blues* (Chicago: University of Chicago Press, 1966), pp. 114–42. See also the fine article by Ayo Bankole, Judith Bush, and Sadek H. Samaan, "The Yoruba Master Drummer," *African Arts* 8, no. 2 (winter 1975): 48–56, 77–78.

40. Fela Anikulapo Kuti, "Carry Me, I Want to Die." A recording of this song is on the album *Fela Ransome-Kuti and the Africa '70 with Ginger Baker*, Signpost Records, SP8401, Atlantic Records Distributor, ST–SP–722532 PR.

41. "An Aesthetic of the Cool: West African Dance," pp. 95–99.

42. *Anthropology of Music*, pp. 190–92. The whole of chapter 10 is particularly rich with examples. Fela Anikulapo Kuti is known not only for satirical social criticism but also for the explicitness of the political criticism in his songs. He has openly ridiculed police and soldiers in "Zombie," and one of his recent songs is "V.I.P.: Vagabonds In Power." See also John Darnton, "Nigeria's Dissident Superstar," *New York Times Magazine*, July 24, 1977, pp. 10–12, 22–24, 26, 28. In the same vein are many of Jamaica's world-famous Reggae musicians, and Westerners who listen to some Reggae lyrics will find it difficult to imagine similar songs on "American Top 40." Even James Brown's "The Payback" was camouflaged with references to a deceitful love relationship, and though many listeners interpreted the song politically, the love and revenge theme may have been all James Brown intended.

43. The Dagomba drum history has been written out and published. See Emmanuel Forster Tamakloe, ed., *A Brief History of the Dagbamba People* (Accra, Ghana: Government Printing Office, 1931).

44. Horoya Band of Kankan, "Boloba," Editions Syliphone Conakry, SLP 17.

45. African Brothers Dance Band (International), "Abusua Nnye Asafo," Afribros, PAB 001. Ramblers (International) Dance Band, "Agyanka Dabre,"

Decca (West Africa) Ltd., WAPS 25. African Brothers Dance Band (International), "San Behwe wo Mma," Afribros, PAB 001; the proverb in the song runs, "You only know how long the frog is when it dies."

46. Royal Brothers Band, "Onyame Nnae," Decca (West Africa) Ltd., GWA 4234.

47. I have heard variations of the phrase several times; it is cited from Andrew C. Denteh, *A Visitor's Guide to Ghanaian Customs and Other Matters* (published by the author, P.O. Box 73, Legon, Ghana, 1967), p. 12.

48. Eastern Star Dance Band, "Baby Pancake," Philips West Africa Records, PF 382793 2F.

49. Fela Anikulapo Kuti and the Africa '70, "Water No Get Enemy," Soundworkshop Records, SWS(LP) 1001.

50. Robert Farris Thompson's article "The Mambo in Mexico," *Jazz Review*, September 1960, pp. 36–38, is a description of the introduction to Mexico of Afro-Cuban Mambo by Perez Prado. Thompson writes (p. 38): "When Justi Barreto wrote the *Newspaper Shirt* mambo in 1950 he succeeded in capturing what it felt like to live in the fifties. The scene is Mexico City in June 1950. A Negro man has fashioned himself a shirt out of newspaper. He studies the material of his shirt, and the cloth of scare headlines frankly worries him. His shirt tells him war is raging in Korea, and he summarizes this news with onomatopoeia: BEEM! BOMB! BOME! BOOM! Perez Prado undercuts his anxiety with a piano solo which tinkles with insouciance. Air raid sirens sound. In the heart of the crisis, the mambo builds up and, to a cowbell-stressed rhythm, blasts out its most affirmative sounds. The man chants praise of his shirt, a chorus answers in call-and-response fashion, and the mambo ends. A capsule allegory; the man does not recoil in fear though he is sensibly alarmed. 'Look,' he says, 'life is delicious and to be savored in spite of doom.' "

See also Keil, *Urban Blues*, pp. 164–90.

51. From the album *Caribbean Folk Music*, recorded by Thomas J. Price, edited by Harold Courlander, Ethnic Folkways Library Album no. FE 4533.

52. Polydor, PD 6039.

53. The name was originally taken from the hero of a widely seen Italian-made cowboy movie, though recently "Sartana" often comes out as "Santana" after the American Latin-Soul musicians—an adaptation to the changing times which also reflects how modern nicknames partake of the sentiments of praise-naming.

54. Dynatone Publishing Co./Belinda Music, Inc., Polydor, PD 2–3007.

55. Detailed discussions of talking drums may be found particularly in John F. Carrington, *Talking Drums of Africa* (London: Carey Kingsgate Press, 1949), and by the same author, *A Comparative Study of Some Central African Gong-Languages* (Brussels: Institut Royale Colonial Belge, 1949). See also Nketia, *Drumming in Akan Communities*, and R. S. Rattray, *Ashanti* (Oxford: Clarendon Press, 1923), pp. 242–86.

56. Although I am conversant in Twi, I do not speak any African languages fluently enough to understand the drum languages. My illustrations in this section come from what various people told me without my being able to verify them with my own direct knowledge. For literary reasons, however, I have chosen to use these illustrations rather than any of the ones provided by authorities like Nketia or Carrington (see above, n. 55). As a further note, I should add that while,

loosely speaking, many readers will identify *tone* with *pitch*, musicologically the concept of *tonality* implies what most readers probably understand by *key*, and *tone* implies harmonic relations of secondary tones among the notes. Generally, therefore, I have used the word *pitch* in many contexts where other writers have used the word *tone*, but I would not claim strict musicological fidelity in the following discussion because the intervals in the illustrations are to be understood as not even approximate but rather purely schematic. Also, it is probably worthwhile at this point to reiterate that I have modified spellings to avoid nonstandard typographical characters.

57. "Drum-Signaling in a West African Tribe," *Word* 1 (1945): 233.

58. Ames, Gregersen, and Neugebauer, "Taaken Sàmàarii," pp. 12–31.

59. Jerry Hansen and the Ramblers Dance Band, "Yiadom Boakye," Decca (West Africa) Ltd., WAP 24.

60. "The Musical Dimension of Perception in the Upper Congo, Zaïre," *African Music* 5, no. 1 (1971): 49.

61. Bangumanga is a victory dance. Three hundred years ago, when Naa Luro defeated the Gonjas in a war, he was searching for someone to praise him, and his eldest daughter, Kachagu, called Lun-zhegu (a "descendent" of the original dondon beater) and asked him to beat a dance for her father so that she and her sisters and mothers could dance. The detailed story of the historical incident is very interesting, particularly the interview between Naa Luro and the Gonja chief, whom the Dagombas call Kalugsi Dagia, before Naa Luro killed him with a spear which passed through Kalugsi Dagia's anus and out his head. When the drum history is being beaten and sung, people gather in an open area outside the chief's house to listen through the night. If the drummers are beating the history of Naa Luro, the story of Naa Luro's Gonja wars can, depending on the knowledgeability of the drummers, be quite involved, and the story of Bangumanga is the climax. When the drummers reach that point, they beat the dance, and the chief's wives and children, who are sitting together, all jump up and dance Bangumanga, carrying swords and baskets (for the spoils). The drum language is *Bem bo ma, be pam bo ma je* ("They will search for me, but they will not see me"). One false meaning is *Man daa yeli, mam bi lan yeli* ("I said it; I don't say it again"). The meaning is a "secret" because of the seriousness of war. In its truth, Bangumanga recalls the blood that was shed in the war, and so too blood must be shed in respect of the dead: animals are killed in sacrifice before drummers will beat the history, and I also killed animals before I learned the meaning of Bangumanga, as I did when I learned Zhem.

62. According to the Dogon people, the two skins of the dondon are the ears of Nummo, the givers of Words, the spirits which issued from the intercourse of God and the earth. In Dogon cosmogony as related by a Dogon elder, the dondon is an aspect of the Third Word and the gift of civilization. In his conversation with the anthropologist, the elder held his hands apart and laced his fingers with thread as a dondon is laced. "The palms of his hands represented the skins of the drum, and thus to play on the drum was, symbolically, to play on the hands of Nummo. . . . Cupping his hands behind his ears, Ogotemmêli explained that the spirit had no external ears but only auditory holes. 'His hands serve for ears,' he said; 'to enable him to hear he always holds them on each side of his head. To tap

the drum is to tap Nummo's palms, to tap, that is, his ears"—Marcel Griaule, *Conversations with Ogotemmêli: An Introduction to Dogon Religious Ideas*, trans. Ralph Butler, Audrey I. Richards, and Beatrice Hook (London: International African Institute and Oxford University Press, 1965), p. 64.

63. Jones, *Studies in African Music*, 1: 67, 68.

64. This phenomenon is very common among drummers in various tribes, though the specific syllables, of course, vary depending on the drum. In fact, I have never met an African drummer who could not "speak" the rhythms he was playing. Jazz scatting is a bit comparable, and for a fine recording of a Latin drummer saying his improvisations aloud, an interested reader might listen to Orestes Vilato play the timbales in "Descarga '73," on the album *Tipica '73*, Inca Records, SLP 1031.

65. Jones, *Studies in African Music*, 1: 67.

66. Ibid., 68.

67. Mezz Mezzrow made the same observation regarding jazz drumming, and he says he helped Gene Krupa learn it: "I would sit there with Gene for hours, just beating out the rhythms of Zutty Singleton or Johnny Wells for hours until my hands were swole double. I'd show him the secret that Dave Tough had dug, that there was a tonal pattern of harmony to be followed and that what seemed like a steady beat was really a sequence of different sounds accented at the right intervals, with just the correct amount of vibrations coming from the snare and bass so that the other musicians who were improvising got the foundation to carry on and be more inventive." Mezz Mezzrow and Bernard Wolfe, *Really the Blues* (Garden City, N.Y.: Doubleday, Anchor Books, 1972), p. 127.

68. A few of my friends told me that certain languages, because of especially clear distinctions of the relative pitch of words or especially percussive qualities of speech patterns, may lend themselves more easily to musical expression, and that they "feel it more" when the singing is, for example, in Ga or Yoruba as opposed to Twi. John F. Carrington suggests the same thing in his brief article, "Tone and Melody in a Congolese Popular Song," *African Music* 4, no. 1 (1966/1967): 39. Personally, singing in any language sounds nice to me.

69. J. H. Kwabena Nketia, "Traditional Music of the Ga People," *African Music* 2, no. 1 (1958): 23.

70. Ladzekpo and Pantaleoni ("Takada Drumming," p. 17) say that there is a kind of harmony in a drum ensemble created by "the faint ringing overtones that wax and wane with the alternation of bounced and stopped strokes of the sticks on the chorus drums, especially when the center area of the head is used consistently." Such an observation is even easier to make, of course, regarding the Dagomba supporting drums.

71. "The Techniques of Ewe Drumming," p. 288.

72. For illustrative discussions of this issue in several contexts, see 'Tunji Vidal, "Oriki in Traditional Yoruba Music," *African Arts* 3, no. 1 (autumn 1969): 56–59; Jones, *Studies in African Music*, 1: 232–51; and a more qualified discussion by Paul Richards, "A Quantitative Analysis of the Relationship between Language Tone and Melody in a Hausa Song," *African Language Studies* 13 (1972): 137–61.

73. "Takada Drumming," p. 18. See also the interesting discussion in Nketia, *Drumming in Akan Communities*, pp. 158–70.
74. I am indebted to C. K. Ganyo of the Arts Council of Ghana and also to Seth Y. Nakey of the University of Ghana Music Ensemble for the drum language of the turning and half-turning phrases, and to Freeman Donkor for the drum language of the supporting drums.

Chapter 3   Style in Africa
1. In the following discussion, I will be presenting my interpretation of the various elements of African musical style—repetition, change, accentuation, precision, and so on—by focusing on Takai and Agbekor, with which readers are already somewhat familiar. I hope that readers will try to get a feeling for the perspectives I advance by listening to as wide a variety of African musical idioms as recordings and experience make available. I decided to eliminate many possible notational examples from this discussion in the interest of greater clarity of exposition, but I have based my discussion and conclusions on the full range of my experience, which includes practical training or observation of dozens of cultural styles. As I abstracted my notions, I searched for unifying and common aspects of aesthetic concern in the many traditions and idioms I kept in mind, and I would hope that my objectivity in this search could be verified as easily in the streets of Douala as in the streets of Tamale, in the nightclubs of Kinshasa as in the nightclubs of Lagos, Accra, or Abidjan. As I stated in my Introduction, I hope that this book can be a starting point for readers who want to move to a better understanding of African music in general, and my interest is that readers will enjoy their understanding of the meaning of African aesthetic concerns through whatever music reaches them best.
2. *Studies in African Music*, 1: 102.
3. John Pemberton, "Eshu-Elegba: The Yoruba Trickster God," *African Arts* 9, no. 1 (October 1975): 23.
4. John Blacking, "Tonal Organization," p. 11. In a private communication, Blacking acknowledged Hindemith as the source of the statement, of which the quotation is a paraphrase.
5. "African Influence," p. 213.
6. *Studies in African Music*, 1: 38.
7. In our music, the vertical lines would tend to be more or less evenly spaced or comprehensible as divisions of a single denominator, based on the time signature and the beginning of the bar.
8. There is no rubato involved, of course. This effect is what Cudjoe was talking about with his notion of "expanding and contracting" time signatures.
9. "African Influence," pp. 213–14.
10. In the discussion, quoted in chapter 2, of the musician elaborating his beating while relying on his audience's supplying "subjective beats."
11. Most commentators had viewed rhythmic repetition as an indication of "primitiveness," and similarly, Western religious biases led many to interpret the aesthetic effect of rhythmic music as primarily emotional and "ecstatic." For an example see Hornbostel, "African Negro Music," p. 38. For further discussion of this issue, see pp. 140–41.
12. "African Influence," p. 217.

13. I know several conga drummers in Highlife bands who distinguish themselves from Latin conga drummers by the fact that they do not slap in many syncopated accents unless in a brief solo, nor do they shift meters with rubato-like beating. Those drummers who do are characterized as "modern"; my own teacher, Seth Ankrah of the Ramblers Dance Band, was extremely modern among Accra drummers, but he nonetheless built most of his style on his childhood experience as a Ga Kpanlogo drummer. He was a fine teacher and a great drummer, yet I sometimes found his style difficult to follow because of the delicate balance he maintained between steadiness and virtuosity. In general, Highlife drummers say that Highlife dancing should be smooth, and since most people dance to the conga drums, the drummers do not want to use irregular rhythms or to focus on improvised accents more than on their steady beat. Most conga drummers for top African bands exemplify this point.

14. Available literary records of indigenous African artistic criticism are few, and in general one may search and find only fragmented examples. Judging from my experience, the points raised in Ibrahim Abdulai's lecture may be applied in almost any African musical context. Differences for specific dances and culture areas exist, of course, but the general applicability of Ibrahim's comments is more remarkable. One good collection of complementary "ethnocriticism" may be found in the Appendix ("Texts of Artistic Criticism of the Dance in Tropical Africa") of Robert Farris Thompson, *African Art in Motion: Icon and Act in the Collection of Katherine Coryton White* (Los Angeles: University of California Press, 1974), pp. 251–75. Significantly, by using videotapes of dances, Thompson also found that criticism from outside the cultures where he taped corresponded to criticisms from indigenous commentators. See also pp. 122–23, and Appendix, pp. 173–82.

15. As usual, the Germans have a word for it: *Spätstil*, or late style, is a concept which refers to the works of old artists, and particularly to certain odd masterpieces—Shakespeare's *The Tempest* and Mozart's *The Magic Flute* are cases in point—in which the artists, facing mortality, do not attempt to break free from the formal constrictions of their art but rather create astounding pieces within the limitations of the genres in which they have worked all their lives and to which they return with a respect for convention paradoxically combined with outlandish motifs, motifs which in the context of this essay we might characterize as "offbeat." Again in the context of this essay, it is not insignificant that late works pose very tricky problems for traditional Western art criticism and appreciation. Gottfried Benn discusses late style in his essay "Artists and Old Age," in *Primal Vision: Selected Writings of Gottfried Benn*, ed. E. B. Ashton (New York: New Directions, 1971), also appearing in *Partisan Review* 22, no. 3 (summer 1955): 297–319.

An extremely interesting and especially valuable discussion of late style can be found in Thomas Mann, *Doctor Faustus: The Life of the German Composer Adrian Leverkühn as Told by a Friend*, trans. H. T. Lowe-Porter (New York: Random House, Vintage Books, 1971), chap. 8, in the context of a lecture given by one of the characters of the novel, Wendell Kretschmar, on why Beethoven had not written a third movement to the Piano Sonata No. 32 in C minor, Opus 111. (A fine recording of this sonata by Wilhelm Kempff is available on Deutsche Grammophon SLPM 138945.) An abridgement of Kretschmar's exposition (pp. 52–53) focuses on "the monstrous movement of variations which forms the second part of this sonata. The theme of this movement goes through a hundred vicissitudes, a hundred worlds of rhythmic contrasts, at length outgrows itself, and is finally lost in giddy heights that one might call other-worldly or abstract. And in just that very way Beethoven's art had overgrown itself, risen out of the habitable regions of tradition, even before the startled gaze of human eyes, into spheres of the entirely and utterly and nothing-but personal. . . .

"So far, so good, said Kretschmar. And yet again, good or right only conditionally and incompletely. For one would usually connect with the conception of the merely personal, ideas of limitless subjectivity and of radical harmonic will to expression, in contrast to polyphonic objectivity (Kretschmar was concerned to have us impress upon our minds this distinction between harmonic subjectivity and polyphonic objectivity) and this equation, this contrast, here as altogether in the masterly late works, would simply not apply. As a matter of fact, Beethoven had been far more 'subjective,' not to say far more 'personal,' in his middle period than in his last, had been far more bent on taking all the flourishes, formulas, and conventions, of which music is certainly full, and consuming them in the personal expression, melting them into the subjective dynamic. The relation of the later Beethoven to the conventional, say in the last five piano sonatas, is, despite all the uniqueness and even uncanniness of the formal language, quite different, much more complaisant and easy-going. Untouched, untransformed by the subjective, convention often appeared in the late works, in a baldness, one might say exhaustiveness, an abandonment of self, with an effect more majestic and awful than any reckless plunge into the personal. In these forms, said the speaker, the subjective and the conventional assumed a new relationship, conditioned by death. . . .

"Where greatness and death come together, he declared, there arises an objectivity tending to the conventional, which in its majesty leaves the most domineering subjectivity far behind, because therein the merely personal—which had after all been the surmounting of a tradition already brought to its peak—once more outgrew itself, in that it entered into the mythical, the collectively great and supernatural.

"He did not ask if we understood that, nor did we ask ourselves."

16. "He who wills repetition is matured in seriousness. . . . If the young man had believed in repetition, of what might he not have been capable? What inwardness he might have attained." Søren Kierkegaard, *Repetition: An Essay in Experimental Psychology*, trans. Walter Lowrie (New York: Harper & Row, Harper Torchbooks, 1964), pp. 35, 49.

17. *Studies in African Music*, 1: 24.

18. "Motion and Feeling through Music," *Journal of Aesthetics and Art Criticism* 24 (1966): 347. Certain aspects of this distinction of gestural timing may also be related to notions of precision. For an interesting comparison we can look at snare drumming in the Ancient Fife and Drum Musters held throughout the United States. The snare drumming displayed in musters is built up from combinations of the nearly thirty "rudiments" basic to Western snare drumming technique: flams, paradiddles, ratamacues, five-stroke rolls, seven-stroke rolls, nine-stroke rolls, and so on. In competitions, for example, drummers are expected to follow sticking patterns consistently, and if the rudiment is to be played in the

open position (slowly) and then closed (played faster), the hands and sticks should be raised on each stroke to exactly the same level and then gradually and consistently lowered. African drummers do not concern themselves at all with such military precision on the fine points of technique; precision is important to them for reasons of formal clarity, and it would never matter to them how a drummer played or even whether he played his part with one hand or two, as long as the sound was right. And they are more interested in the forceful clarity of the rhythms they select than the precision clarity of their technique.

19. The voice and the attitude James Brown brings to his lyrics are also important.

20. Jones, *Studies in African Music*, 1: 193.

21. See also Cudjoe, "The Techniques of Ewe Drumming," p. 288.

22. *Studies in African Music*, 1: 175.

23. See notation, p. 56.

24. Jones, *Studies in African Music*, 1: 183–85.

25. There was one friend of mine interested in jazz who pointed to Charlie Parker's original solo in "A Night in Tunisia" as a watershed in the development of jazz. In that solo, Parker achieved a remarkable technical feat and set a standard for other jazzmen who, according to my critical friend, subordinated their sense of expression to their interest in technical display. The balance that Parker and the jazzmen he influenced had always struck between their virtuosity and their communicative purpose shifted toward a conception which was closer to Western "art" music. Probably my friend was taking that solo as a symbol for Parker's career, which is often taken to mark the end of the swing era and the beginning of more personal and expressive jazz. Personally, I am not sure of the extent to which this perspective is applicable because many of the great jazz artists seem to me to approach their music in the same way as many of the African musicians I have heard. Nevertheless, such a perspective does indicate a dimension through which questions of "authenticity," for whatever they are worth, may be approached. I have not seen such a perspective fully articulated in jazz criticism, and I feel that it offers at least a viable alternative to judging jazz in terms of purely formal qualities or individual artists' stylistic development. Certainly it is possible for a piece of music to have complexly organized rhythms or even African percussive instrumentation and still be far removed from the sensibility defined in this study, in which the musician's attitudes toward his audience and toward the traditional forms of his genre are such crucial concerns. Then again, jazz, though it does manifest many of the structural characteristics of African traditional music, is played in a very different context. (A nice brief essay on the development of modern jazz drumming is Robert Palmer's liner notes for *The Drums*, Impulse Records, ASH–9272–3.) To my mind, the standards and artistic norms of African "jazz" are set by Fela Anikulapo Kuti, African Brothers, Orchestra O.K. Jazz, Camayenne Sofa, and the many other musicians making music in African urban settings. All in all, African "jazz" is still dance music.

26. "Diola-Fogny Funeral Songs and the Native Critic," *African Language Review* 8 (1969): 181, 178.

27. See above, chap. 2, n. 61.

28. *Religion and Medicine among the Ga People* (London: Oxford University Press, 1937), p. 5.

29. *Voodoo in Haiti*, trans. Hugo Charteris (New York: Oxford University Press, 1959), p. 187.

30. Serge Bramly, *Macumba: The Teachings of Maria-José, Mother of the Gods*, trans. Meg Bogin (New York: St. Martin's Press, 1977), p. 47.

31. "An Aesthetic of the Cool: West African Dance," p. 91.

32. Extremely interesting comparative material on the issue of artistic influence in Western contexts may be found in Hartman, "Toward Literary History," in *Beyond Formalism*; and in Harold Bloom, *The Anxiety of Influence: A Theory of Poetry* (New York: Oxford University Press, 1973).

33. Amoah Azangeo, the musician who so impressed Les McCann at the Soul to Soul Concert in Accra in 1971, is a Frafra rattle player. Amoah had been in Accra a short time prior to the concert, demonstrating his skills to rather mixed responses, and Les McCann, I imagine, must have seen Amoah and invited him to participate with the Les McCann-Eddie Harris group. The producers of the film *Soul to Soul*, I further imagine, must have then decided to stage the section of the film which depicts Amoah on his trip from Bolgatanga to Accra, supposedly to see the Soul to Soul Concert. On that trip, Amoah stops in Tamale and, in the place where I used to take my morning lessons, comes upon a performance of the Takai dancers, moving around Ibrahim and the other drummers inside the circle. Amoah enters the circle and joins the drummers with his rattle, jamming, and Ibrahim is the one who has the funny look on his face, no doubt wondering what in the world a Frafra rattle player like Amoah could be doing inside the circle with the Dagomba Takai musicians. Ibrahim had mentioned something about being hired to play for some people who took films, but I had no idea it was the production company of *Soul to Soul*. It was only a few weeks after I returned to the United States, while I was strolling around New York City alone one night with nothing in particular to do, that I came across a theater showing the film about the concert, and having been there, I decided to go in to see what it looked like. When I saw Ibrahim and a great many of my friends, one of them playing a gongon which I had bought and brought back with me, I nearly went crazy with excitement. After the film ended, I was happily babbling to various people in the audience, "Those were all my friends! That one man was playing my drum!" I received some very curious looks from people who hurried out into the street. Truth is stranger than fiction.

34. The fiddles are called *goonji*. According to Ibrahim Abdulai, "The goonji comes from the Guruma people. Today we have the Gurumas around Chereponi in Togo, but in the olden days they were around Mali. When they came to Togo and settled, the first place they settled was in the Mamprusi land. They married Mamprusi wives and brought forth children, and they were playing the goonji. And a time came when the Mamprusis too became goonji players. So it is the Gurumas who have goonjis but those who don't know say it is the Mamprusis. And those who are playing it here came from the Mamprusis and settled here, and it was in the time of Naa Ziblim Bandamda. The wives they brought were bringing forth, and their children were marrying Dagomba women and bringing forth, and now they have become Dagombas." For pictures of similar fiddles, see Bebey, *African Music*, pp. viii, 42, and 43.

35. Atikatika also has a "political" name stemming from its formative period during the national and regional power struggles following the overthrow of

Nkrumah in the late 1960s and the chieftaincy crisis in Dagbon in the early 1970s. *Kpara ni jansi*: *be nman taba* means "Baboons and monkeys: they resemble one another." An example of a typical Atikatika song: the leader sings, "An airplane has got a punctured tire"; the chorus replies, "That is the trouble of the people in the sky." The children are not concerned with the problems of the elite. They also think nothing of attacking local figures like school headmasters or prominent businessmen. Some people find Atikatika songs so funny that they can stand and watch the children for hours; others find the gossip so outrageous that they wonder what today's children are coming to.

36. I have never seen anything like the following happen in Tamale, but the story is interesting. I was on a trip which took me through Niamey, the capital of Niger, and I was walking around when I heard some music. As usual, I went to see what was happening, and down an alley, surrounded by a small group of people, were a number of musicians. They had five gongons and the beating was great, and there was a singer who began singing at me as soon as I arrived. I was watching him for some time, and he seemed to be singing more aggressively in my direction; I finally realized that his song was "praising" me and that I had to find my pocket. As it turned out, I was lucky. After the singer had touched everybody in the circle, he directed his singing to a man who had set up a small table and was selling cigarettes. The man would hear none of it, and while the singer sang on, two of the gongon beaters brought their drums to either side of the man's head and beat furiously until the man came across with some of the money he had been making. It had been too much for him, though; he picked up his table and stumbled away, his head twitching.

37. This particular phrase was suggested to me by Robert Thompson in a conversation.

38. These are two of the translations I have been given for the Dagbani phrase *be ni nyemya*.

39. The Dagbani is *Dema* (music) *maari* (cools) *suhu* (the heart).

40. Interested readers can find a picture of a kora in Roderic Knight, "Towards a Notation and Tabulature for the Kora," *African Music* 5, no. 1 (1971): 26. There are many fine pictures of the kora and related instruments in Bebey, *African Music*, especially pp. 59 and 148.

41. "An Aesthetic of the Cool: West African Dance." Thompson's work as a whole stands out as a major contribution to the scholarly understanding of African art, and I hope that my continuous use throughout this book of material drawn from his writings will indicate the affinity I feel exists between the themes which have emerged from his work as an art historian and the considerations which I have found relevant in my research as a social scientist. Within the history of African musicological scholarship, Jones's work brought out many significant features of African music, notably rhythmic conflict, and Jones's writings indicate that he was beginning to grasp the significance of repetition as a basis of formal clarity along with the converse notion of continuity within improvisational change, but it was Thompson who elucidated and expanded Waterman's breakthrough notion of mediation in African musical forms, and he has also been primarily responsible for bringing the concept of "coolness" as an ethical modality into Western discussions of African art in general. African dance music is sometimes referred to as "hot" in the sense of dynamic and exciting. (See Richard Alan

Waterman, " 'Hot' Rhythm in Negro Music," *Journal of the American Musico-logical Society* 1 [spring 1948]: 24–25; this "hot" concept has been picked up by Merriam as a descriptive referent in several of his articles.) Thompson, in re-ferring to coolness as a mode of communication and a moral concept, has fol-lowed, to my mind, a more philosophically authentic notion of aesthetics, com-bining artistic criticism of creative modes with social analysis of cultural patterns. Thompson's latest book offers an outstanding presentation and synthesis of his perspective on aesthetics and ethics in African art (*African Art in Motion*, espe-cially the short descriptive essays in chapter 3).

42. Chief Defang Tarhmben, cited in Thompson, *African Art in Motion*, p. 262.

43. "An Aesthetic of the Cool: West African Dance," pp. 93–94. The relation-ship of rhythms and dance steps is also mentioned by Robin Horton, "The Kala-bari *Ekine* Society: A Borderland of Religion and Art," *Africa* 33 (1963): 96–99; by J. H. Kwabena Nketia, "The Interrelations of African Music and Dance," *Studia Musicologica* 7 (1965): 91–101; by Philip Gbeho, "African Music Deserves Generous Recognition," *West Africa Review* 22 (1951): 911; and by several other scholars.

44. Anthropologists have also looked at dancing and noted community soli-darity, though they have not based their observations on aesthetic considerations and thus have tended from the first to emphasize the collective dimensions of both the activity of dancing and the expression of feelings. See E. E. Evans-Pritchard, "The Dance," *Africa* 1 (1928): esp. 458–60.

45. "An Aesthetic of the Cool: West African Dance," p. 85.

46. In 1915 Billy Sunday delivered a sermon called "Dancing, Drinking, Card-playing," from which the following passages are excerpted. "I have a message that burns its way into your soul and into my heart. My words may be strong, but if they are you must remember they are blood-red with conviction. With the cry of lost souls ringing in my ears, I cannot remain still. I must cry out. . . . You sow the dance and you reap a crop of brothels. . . . If you don't care whether your children go to the dance, and I do care, you make it that much harder for me to keep my children right. But I will keep them right if I have to slap my next door neighbor in the face. . . . I am asked to give a reason to the unsaved, why they should not do it [the dance]. The church of God forbids it. The greatest and most spiritual churches forbid it, and are against it. Catholic, Presbyterian, Congregational, the United Brethren and the Christian are all against it. The Methodist church was raised up for the very purpose of counteracting the dance in the church. . . . I have never known a Baptist or Congregational preacher worth a snap of the finger who didn't cry out against the dance. That was on their own initiative, too. You tell us that young people must sow their wild oats. Oh, away with such spiritual rot. You can't sow sin and reap virtue. If there were nothing but card players and dancers in the church, it would stink and rot out. The lowest rascal in any community is a dancing Methodist. . . . The dancing Christian never was a soul winner. The dance is simply a hugging match set to music. The dance is a sexual love feast. This crusade against the dance is for everybody, not merely for the preacher or the old man or woman who couldn't dance if they wanted to, but for everybody interested in morals, whether in the church or out of the church. . . . My wife and I have been at the bed-side of a girl who was dying in a house of ill-fame. She said the reason for her downfall

had been the dance, which she began when fifteen years old. She used to attend Sunday school. When we asked her if she had any message for the girls, she cried, 'Tell the girls and warn them to let the dance alone.' . . . I have more respect for a saloonkeeper than for a dancing teacher. I don't believe the saloons will do as much to damn the morals of young people as the dancing school. That is my position. I don't care anything about yours. Professor Faulkner said he knew of one private dancing school that sent six girls into houses of ill-fame in about three months. He talked with 200 girls and found that 165 fell as the result of the dance, twenty by drink, ten by choice and seven from poverty. Where do you find the most accomplished dancers? In the brothels. Why? They were taught in dancing schools. . . . I believe the dance is founded on sexual preference and I believe that passion makes the dance popular. You say you don't believe it! You make men dance by themselves, and it'll kill the dance in two weeks. . . . When you die you don't send for the dancing master to pray over you. . . . People say to me: 'Well, didn't they dance in the Bible?' Yes, they danced in the Bible, and they committed adultery, too; and they got punished." From Clyde E. Fant, Jr., and William M. Pinson, Jr., eds., *20 Centuries of Great Preaching: An Encyclopedia of Preaching*, vol. 7, *Watson [Maclaren] to Rufus Jones, 1850–1950* (Waco, Texas: Word Books, 1971), pp. 280–93.

47. The mutual relationship of drummers and dancers also provides some interesting possibilities for interpersonal dynamics, particularly in a dance as professional as Agbekor. One time after I had not played Ewe drums for several months, Gideon visited me and asked me to play Agbekor for him to dance at a funeral in his home town. Although he failed to meet me for a practice session, when we arrived at his town, he announced that I was to play the fast version for a full two hours, and he interrupted my protests with, "You know how to play it, and I know that you can't forget." I knew that, too, but I was worried about toughening the skin of my hands. That day, the dead master drummers helped me to remember, but they were not concerned about my hands, and the skin on my fingertips blistered and broke open after half an hour. The pain was terrible. When I tried to beat the rhythms that would end the dance, Gideon would come up to the drum, take the sticks from my hands, beat the rhythm he wanted to dance, then hand me the sticks and go back to his place.

I got my revenge months later in a similar situation, except that I had been playing conga drums and my hands were tough. The other dancers were fresh, but Gideon was tired after finishing a very strenuous display on three drums. I punished him very well. Every time he would signal me and begin dancing the step which would close the dance, I would go back to the beginning and make the ensemble play faster. One particular rhythm makes the dancers walk forward in a half crouch, as if advancing on an enemy; I concentrated on that beat. There was nothing Gideon could do. Whenever he got close enough to me to try to tell me to stop, I would smile as if I could not understand him, beat the drum and send him back into the dance circle.

48. "An Aesthetic of the Cool: West African Dance," p. 94.

49. See, for example, Erikson, *Youth*, pp. 243–45; and Eldridge Cleaver, *Soul on Ice* (New York: McGraw-Hill, 1968), pp. 191–204.

50. This example is interesting from the standpoint of criticism. Looking at this kind of dancing is useful for recognizing the effect of the music in a different cul-

tural context—and by extension for recognizing significant factors of influence in more authentic contexts like the Latin dance halls—but by all means it would be misguided to interpret the meaning of African dance on the basis of what white American teenagers do with it. A great deal of the white American moral reaction against Afro-American musical idioms (see chap. 1, n. 2) has been based on such an indirect approach to the music. A parallel can be drawn to Picasso's use of African mask motifs in his early cubist period. Using his own understanding of the meaning of the masks for his own artistic purposes, he significantly influenced our ways of looking at African masks. To a great extent, new artistic styles emerge out of the reinterpretation or misinterpretation of earlier artistic works, and as these new styles find a place in our own cultural heritage, we may often find it extremely difficult to relate to the aesthetic meaning of an artwork within its original context. In the kind of art interpretation exemplified by this study, practical training and experience were essential and, it is hoped, adequate measures undertaken to avoid such biases. The issue has been addressed most particularly, with regard to the visual arts, by André Malraux in *The Voices of Silence* and in *The Metamorphosis of the Gods*, trans. Stuart Gilbert (Garden City, N.Y.: Doubleday, 1960). Other relevant though abstruse studies of historical innovation and influence, from quite different perspectives, are offered by Bloom, *The Anxiety of Influence*; Hartman, "Toward Literary History," in *Beyond Formalism*; and George Kubler, *The Shape of Time: Remarks on the History of Things* (New Haven: Yale University Press, 1962).

51. They know where it's at, but they don't know what it is, as Kesey says.

52. "An Aesthetic of the Cool: West African Dance," p. 95.

53. Cited in Thompson, *African Art in Motion*, p. 263.

54. "An Aesthetic of the Cool: West African Dance," p. 98.

55. Ibid., pp. 85–86.

56. See, for example, Meyer Fortes, "Ritual Festivals and Social Cohesion in the Hinterlands of the Gold Coast," *American Anthropologist* 38 (1936): 590–604.

Chapter 4   Values in Africa

1. The admirable artistic integrity of an African musical situation is sometimes romanticized into a broad equation of "Art," "Life," and "Oneness" and then elaborated into an implicit critique of other cultural styles. But the value judgements involved in such comparisons do not help characterize the different kinds of actual interactional configurations that distinguish people's social life. All ongoing cultures, of course, are "living," "genuine," and "authentic," and music everywhere is related to its culture; it is the character of art as a mediator which varies. Acknowledging the depth of African music's role in African culture, even with the best intentions, does not reach deeply enough into the greatness of the music's achievement. In my Introduction I discussed some of the issues of cultural relativism in artistic criticism as interpretive problems in finding the proper level of abstraction. In other words, how does one formulate understanding of the music? In his speech to me about the meaning of my studies, Ibrahim Abdulai touched many of the same themes of my Introduction as he addressed issues in the problem of understanding. We can say that African music serves

functions which other cultures relegate to other types of institutions, and we have seen that there are some parallels between Western traditions of learning and African traditions of music. As for the incongruities that led me to begin this book with reference to the multiple ironies of Nietzsche's *Birth of Tragedy*, these incongruities are there on the fundamental level of the distinction between understanding as aesthetics and understanding as metaphysics. To give credit to both modalities has been one of my tasks in the writing of this book, and the multiple ironies of that task have continued throughout to recall the fundamental formal contradiction, that Africans have elevated and may thus seem to rely on aesthetic rather than metaphysical conceptions to ground a number of their social and existential concerns. I once asked a group of Africans responsible for presenting the dances of their cultures to Americans on what basis they selected the information for their program notes. They were providing historical and ethnographic data on various dances, but they were not providing any introductory advice that might enable an audience to watch for and appreciate the aesthetic subtleties of the performances, for instance, the relationship of drumming and dance or the controlling of improvisational changes. They said they were saying what people wanted to hear, that the orthodox ethnographic elaborations of their notes would make the dances more respectable to Americans. One remarked, "These people, you see, they believe in words"; and everyone laughed.

2. Education in the classical sense: see Werner Jaeger, *Paideia: The Ideals of Greek Culture*, trans. Gilbert Highet (Oxford: Basil Blackwell, 1939).

3. A relevant poem is "What Bert Say," by David Henderson, in *De Mayor of Harlem* (New York: E. P. Dutton, 1970), p. 64.

4. I am indebted to Howard Mayer for pointing out to me the interesting imagery in the words of an early Christian spokesman—a convert—from Africa: "Now consider what kind of man he is, . . . who relates, not to mere pleasure, but to the preservation of his bodily self all such rhythms whose source is in the body and in the responses to the affects of the body, and who brings into use, *redigit*, the residue from such rhythms retained in the memory, and others operating from, *de*, other souls in the vicinity, or extruded in order to attach, *adiugere*, to the soul those other souls, or their residue retained in memory, not for its own proud ambition to excel, but for the advantage of those other souls themselves; and who employs that other rhythm, which presides, with an examiner's control, over such rhythms of either kind which subsist in the transience of perception, not for the purpose of satisfying an unjustifiable and harmful curiosity, *curiositas*, but only for essential proof or disproof—such a man, surely, performs every rhythm without being entrapped in their entanglements. His choice is that bodily health should not be obstructed, *ut non impediatur*, and he refers every action to the advantage of his neighbour, whom by the bond of nature he must love as himself. He would obviously be a great man and a great gentleman, *humanissimus*." St. Augustine of Hippo, *De Musica*, trans. W. F. Jackson Knight, in Albert Hofstadter and Richard Kuhns, eds., *Philosophies of Art and Beauty: Selected Readings in Aesthetics from Plato to Heidegger* (New York: Random House, Modern Library, 1964), p. 195.

5. "African Traditional Thought and Western Science," part 1, *Africa* 37 (1967): 61–62. In this article, Horton speculates that an African's immediate world view, his everyday working model of what is happening and how to act, is

perhaps closer to the sophistication of Western social science than is the immediate world view of a typical Westerner. Discussing Meyer Fortes's work, Horton writes, "Perhaps the most significant comment on Fortes' work in this field was pronounced, albeit involuntarily, by a reviewer of 'Oedipus and Job'. 'If any criticism of the presentation is to be made it is that Professor Fortes sometimes seems to achieve an almost mystical identification with the Tallensi world view and leaves the unassimilated reader in some doubt about where to draw the line between Tallensi notions and Cambridge concepts!' Now the anthropologist has to find *some* concepts in his own language roughly appropriate to translating the 'notions' of the people he studies. And in the case in question, perhaps only the lofty analytic 'Cambridge' concepts did come anywhere near to congruence with Tallensi notions. This parallel between traditional African religious 'notions' and Western sociological 'abstractions' is by no means an isolated phenomenon. Think for instance of individual guardian spirits and group spirits—two very general categories of African religious thought. Then think of those hardy Parsonian abstractions—psychological imperatives and sociological imperatives. It takes no great brilliance to see the resemblance." (P. 63) (During several trips to Taleland, I became friends with the present Tongo Ra-Na, who was a young man when Fortes did his work. He and many of his elders and children remember Fortes quite well, and they told me that as the original elders with whom Fortes worked died, Fortes, who had sat with them, became "more" than an elder to the new elders coming up, and he would correct them occasionally on issues of Tallensi custom.) In another article, "Destiny and the Unconscious in West Africa," *Africa* 31 (1961): 110–16, Horton draws parallels between African conceptions of multiple souls and the Freudian model of the personality. The difference, of course, is that the African concepts are *working* models of action and not theoretical structures. The sophistication of traditional African social models and wisdom is an aspect of societies which value social understanding and even institutionalize respectability and decision-making, among other things, in their elders who are distinguished by insight into social affairs and cultural traditions. Possibly the point is so fundamental to the anthropological enterprise that it has not seemed to require emphasis. Still, we would probably not be able to recognize and appreciate the values of other cultures if we were not also able to find or reconstitute these values in some form within our own heritage.

6. Compare Herbert Marcuse's discussion of language and meaning in *One-Dimensional Man: Studies in the Ideology of Advanced Industrial Society* (Boston: Beacon Press, 1964), chaps. 3 and 4, and also Jacques Lacan's similar discussion of metaphor and metonymy in "The Insistence of the Letter in the Unconscious." Marcuse says that in the space between words, meaning enters when systemic, fixed metaphors conflict, when the gap between signifier and signified, God and man, or man and man is opened to reveal "Being," and Lacan also uses linguistic and literary arguments to describe self-consciousness as a dialectical process in which metonymy opens subjectivity to its own Being. Both discussions, among many similar ones, are suggestive of ways in which Western philosophical literature on alienation is addressed in the aesthetics of African music.

7. This interpretation is from a traditional point of view. In Ghana the motto is derived generally from the Akan *gye Nyame*, represented on *adinkra* cloth

by an abstract symbol and on linguists' staffs by a clenched fist with the thumb or finger up. In Kofi Antubam's translation, the proverb of the finitude of the world and the omnipotence of God is "This great panorama of creation originated from the unknown past; no one lives who saw its beginning. No one lives who will see its end except God" (Kofi Antubam, *Ghana's Heritage of Culture* [Leipzig: Koehler & Amelang, 1963], pp. 159–60). Outside the Akan area, the Ewes say *Negbe Mawu ko atenu awoe*, and the Gas say *Be dza Nyomo pe ba nye efe*. A possible alternative interpretation for Islamic areas, suggested to me by Willem A. Bijlefeld, who knew the motto in Nigeria, would be to trace the motto "Except God" to the most adequate translation in African languages of the first part of the Muslim profession of faith: "There is no God (but God). . . ." From an orthodox Muslim point of view, Koranic law manifests God's involvement with the world, but the central idea of submission in the very word *Islam* ultimately removes God from human understanding, and the religious meaning of the motto would not be greatly different in syncretist Muslim areas.

8. Bohannan, "Artist and Critic," p. 248.

9. Signal drums, of course, have meaning, but they are not likely to be considered musical, nor do they provide focus for a social occasion.

10. Western notions of purity of heart as "to will one thing" are perhaps the spiritual and moral antithesis of the African approach, in which purity of heart is manifest in mediation and the balancing of differences. See also Robert Farris Thompson, "An Aesthetic of the Cool," *African Arts* 7, no. 1 (fall 1973): 40–43, 64–67, 89.

11. The relationship of host and guest is a good and almost universal example of the way conventions add clarity to situations. On a different continent, E. M. Forster made the point beautifully:

"He was dressing after a bath when Dr. Aziz was announced. Lifting up his voice, he shouted from the bedroom 'Please make yourself at home.' The remark was unpremeditated like most of his actions; it was what he felt inclined to say.

"To Aziz it had a definite meaning. 'May I really, Mr. Fielding? It's very good of you,' he called back; 'I like unconventional behavior so extremely.' " *A Passage to India* (New York: Harcourt, Brace & World, Harvest Books, 1952), p. 63.

12. An example is the ambivalent ideal which our tradition elevates between passionate love and marriage; see Denis de Rougemont, *Love in the Western World*, trans. Montgomery Belgion, rev. ed. (Greenwich, Conn.: Fawcett Publications, Fawcett Premier Books, 1966). And of course the most profound example is the distinction we may pose between our "self" and our "real" self or soul or Being.

13. Max Gluckman has been among the anthropologists who have stressed the role of African rituals in patterning and clarifying social relationships around points of conflict, difference, and opposition. See *Custom and Conflict in Africa* (Oxford: Basil Blackwell, 1955) and the collection edited by him, *Essays on the Ritual of Social Relations* (Manchester: Manchester University Press, 1962). See also Fallers's statement above, chapter 1, n. 4. Among social interactionists, Erving Goffman has written much about the characteristic processes at work when Westerners encounter different types of situations. See his essays "On Face-Work" and "Where the Action Is," both in *Interaction Ritual*. In sociological terms,

African world views reflect a "conflict model" of social relations; for a discussion of the analytical and pragmatic utility of such a model, see Lewis Coser, *The Functions of Social Conflict* (Glencoe, Ill.: Free Press, 1956).

14. In this instance, I should note, perhaps, that I use the word *individuation* without reference to the specialized significance which several scholars, particularly in the field of analytical psychology, have given the term. From the perspective I developed in my study of music, in Africa the formal and ceremonial dimensions of social life support rather than stifle the full development of personality. In an African context, it is usually very difficult to find ideological or consensual conformity.

15. Dance is the metaphor for participation in these comments from Ibrahim Abdulai: "Music and dancing help us to be happy. There is someone and his somebody dies, and as his somebody dies, his heart will be spoiled. And if they are able to play and dance, his heart will come to the dance and he will throw away his spoiled heart. And this alone is something that makes us happy. You are sitting down and you are poor. And when you are poor, you sit down and you are thinking. And they bring some playing and dance. If you are somebody who is not a useless person, your heart will be on the dance. Unless they finish with the dancing before the worry about your poorness will come to you. And somebody can be sitting down and worries will be having him, and it is his heart thinking. The sickness of the heart is hard. When it comes to somebody, he is sitting down and his heart is not sleeping. But if they dance, he can collect the worried heart and throw it away. It is inside the dance that laughter laughs. And the time there is laughter, it is from the dance that the laugh comes. Somebody can come out to dance, and all his dance speaks laughter. Somebody can come out to dance, and his dancing will be watching. Watching like what? As he is dancing, you will say that if you watch him, maybe you too will be able to dance like him. Everyone has got the dance his heart likes, and that is why the dances are many in Dagbon. And if you have some worry and you look at all this, you'll see that your worry will become a bit small.

"Yesterday where we went, they are maalams [people learned in Islam]. There are some maalams, when their person dies, the drum will not cry there. Nothing will cry. No dance will dance. It is the way they live. And it will be only worry that will add to them always. But yesterday where we went, it wasn't like a maalam's funeral. They collected their maalam's way and put it aside and entered into the dance. Yesterday, there was a certain maalam there: when he stands and gets papers, he can write the whole Quran. That is his work. But yesterday he danced. And no one has ever seen his dance, and it made everybody surprised. But just two days ago, his brother died. The dance he danced, the worry will leave him. This morning when everyone came, they were saying, 'Yesterday Maalam Issah danced; Maalam Issah danced.' Everybody was happy. Even the ones who did not see him dance became happy, not to talk of those who saw him dance. That is why we like dancing, and that is why we take it and give it to our children. It is something that adds to us, and it makes everyone happy."

16. Bad-minded people who look to criticize things and who do not try to see something good or valuable in what they find are addressed in an Akan proverb, "The result of continually chasing a chicken is that your hand touches some dirty ground" (cited in Antubam, *Ghana's Heritage of Culture*, p. 172); or to re-

phrase an American saying, what you saw is what you got. People sometimes complain of being "troubled" by bad mind when they are suspicious or depressed.

17. All the great religious traditions, of course, address all the major concerns of life. The distinctions among religions are much the same as those among cultures, that is, in the way they elevate and concentrate on certain tendencies or complexes of questions and in the way these concerns are integrated into the institutions and patterns of people's lives. For brief descriptions of this typological approach, see Clifford Geertz, "Religion as a Cultural System," in *The Interpretation of Cultures*; or Erik H. Erikson, *Childhood and Society*, 2d ed., rev. and enl. (New York: W. W. Norton, 1963), pp. 285 ff.

18. They do not project the "objective" view of chaos and creation so prevalent in Western religious conceptions, nor does their religious imagery reflect themes of dominance and submission to the laws of God or the "natural" order.

19. The enthnomusicologist Alan Lomax, working with the types of data I discussed in chapter 2, made one of the first attempts to use music as a basis for broad sociological generalizations. In African societies, Lomax maintained, an individual's movement to higher status in one or more of the several interlocking groups of which he is a member "provides an exact analogy to the emergence of a talented individual in the African musical group. African music is full of spaces. The loose structure of this musical situation gives the individual dancer, drummer, or singer the leeway to exhibit his personality in a moment of virtuosic display. . . . The strong rhythmic bias of African music also represents this many-goaled, many-headed, group-oriented culture. African rhythm is usually anchored . . . , but around and through this positive, thrusting, rhythmic unity plays a variety of contrasting counter-rhythms on numbers of instruments that give voice to the diverse groups and personalities bound together in tribal unity." "Song Structure and Social Structure," *Ethnology*, 1 (1962), 448.

20. The Gonja people around Tamale and in their land, for example, had no problem in calling Dagomba drummers to play for their Damba Festival. The situation would perhaps be parallel to having a British Army band play "Hail to the Chief" at a presidential inauguration or to having a Congregational minister give communion at an Episcopalian service. Ibrahim Abdulai has already described how he learned the dances of other tribes, to the point that he could modify his technique to beat with the correct sound and even use his drum to speak languages he does not understand. The fact that people understand and are happy with his playing also reflects on our discussion of the relative importance of symbolic as opposed to aesthetic factors in musical meaning. One story he told me can serve as an illustration. "There was a certain man who settled at Savelugu for long, and he begot many children. And he died, and we went to play his funeral. We were following the Savelugu drummers because Savelugu is their town. We were playing all the Dagomba dances when some Wangara people came from Techiman, and one woman came out and asked us, 'Don't you know that the dead body was a Wangara?' And we kept quiet and we were all looking at each other. By that time I was sitting down, and somebody called me and said, 'My junior father, you have learned drumming in so many places, and I think you will know how to play the kind of drumming she wants.' And I received a dondon and started beating it. And no one knew how to follow, and the gongon beater did not know how to reply. So I removed my drum from my arm and got

a gongon and taught him how to play. And we were able to play the Wangaras' dance. And the woman said she was very surprised to see that Dagombas could play the Wangaras' dance and that there was no mistake in it. And at that place I was very, very respected."

21. Meyer Fortes's work has been very influential in emphasizing the parent-child relationship as the main concern of African moral systems characterized by "ancestor worship." See for example *Oedipus and Job in West African Religion* (Cambridge: Cambridge University Press, 1959). Afro-Americans affirm the continuity of this traditional moral perspective with their call, supported by musicians and religious leaders, to "Save the Children."

22. The closest parallel to this description in Western paradigms of development seems to be offered by psychoanalytic ego psychology, starting particularly with Freud's discussions of negation, ego formation, and sublimation, and more integratively presented by Anna Freud, *The Ego and the Mechanisms of Defense*, trans. Cecil Baines (New York: International Universities Press, 1946).

23. Again, an interesting sociological discussion is Goffman's essay, "Where the Action Is," is *Interaction Ritual.*

24. "An Aesthetic of the Cool," p. 42.

25. *Black Gods and Kings: Yoruba Art at UCLA* (Los Angeles: University of California Museum and Laboratories of Ethnic Art and Technology, 1971), pp. P/1, 2/2, 20/1.

26. African Brothers Dance Band (International), "Mmobrowa," Afribros, PAB 001.

Bibliography

This bibliography is divided into two sections. It includes all sources which I have cited in notes or which I consulted to formulate and define my own approach. The first section consists of sources, primarily social scientific, which explicitly relate to African music and art and which could constitute a fairly interesting reading list in the area of African music. I should note that I had read only a few of these sources at the time of my own research. Though these works often evidence methodological orientations and discursive styles extremely different from my own, I found them to be useful sources of information, much of which I was able to interpret or reinterpret from my own point of view. Almost needless to say, it would hardly be possible to endorse all the views presented in the selections below. Some works, without substantive relevance to my discussion, were useful for helping me understand the work of a particularly significant author or school of thought, for calling my attention to historical or contemporary issues of scholarly interpretation and debate, or perhaps even for demonstrating, to my mind, the relative adequacy or inadequacy of alternative terminological, methodological, or analytical frames of reference as I prepared my presentation. My decision to provide a fairly extensive rather than a selective bibliography represents an acknowledgment to the many people who have enjoyed and struggled with many of the same issues as I have, perhaps finding kinds of inspiration and insight different from my own, but in so doing, revealing some of the potential that the study of music has for the study of humanity.

The second section of the bibliography has no topical point of unity. Many of the sources were cited for various purposes in notes; a few are more general works on African societies or history; but in general, most are not directly concerned with African music. Following some of the themes raised in my Introduction, I have tried to list some of the sources which gave me methodological confidence or which informed my interpretive sensibility, and as such, the section may have some practical value for students interested in pursuing interdisciplinary efforts. Whether or not any theoretical connections may exist or be established among the various disciplinary approaches indicated below, in substantive investigation, any given subject matter seems to have its own way of relating these distinctive approaches; in terms of method, design, and content, this essay on African music, to a considerable extent, offers a reflection on these sources. While I feel that the validity of my interpretation can and should be measured in musical situations, I believe that these sources contributed greatly toward my understanding of my own efforts during fieldwork and during the preparation of this essay.

1. African Music and Art

Akpabot, Samuel. "Standard Drum Patterns in Nigeria," *African Music* 5, no. 1 (1971): 37–39.

————. "Theories in African Music," *African Arts* 6, no. 1 (autumn 1972): 59–62.

————. *Ibibio Music in Nigerian Culture*. [East Lansing]: Michigan State University Press, 1975.

Ames, David W. "Professionals and Amateurs: The Musicians of Zaria and Obimo," *African Arts/Arts d'Afrique* 1, no. 2 (winter 1968): 40–45, 80, 82–84.

————. "Igbo and Hausa Musicians: A Comparative Examination," *Ethnomusicology* 17 (1973), 250–78.

————; Gregersen, Edgar A.; and Neugebauer, Thomas. "Taaken Sàmàarii: A Drum Language of Hausa Youth," *Africa* 41 (1971): 12–31.

Antubam, Kofi. *Ghana's Heritage of Culture*. Leipzig: Koehler & Amelang, 1963.

Armstrong, Robert P. *The Affecting Presence: An Essay in Humanistic Anthropology*. Urbana: University of Illinois Press, 1971.

d'Azevedo, Warren L., ed. *The Traditional Artist in African Societies*. Bloomington: Indiana University Press, 1973.

Ballantine, Christopher. "The Polyrhythmic Foundation of a Tswana Pipe Melody," *African Music* 3, no. 4 (1965): 52–67.

Bane, K. A. "Comic Play in Ghana," *African Arts/Arts d'Afrique* 1, no. 4 (summer 1968): 30–34, 101.

Bankole, Ayo; Bush, Judith; and Samaan, Sadek H. "The Yoruba Master Drummer," *African Arts* 8, no. 2 (winter 1975): 48–56, 77–78.

Bebey, Francis. *African Music: A People's Art*. Translated by Josephine Bennet. New York: Lawrence Hill, 1975.

Becker, Howard S. *Outsiders: Studies in the Sociology of Deviance*. New York: Free Press, 1963.

Beier, Ulli. "The Talking Drums of the Yoruba," *African Music* 1, no. 1 (1954): 29–31.

————, ed. *Introduction to African Literature: An Anthology of Critical Writing from "Black Orpheus"*. Evanston, Ill.: Northwestern University Press, 1970.

Berger, Morroe. "Jazz: Resistance to the Diffusion of a Culture Pattern," *Journal of Negro History* 32 (1947): 461–94.

Berrian, Albert H., and Long, Richard A., eds. *Négritude: Essays and Studies*. Hampton, Va.: Hampton Insititute Press, 1967.

Blacking, John. "Some Notes on a Theory of Rhythm Advanced by Erich von Hornbostel," *African Music* 1, no. 2 (1955): 12–20.

————. "Problems of Pitch, Pattern and Harmony in the Ocarina Music of the Venda," *African Music* 2, no. 2 (1959): 15–23.

————. "Review of *Studies in African Music*," *African Music* 2, no. 2 (1959): 88–89.

————. "Musical Expeditions of the Venda," *African Music* 3, no. 1 (1962): 54–78.

————. "The Role of Music in the Culture of the Venda of the Northern Transvaal," in *Studies in Ethnomusicology*, vol. 2, edited by M. Kolinski. New York: Oak Publications, 1965.

————. "Tonal Organization in the Music of Two Venda Initiation Schools," *Ethnomusicology* 14 (1970): 1–56.

————. "Music and the Historical Process in Vendaland," in *Essays on Music and History in Africa*, edited by Klaus P. Wachsmann. Evanston, Ill.: Northwestern University Press, 1971.

————. "Man and Music," *Times Literary Supplement*, November 19, 1971, pp. 1443–44.

Blum, Odette. "Dance in Ghana," *Dance Perspectives*, no. 56 (winter 1973).

Bohannan, Paul. "Artist and Critic in an African Society," in *The Many Faces of Primitive Art: A Critical Anthology*, edited by Douglas Fraser. Englewood Cliffs, N.J.: Prentice-Hall, 1966.

Bramly, Serge. *Macumba: The Teachings of Maria-José, Mother of the Gods*. Translated by Meg Bogin. New York: St. Martin's Press, 1977.

Bravmann, René A. *Islam and Tribal Art in West Africa.* London: Cambridge University Press, 1974.

Carrington, John F. *A Comparative Study of Some Central African Gong-Languages.* Brussels: Institut Royale Colonial Belge, 1949.

_____. *Talking Drums of Africa.* London: Carey Kingsgate Press, 1949.

_____. "Tone and Melody in a Congolese Popular Song," *African Music* 4, no. 1 (1966/1967): 38–39.

_____. "The Musical Dimension of Perception in the Upper Congo, Zaïre," *African Music* 5, no. 1 (1971): 46–51.

Cleaver, Eldridge, *Soul on Ice.* New York: McGraw-Hill, 1968.

Collins, E. J. "Comic Opera in Ghana," *African Arts* 9, no. 2 (January 1976): 50–57.

_____. "Ghanaian Highlife," *African Arts* 10, no. 1 (October 1976): 62–68, 100.

_____. "Post-War Popular Band Music in West Africa," *African Arts* 10, no. 3 (April 1977): 53–60.

Courlander, Harold. *The Drum and the Hoe: Life and Lore of the Haitian People.* Berkeley and Los Angeles: University of California Press, 1960.

_____. "Notes on Caribbean Folk Music," from the album *Caribbean Folk Music,* recorded by Thomas J. Price, edited by Harold Courlander. Ethnic Folkways Library Album no. FE 4533.

Crowley, Daniel J. "Towards a Definition of Calypso" (part 1), *Ethnomusicology* 3 (1959): 57–66.

Cudjoe, S. D. "The Techniques of Ewe Drumming and the Social Importance of Music in Africa," *Phylon* 14 (1953): 280–91.

Cutter, Charles. "The Politics of Music in Mali," *African Arts/Arts d'Afrique* 1, no. 3 (spring 1968): 38–39, 74–77.

Dam, Theodore van. "The Influence of the West African Songs of Derision in the New World," *African Music* 1, no. 1 (1954): 53–56.

Darnton, John. "Nigeria's Dissident Superstar," *New York Times Magazine,* July 24, 1977, pp. 10–12, 22–24, 26, 28.

Deren, Maya. *Divine Horsemen: The Living Gods of Haiti.* London: Thames and Hudson, 1953.

Drewal, Margaret Thompson, and Drewal, Henry John. "Gelede Dance of the Western Yoruba," *African Arts* 8, no. 2 (winter 1975): 36–45, 78.

Euba, Akin. "Islamic Musical Culture among the Yoruba: A Preliminary Survey," in *Essays on Music and History in Africa,* edited by Klaus P. Wachsmann. Evanston, Ill.: Northwestern University Press, 1971.

Evans-Pritchard, E. E. "The Dance," *Africa* 1 (1928): 446–62.

Gadzekpo, B. Sinedzi. "Making Music in Eweland," *West African Review* 23 (1952): 817–21.

Gbeho, Philip. "African Music Deserves Generous Recognition," *West African Review* 22 (1951): 910–13.

————. "Africa's Drums Are More than Tom-toms," *West African Review* 22 (1951): 1150–52.

————. "Beat of the Master Drum," *West African Review* 22 (1951): 1263–65.

————. "Cross-Rhythm in African Music," *West African Review* 23 (1952): 11–13.

————. "The Indigenous Gold Coast Music," *African Music Society Newsletter* 1, no. 5 (1952): 30–34.

————. "Music of the Gold Coast," *African Music* 1, no. 1 (1954): 62–64.

Gibling, R. Styx. "Notes on the Latin American National Dances," *African Music Society Newsletter* 1, no. 4 (1951): 32–37.

Harper, Peggy. "A Festival of Nigerian Dances," *African Arts/Arts d'Afrique* 3, no. 2 (winter 1970): 48–53.

Herzog, George. "Drum-Signaling in a West African Tribe," *Word* 1 (1945): 217–38.

Hirschberg, Walter. "Early Historical Illustrations of West and Central African Music," *African Music* 4, no. 3 (1969): 6–18.

Hornbostel, E. M. von. "African Negro Music," *Africa* 1 (1928): 30–62.

Horton, Robin. "The Kalabari *Ekine* Society: A Borderland of Religion and Art," *Africa* 33 (1963): 94–114.

Imperato, Pascal James. "Contemporary Adapted Dances of the Dogon," *African Arts* 5, no. 1 (autumn 1971): 28–33, 68–72, 84.

Jahn, Janheinz. *Muntu: An Outline of the New African Culture.* Translated by Marjorie Grene. New York: Grove Press, 1961.

————. *Neo-African Literature: A History of Black Writing.* Translated by Oliver Coburn and Ursula Lehrburger. New York: Grove Press, 1968.

Jones, A. M. "African Music," *African Affairs* 48 (1949): 290–97.

————. "What's in a Smile?" *African Music Society Newsletter* 1, no. 3 (1950): 13–16.

————. "Blue Rhythm and Hot Notes," *African Music Society Newsletter* 1, no. 4 (1951): 9–12.

————. "African Rhythm," *Africa* 24 (1954): 26–47.

————. "East and West, North and South," *African Music* 1, no. 1 (1954): 57–62.

_____. "Drums Down the Centuries," *African Music* 1, no. 4 (1957):
4–10.

_____. "On Transcribing African Music," *African Music* 2, no. 1
(1958): 11–14.

_____. *African Music in Northern Rhodesia and Some Other Places.*
Occasional Papers of the Rhodes-Livingstone Museum, no. 4. Living-
stone, Northern Rhodesia [Zambia]: Rhodes-Livingstone Museum,
1958.

_____. *Studies in African Music.* 2 vols. London: Oxford University
Press, 1959.

_____. "African Metrical Lyrics," *African Music* 3, no. 3 (1964):
6–14.

Jones, LeRoi [Imamu Amiri Baraka]. *Blues People: Negro Music in
White America.* New York: William Morrow, 1963.

Jopling, Carol, ed. *Art and Aesthetics in Primitive Societies: A Critical
Anthology.* New York: E. P. Dutton, 1971.

Keil, Charles. *Urban Blues.* Chicago: University of Chicago Press, 1966.

_____. "Motion and Feeling through Music," *Journal of Aesthetics
and Art Criticism* 24 (1966): 337–49.

King, Anthony. *Yoruba Sacred Music from Ekiti.* Ibadan, Nigeria: Ibadan University Press, 1961.

_____. "Employments of the 'Standard Pattern' in Yoruba Music,"
African Music 2, no. 3 (1961): 51–54.

Knight, Roderic. "Towards a Notation and Tabulature for the Kora,"
African Music 5, no. 1 (1971): 23–39.

Kubik, Gerhard. "The Phenomenon of Inherent Rhythms in East and
Central African Instrumental Music," *African Music* 3, no. 1 (1962):
33–42.

Ladzekpo, S. Kobla. "The Social Mechanics of Good Music: A Description of Dance Clubs among the Anlo Ewe-Speaking People of Ghana,"
African Music 5, no. 1 (1971): 6–22.

_____, and Pantaleoni, Hewitt, "Takada Drumming," *African Music*
4, no. 4 (1970): 6–31.

Leach, Edmund. "Aesthetics," in E. E. Evans-Pritchard et al., *The Institutions of Primitive Society: A Series of Broadcast Talks.* Glencoe,
Ill.: Free Press, 1954.

Leuzinger, Elsy. *Africa: The Art of the Negro Peoples.* Translated by
Ann E. Keep. New York: McGraw-Hill, 1960.

Lomax, Alan. "Folk Song Style: Musical Style and Social Context,"
American Anthropologist 61 (1959): 927–54.

—————. "Song Structure and Social Structure," *Ethnology* 1 (1962): 425–51.

Mbunga, Steven. "Music Reform in Tanzania," *African Ecclesiastical Review* 10, no. 1 (1968): 47–54.

Mensah, Atta Annan. "The Music of Zumaile Village, Zambia," *African Music* 2, no. 4 (1970): 96–102.

Merriam, Alan P. "African Music Re-Examined in the Light of New Materials from the Belgian Congo and Ruanda Urundi," *African Music Society Newsletter* 1, no. 6 (1953): 57–64.

—————. "Song Texts of the Bashi," *African Music* 1, no. 1 (1954): 44–52.

—————. "Songs of the Ketu Cult of Bahia," *African Music* 1, no. 3 (1956): 53–67.

—————. "African Music," in *Continuity and Change in African Cultures*, edited by William R. Bascom and Melville J. Herskovits. Chicago: University of Chicago Press, 1959.

—————. "Ethnomusicology: Discussion and Definition of the Field," *Ethnomusicology* 4 (1960): 107–14.

—————. "The African Idiom in Music," *Journal of American Folklore* 75 (1962): 120–30.

—————. "Purposes of Ethnomusicology: An Anthropological View," *Ethnomusicology* 7 (1963): 206–13.

—————. *The Anthropology of Music.* Evanston, Ill.: Northwestern University Press, 1964.

—————. "The Ethnographic Experience: Drum-making among the Bala (Basongye)," *Ethnomusicology* 13 (1969): 74–100.

—————, and Garner, Fradley H. "Jazz—The Word," *Ethnomusicology* 12 (1968): 373–96.

—————, and Mack, Raymond W. "The Jazz Community," *Social Forces* 38 (1960): 211–22.

Métraux, Alfred. *Voodoo in Haiti.* Translated by Hugo Charteris. New York: Oxford University Press, 1959.

Mezzrow, Mezz, and Wolfe, Bernard. *Really the Blues.* Garden City, N.Y.: Doubleday, Anchor Books, 1972.

Moyana, Tafirenyika. "Muchongoyo: A Shangani Dance," *African Arts* 9, no. 2 (January 1976): 40–42.

Mubitana, Kafungulwa. "Wiko Masquerades," *African Arts* 4, no. 3 (spring 1971): 58–62.

Mueller, John H. "A Sociological Approach to Musical Behavior," *Ethnomusicology* 7 (1963): 216–20.

Mveng, E. *L'Art d'Afrique noire: Liturgie cosmique et langage religieux.* Paris: Maison Mame, 1964.

Neto, Paulo de Carvalho. "The Candombe: A Dramatic Dance from Afro-Uruguayan Folklore," *Ethnomusicology* 6 (1962): 164–74.

Nettl, Bruno. *Music in Primitive Cultures.* Cambridge, Mass.: Harvard University Press, 1956.

Njungu, Agrippa N. "The Music of My People," *African Music* 2, no. 3 (1961): 48–50.

_____. "Music of My People: Dances in Barotseland," *African Music* 2, no. 4 (1961): 77–80.

Nketia, J. H. Kwabena. "The Role of the Drummer in Akan Society," *African Music* 1, no. 1 (1954): 34–43.

_____. *Funeral Dirges of the Akan People.* Achimota, Ghana, and Exeter: James Townsend and Sons, 1955.

_____. "Modern Trends in Ghana Music," *African Music* 1, no. 4 (1957): 13–17.

_____. "Traditional Music of the Ga People," *African Music* 2, no. 1 (1958): 21–27.

_____. "Organization of Music in Adangme Society," *African Music* 2, no. 1 (1958): 28–30.

_____. "The Contribution of African Culture to Christian Worship," *International Review of Missions* 47 (1958): 265–78.

_____. "Drums, Dance, and Song," *Atlantic Monthly*, April 1959, pp. 69–72.

_____. "The Problem of Meaning in African Music," *Ethnomusicology* 6 (1962): 1–7.

_____. *Drumming in Akan Communities of Ghana.* London: University of Ghana and Thomas Nelson and Sons, 1963.

_____. "Unity and Diversity in African Music: A Problem of Synthesis," in *The Proceedings of the First International Congress of Africanists*, edited by Lalage Brown and Michael Crowder. Accra: International Congress of Africanists and Longmans, 1964.

_____. "The Interrelations of African Music and Dance," *Studia Musicologica* 7 (1965): 91–101.

_____. "Music in African Cultures: A Review of the Meaning and Significance of Traditional African Music." Mimeographed. Legon, Accra, Ghana: Institute of African Studies, University of Ghana, 1966.

_____. "History and Organization of Music in West Africa," in *Essays on Music and History in Africa*, edited by Klaus P. Wachsmann. Evanston, Ill.: Northwestern University Press, 1971.

————. "Sources of Historical Data on the Musical Cultures of Africa." Mimeographed. Legon, Accra, Ghana: Institute of African Studies, University of Ghana, 1972.

————. *Music of Africa.* New York: W. W. Norton, 1974.

Nurse, George T. "Popular Songs and National Identity in Malawi," *African Music* 3, no. 3 (1964): 101–6.

Oderigo, Néstor R. Ortiz. "Negro Rhythm in the Americas," *African Music* 1, no. 3 (1956): 68–69.

Ojo, J.R.O. "Ogboni Drums," *African Arts* 6, no. 3 (spring 1973): 50–52, 84.

Osafo, F. Onwona. "An African Orchestra in Ghana," *African Music* 1, no. 4 (1957): 11–12.

Otten, Charlotte M., ed. *Anthropology and Art: Readings in Cross-Cultural Aesthetics.* American Museum Sourcebooks in Anthropology. Garden City, N.Y.: Natural History Press, 1971.

Palmer, Robert. *The Drums,* liner notes, Impulse Records, ASH–9272–3.

Pantaleoni, Hewitt. "The Rhythm of Atsiã Dance Drumming Among the Anlo (*Eve*) of Anyako." Ph.D. dissertation, Wesleyan University, 1972.

Pemberton, John. "Eshu-Elegba: The Yoruba Trickster God," *African Arts* 9, no. 1 (October 1975): 20–27, 66–70, 90–92.

Ranger, T. O. *Dance and Society in Eastern Africa, 1890–1970: The Beni "Ngoma."* London: Heinemann Educational Books, 1975.

Rattray, R. S. *Ashanti.* Oxford: Clarendon Press, 1923.

————. *Religion and Art in Ashanti.* Oxford: Clarendon Press, 1927.

Richards, Paul. "A Quantitative Analysis of the Relationship between Language Tone and Melody in a Hausa Song," *African Language Studies* 13 (1972): 137–61.

Sapir, J. David. "Diola-Fogny Funeral Songs and the Native Critic," *African Language Review* 8 (1969): 176–91.

Schneider, Marius. "Tone and Tune in West African Music," *Ethnomusicology* 5 (1962): 204–15.

Senghor, Léopold Sédar. "Standards critiques de l'art Africain," *African Arts/Arts d'Afrique* 1, no. 1 (autumn 1967): 6–9, 52.

Serwadda, Moses, and Pantaleoni, Hewitt. "A Possible Notation for African Dance Drumming," *African Music* 4, no. 2 (1968): 47–52.

Smith, Edna M. "Popular Music in West Africa," *African Music* 3, no. 1 (1962): 11–17.

————. "Musical Training in Tribal West Africa," *African Music* 3, no. 1 (1962): 6–10.

Smith, M. G. "The Social Function and Meaning of Hausa Praise Singing," *Africa* 27 (1957): 26–45.

Stearns, Marshall W. *The Story of Jazz.* New York: New American Library and Oxford University Press, Mentor Books, 1958.

Tamakloe, Emmanuel Forster, ed. *A Brief History of the Dagbamba People.* Accra, Ghana: Government Printing Office, 1931.

Thieme, Darius L. "Research in African Music: Accomplishments and Prospects," *Ethnomusicology* 7 (1963): 266–71.

Thiermann, David. "The Mbira in Brazil," *African Music* 5, no. 1 (1971): 90–94.

Thompson, Robert Farris. "The Mambo in Mexico," *Jazz Review*, September 1960, pp. 36–38.

———. "Highlife in Nigeria," *Saturday Review*, August 26, 1961, pp. 34–35.

———. "Portrait of the Pachanga: The Music, the Players, the Dancers, *Saturday Review*, October 28, 1961, pp. 42–43, 54.

———. "An Aesthetic of the Cool: West African Dance," *African Forum* 2, no. 2 (fall 1966): 85–102.

———. "New Voice from the Barrios," *Saturday Review*, October 28, 1967, pp. 53–55, 68.

———. "Esthetics in Traditional Africa," *Art News*, January 1968, pp. 44–45, 63–66.

———. "The Sign of the Divine King," *African Arts/Arts d'Afrique* 3, no. 3 (spring 1970): 8–17, 74–78.

———. *Black Gods and Kings: Yoruba Art at UCLA*, Los Angeles: University of California Museum and Laboratories of Ethnic Art and Technology, 1971.

———. "An Aesthetic of the Cool," *African Arts* 7, no. 1 (fall 1973): 40–43, 64–67, 89.

———. *African Art in Motion: Icon and Act in the Collection of Katherine Coryton White.* Los Angeles: University of California Press, 1974.

Tracey, Hugh. *Chopi Musicians: Their Music, Poetry, and Instruments.* London: Oxford University Press, 1948.

———. "The Art of Africa: The Visual and the Aural," *African Music* 3, no. 1 (1962): 20–32.

Vidal, 'Tunji. "Oriki in Traditional Yoruba Music," *African Arts/Arts d'Afrique* 3, no. 1 (autumn 1969): 56–59.

———. "Lagos State Music and Dance," *African Arts* 9, no. 2 (January 1976): 35–39, 80.

Wachsmann, Klaus P., ed. *Essays on Music and History in Africa.* Evanston, Ill.: Northwestern University Press, 1971.

Waterman, Richard Alan. " 'Hot' Rhythm in Negro Music," *Journal of the American Musicological Society* 1 (spring 1948): 24–37.

———. "African Influence on the Music of the Americas," in *Acculturation in the Americas,* edited by Sol Tax. Proceedings and Selected Papers of the 29th International Congress of Americanists, vol. 2. Chicago: University of Chicago Press, 1952.

———. "On Flogging a Dead Horse: Lessons Learned from the Africanisms Controversy," *Ethnomusicology* 7 (1963): 83–87.

Weman, Henry. *African Music and the Church in Africa.* Translated by Eric J. Sharpe. Uppsala: Svenska Institutet För Missionsforskning, 1960.

Zemp, Hugo. *Musique Dan: La musique dans la pensée et la vie sociale d'une société africaine.* Paris: Mouton and École Practique des Hautes Etudes, 1971.

2. Miscellaneous

Apel, Willi, and Daniel, Ralph T. *The Harvard Brief Dictionary of Music.* New York: Pocket Books, 1961.

Armah, Ayi Kwei. *The Beautyful Ones Are Not Yet Born.* New York: Macmillan, 1969.

Aron, Raymond. *German Sociology.* Translated by Mary and Thomas Bottomore. Glencoe, Ill.: Free Press, 1957.

———. *Main Currents of Sociological Thought.* 2 vols. Translated by Richard Howard and Helen Weaver. Garden City, N.Y.: Doubleday, Anchor Books, 1970.

Bacon, Francis. *The Advancement of Learning.* London: Oxford University Press, 1926.

Bayer, Raymond. "The Essence of Rhythm," in *Reflections on Art: A Source Book of Writings by Artists, Critics, and Philosophers,* edited by Susanne K. Langer. Baltimore: Johns Hopkins University Press, 1958.

Becker, Howard S. *Sociological Work: Method and Substance.* Chicago: Aldine, 1970.

Benedict, Ruth. *Patterns of Culture.* Boston: Houghton Mifflin, 1934.

———. "Continuities and Discontinuities in Cultural Conditioning," in *A Study of Interpersonal Relations,* edited by Patrick Mullahy. New York: Hermitage Press, 1949.

Benn, Gottfried. "Artists and Old Age," in *Primal Vision: Selected Writings of Gottfried Benn*, edited by E. B. Ashton. New York: New Directions, 1971. Also in *Partisan Review* 22, no. 3 (summer 1955): 297–319.

Berger, Peter L. *Invitation to Sociology: A Humanistic Perspective.* Garden City, N.Y.: Doubleday, Anchor Books, 1963.

Bijlefeld, Willem A. *De Islam als na-Christelijke Religie.* The Hague: van Keulen N.V., 1959.

Birdwhistell, Ray L. *Kinesics and Context: Essays on Body Motion Communication.* Philadelphia: University of Pennsylvania Press, 1970.

Blair, H. A., and Duncan-Johnstone, A.C., eds. *Enquiry into the Constitution and Organization of the Dagbon Kingdom.* Accra, Ghana: Government Printing Office, 1931.

Bloom, Harold. *The Anxiety of Influence: A Theory of Poetry.* New York: Oxford University Press, 1973.

Blumer, Herbert. *Symbolic Interactionism: Perspective and Method.* Englewood Cliffs, N.J.: Prentice-Hall, 1969.

Bohannan, Paul, and Curtin, Philip. *Africa and Africans.* Rev. ed. Garden City, N. Y.: American Museum of Natural History and Natural History Press, 1971.

Buber, Martin. *I and Thou.* 2d ed. Translated by Ronald Gregor Smith. New York: Charles Scribner's Sons, 1958.

————. *The Knowledge of Man: Selected Essays.* Translated by Maurice Friedman and Ronald Gregor Smith. Edited by Maurice Friedman. New York: Harper & Row, 1965.

Burke, Kenneth. *Permanence and Change: An Anatomy of Purpose.* 2d rev. ed. Library of Liberal Arts. Indianapolis: Bobbs-Merrill, 1965.

Campbell, Joseph. *The Masks of God.* 4 vols. New York: Viking Press, 1969.

Casagrande, Joseph B., ed. *In the Company of Man: Twenty Portraits of Anthropological Informants.* New York: Harper & Row, Harper Torchbooks, 1964.

Cassirer, Ernst. *Language and Myth.* Translated by Susanne K. Langer. New York: Dover Publications, 1953.

Castenada, Carlos. *Journey to Ixtlan: The Lessons of Don Juan.* New York: Simon and Schuster, Touchstone Books, 1972.

Cole, Michael; Gay, John; Glick, Joseph A.; Sharp, Donald W., et al. *The Cultural Context of Learning and Thinking: An Exploration in Experimental Anthropology.* New York: Basic Books, 1971.

Collingwood, R. G. *The Principles of Art.* Oxford: Clarendon Press, 1938.

Comhaire, J. "Some Aspects of Urbanization in the Belgian Congo," *American Journal of Sociology* 62 (1956): 8–13.

Coser, Lewis. *The Functions of Social Conflict.* Glencoe, Ill.: Free Press, 1956.

Croce, Benedetto. *Aesthetic: As Science of Expression and General Linguistic.* Rev. ed. Translated by Douglas Ainslie. New York: Noonday Press, 1922.

Cruse, Harold. *The Crisis of the Negro Intellectual.* New York: William Morrow, 1967.

———. *Rebellion or Revolution?* New York: William Morrow, Apollo Editions, 1968.

Davidson, Basil. *The African Genius: An Introduction to African Social and Cultural History.* Boston: Atlantic Monthly Press of Little, Brown, 1969.

Denteh, Andrew C. *A Visitor's Guide to Ghanaian Customs and Other Matters.* Published by the author, P.O. Box 73, Legon, Ghana, 1967.

Denzin, Norman K. *The Research Act: A Theoretical Introduction to Sociological Methods.* Chicago: Aldine, 1970.

Devereux, George. *From Anxiety to Method in the Behavioral Sciences.* The Hague: Mouten, 1967.

Eisenstadt, S. N. *From Generation to Generation: Age Groups and Social Structure.* London: Free Press of Glencoe and Collier-Macmillan, 1964.

Eliade, Mircea. *Patterns in Comparative Religion.* Translated by Rosemary Sheed. Cleveland: World, Meridian Books, 1963.

Erikson, Erik H. *Young Man Luther: A Study in Psychoanalysis and History.* New York: W. W. Norton, 1962.

———. *Childhood and Society.* 2d ed., rev. and enl. New York: W. W. Norton, 1963.

———. *Insight and Responsibility: Lectures on the Ethical Implications of Psychoanalytic Insight.* New York: W. W. Norton, 1964.

———. *Youth: Identity and Crisis.* New York: W. W. Norton, 1968.

Erikson, Kai T. *Wayward Puritans: A Study in the Sociology of Deviance.* New York: John Wiley & Sons, 1966.

———. "Sociology: That Awkward Age," *Social Problems* 19 (1972): 431–36.

Evans, Bergen, and Evans, Cornelia. *A Dictionary of Contemporary American Usage.* New York: Random House, 1957.

Evans-Pritchard, E. E. *Witchcraft, Oracles and Magic among the Azande*. Oxford: Clarendon Press, 1937.

————. *Nuer Religion*. Oxford: Clarendon Press, 1956.

————. *Essays in Social Anthropology*. New York: Free Press of Glencoe and Macmillan, 1963.

————. *Theories of Primitive Religion*. Oxford: Clarendon Press, 1965.

————, et al. *The Institutions of Primitive Society: A Series of Broadcast Talks*. Glencoe, Ill.: Free Press, 1954.

————, et al. "The State of Anthropology," *Times Literary Supplement*, July 6, 1973.

Fallers, Lloyd. "Social Stratification and Economic Processes in Africa," in *Class, Status, and Power: Social Stratification in Comparative Perspective*, edited by Reinhard Bendix and Seymour Martin Lipset. 2d ed. New York: Free Press, 1966.

Fanon, Frantz. *The Wretched of the Earth*. Translated by Constance Farrington. New York: Grove Press, 1963.

Feldman, A. Bronson. "Mental Economy and Political Economy," in *Psychoanalysis and the Future*, edited by Theodore Reik. New York: National Psychological Association for Psychoanalysis, 1957.

Ferguson, Phyllis, and Wilkes, Ivor. "Chiefs, Constitutions, and the British in Northern Ghana," in *West African Chiefs: Their Changing Status under Colonial Rule and Independence*, edited by Michael Crowder and Obaro Ikime. New York: African Publishing Corp., 1970.

Field, M. J. *Religion and Medicine among the Ga People*. London: Oxford University Press, 1937.

————. *Search for Security: An Ethno-psychiatric Study of Rural Ghana*. New York: W. W. Norton 1970.

Forde, Daryll, ed. *African Worlds: Studies in the Cosmological Ideas and Social Values of African Peoples*. London: International African Institute and Oxford University Press, 1954.

Forster, E. M. *A Passage to India*. New York: Harcourt, Brace & World, Harvest Books, 1952.

Fortes, Meyer. "Ritual Festivals and Social Cohesion in the Hinterlands of the Gold Coast," *American Anthropologist* 38 (1936): 590–604.

————. "Mind," in E. E. Evans-Pritchard et al., *The Institutions of Primitive Society: A Series of Broadcast Talks*. Glencoe, Ill.: Free Press, 1954.

————. *Oedipus and Job in West African Religion*. Cambridge: Cambridge University Press, 1959.

————, and Dieterlen, G. *African Systems of Thought: Studies Presented and Discussed at the Third International African Seminar in*

Salisbury, December, 1960. London: International African Institute and Oxford University Press, 1965.

Freilich, Morris, ed. *Marginal Natives: Anthropologists at Work.* New York: Harper & Row, 1970.

Freud, Anna. *The Ego and the Mechanisms of Defense.* Translated by Cecil Baines. New York: International Universities Press, 1946.

Freud, Sigmund. *The Interpretation of Dreams.* [1900] Translated by James Strachey. New York: Basic Books, Avon Books, 1965.

————. *The Psychopathology of Everyday Life.* [1901] Vol. 6 of *The Standard Edition of the Complete Psychological Works of Sigmund Freud.* Translated by James Strachey in collaboration with Anna Freud. London: Hogarth Press and the Institute of Psycho-analysis, 1951.

————. *Jokes and their Relation to the Unconscious.* [1905] Vol. 7 of *The Standard Edition of the Complete Psychological Works of Sigmund Freud.* Translated by James Strachey in collaboration with Anna Freud. London: Hogarth Press and the Institute of Psycho-analysis, 1951.

————. *Inhibitions, Symptoms, and Anxiety.* [1926] Vol. 20 of *The Standard Edition of the Complete Psychological Works of Sigmund Freud.* Translated by James Strachey in collaboration with Anna Freud. London: Hogarth Press and the Institute of Psycho-analysis, 1951.

————. *Collected Papers.* Translation under the supervision of Joan Riviere, Alix Strachey, and James Strachey. 5 vols. New York: Basic Books, 1959.

Gans, Herbert J. *The Urban Villagers: Group and Class in the Life of Italian-Americans.* New York: Free Press, 1962.

Garfinkel, Harold. *Studies in Ethnomethodology.* Englewood Cliffs, N.J.: Prentice-Hall, 1967.

Geertz, Clifford, ed. *Old Societies and New States: The Quest for Modernity in Asia and Africa.* New York: Free Press of Glencoe and Collier-Macmillan, 1963.

————. *Peddlars and Princes.* Chicago: University of Chicago Press, 1963.

————. *The Interpretation of Cultures.* New York: Basic Books, 1973.

Glaser, Barney S., and Strauss, Anselm L. *The Discovery of Grounded Theory: Strategies for Qualitative Research.* Chicago: Aldine, 1967.

Gluckman, Max. *Custom and Conflict in Africa.* Oxford: Basil Blackwell, 1955.

————, ed. *Essays on the Ritual of Social Relations.* Manchester: Manchester University Press, 1962.

Goffman, Erving. *The Presentation of Self in Everyday Life*. Garden City, N.Y.: Doubleday, Anchor Books, 1959.

_____. *Asylums: Essays on the Social Situation of Mental Patients and Other Inmates*. Garden City, N.Y.: Doubleday, Anchor Books, 1961.

_____. *Encounters: Two Studies in the Sociology of Interaction*. Indianapolis: Bobbs-Merrill, 1961.

_____. *Behavior in Public Places: Notes on the Social Organization of Gatherings*. New York: Free Press, 1966; London: Collier-Macmillan, 1963.

_____. *Interaction Ritual: Essays on Face-to-Face Behavior*. Garden City, N.Y.: Doubleday, Anchor Books, 1967.

_____. *Strategic Interaction*. Philadelphia: University of Pennsylvania Press, 1969.

_____. *Relations in Public: Microstudies of the Public Order*. New York: Basic Books, 1971.

Gombrich, E. H. *Art and Illusion: A Study in the Psychology of Pictorial Representation*. Bollingen series, vol. 35, no. 5. New York: Pantheon Books, 1960.

_____. "The Evidence of Images," in *Interpretation: Theory and Practice*, edited by Charles S. Singleton. Baltimore: Johns Hopkins University Press, 1969.

Gouldner, Alvin W. *Patterns of Industrial Bureaucracy*. Glencoe, Ill.: Free Press, 1954.

_____. *Wildcat Strike*. Yellow Springs, Ohio: Antioch Press, 1954.

Griaule, Marcel. *Conversations with Ogotemmêli: An Introduction to Dogon Religious Ideas*. Translated by Ralph Butler, Audrey I. Richards, and Beatrice Hook. London: International African Institute and Oxford University Press, 1965.

Hall, Edward T. *The Silent Language*. Greenwich, Conn.: Fawcett Publications, Fawcett Premier Books, 1959.

Hartman, Geoffrey H. *The Unmediated Vision: An Interpretation of Wordsworth, Hopkins, Rilke, and Valéry*. New York: Harcourt, Brace & World, Harbinger Books, 1966.

_____. *Beyond Formalism: Literary Essays, 1958–1970*. New Haven: Yale University Press, 1970.

Heidegger, Martin. *Discourse on Thinking: A Translation of "Gelassenheit."* Translated by John M. Anderson and E. Hans Freund. New York: Harper & Row, 1966.

_____. *Poetry, Language, Thought*. Translations and introduction by Albert Hofstadter. New York: Harper & Row, 1971.

Henderson, David. *De Mayor of Harlem.* New York: E. P. Dutton, 1970.

Herskovits, Melville J. *Dahomey: An Ancient West African Kingdom.* 2 vols. New York: J. J. Augustin, 1938.

―――. *The Myth of the Negro Past.* Boston: Beacon Press, 1958.

―――. "Anthropology and Africa: A Wider Perspective," *Africa* 29 (1959): 225–38.

―――. *The Human Factor in Changing Africa.* London: Routledge and Kegan Paul, 1962.

Hinde, R. A., ed. *Non-Verbal Communication.* Cambridge: Cambridge University Press, 1972. Especially Edmund Leach, "The Influence of Cultural Context on Non-Verbal Communication," and E. H. Gombrich, "Action and Expression in Western Art."

Hodgkin, Thomas. *Nationalism in Colonial Africa.* New York: New York University Press, 1959.

Hofstadter, Albert, and Kuhns, Richard, eds. *Philosophies of Art and Beauty: Selected Readings in Aesthetics from Plato to Heidegger.* New York: Random House, Modern Library, 1964.

Holas, B. *L'Afrique noire.* Religions du Monde. Paris: Bloud & Gay, 1964.

Hopper, Stanley R., and Miller, David L., eds. *Interpretation: The Poetry of Meaning.* New York: Harcourt, Brace & World, Harbinger Books, 1967.

Horton, Donald, and Strauss, Anselm. "Interaction in Audience-Participation Shows," *American Journal of Sociology* 62 (1957): 579–87.

Horton, Robin. "Destiny and the Unconscious in West Africa," *Africa* 31 (1961): 110–16.

―――. "African Traditional Thought and Western Science," 2 parts, *Africa* 37 (1967): 50–71, 155–87.

Howard, Vernon A. "Musical Meaning: A Logical Note," *Journal of Aesthetics and Art Criticism* 30, no. 2 (winter 1971): 215–19.

Jacobs, Glenn, ed. *The Participant-Observer.* New York: George Braziller, 1970. Especially John Horton, "Time and Cool People."

Jaeger, Hans. "Heidegger and the Work of Art," in *Aesthetics Today*, edited by Morris Philipson. New York: World, Meridian Books, 1961.

Jaeger, Werner. *Paideia: The Ideals of Greek Culture.* Translated by Gilbert Highet. Oxford: Basil Blackwell, 1939.

Jahn, Janheinz. *Through African Doors: Experiences and Encounters in West Africa.* Translated by Oliver Coburn. New York: Grove Press, 1962.

————. "Value Conceptions in Sub-Saharan Africa," in *Cross-Cultural Understanding: Epistemology in Anthropology*, edited by F. S. C. Northrop and Helen Livingston. New York: Harper & Row, 1964.

Jahoda, Gustav. *White Man: A Study of the Attitudes of Africans to Europeans in Ghana before Independence*. London: Oxford University Press, 1961.

James, William. *The Varieties of Religious Experience: A Study in Human Nature*. New York: New American Library, Mentor Books, 1958.

Johnstone, John, and Katz, Elihu. "Youth and Popular Music: A Study in the Sociology of Taste," *American Journal of Sociology* 62 (1957): 569–78.

Kierkegaard, Søren. *Repetition: An Essay in Experimental Psychology*. Translated by Walter Lowrie. New York: Harper & Row, Harper Torchbooks, 1964.

King, Noel Q. *Religions of Africa: A Pilgrimage into Traditional Religions*. New York: Harper & Row, 1970.

————. *Christian and Muslim in Africa*. New York: Harper & Row, 1971.

Kluckhohn, Florence. "The Participant-Observer Technique in Small Communities," *American Journal of Sociology* 46 (1940): 331–43.

Kolakowski, Leszek. "The Priest and the Jester," in *The Modern Polish Mind: An Anthology*, edited by Maria Kuncewicz. New York: Grosset & Dunlap and Little, Brown, 1962.

Kris, Ernst. *Psychoanalytic Explorations in Art*. New York: Shocken Books, 1964.

Kroeber, A. L. *Style and Civilizations*. Ithaca, N.Y.: Cornell University Press, 1957.

————, ed. *Anthropology Today: An Encyclopedic Inventory*. Chicago: University of Chicago Press, 1953.

————; Kluckhohn, Clyde; et al. *Culture: A Critical Review of Concepts and Definitions*. Papers of the Peabody Museum of American Archaeology and Ethnology, Harvard University, vol. 47, no. 1. Cambridge, Mass.: Peabody Museum of American Archaeology and Ethnology, 1952.

Kubie, Lawrence S. *Neurotic Distortion of the Creative Process*. New York: Noonday Press, 1958.

Kubler, George. *The Shape of Time: Remarks on the History of Things*. New Haven: Yale University Press, 1962.

Kuhn, Thomas S. *The Structure of Scientific Revolutions*. 2d ed. Chicago: University of Chicago Press, 1970.

Lacan, Jacques. "The Insistence of the Letter in the Unconscious," translated by Jan Miel, *Yale French Studies*, 36–37 (1966): 112–47.

Ladouceur, Paul. "The Yendi Chieftaincy Dispute and Ghanaian Politics," *Canadian Journal of African Studies* 6 (1972): 97–115.

Leeuw, Gerardus van der. *Sacred and Profane Beauty: The Holy in Art.* Translated by David E. Green. New York: Holt, Rinehart and Winston, 1963.

———. *Religion in Essence and Manifestation.* Translated by J. E. Turner. 2 vols. Gloucester, Mass.: Peter Smith, 1967.

Lévi-Strauss, Claude. *The Savage Mind.* Chicago: University of Chicago Press, 1966.

———. *Structural Anthropology.* New York: Doubleday, Anchor Books, 1967.

———. *Tristes Tropiques.* Translated by John Russell. New York: Atheneum, 1972.

Levtzion, Nehemia. *Muslims and Chiefs in West Africa: A Study of Islam in the Middle Volta Basin in the Pre-Colonial Period.* Oxford: Clarendon Press, 1968.

Lévy-Bruhl, Lucien. *The "Soul" of the Primitive.* Translated by Lilian A. Clare. New York: Macmillan, 1928.

Lewis, I. M., ed. *Islam in Tropical Africa: Studies Presented and Discussed at the Fifth International African Seminar, Ahmadu Bello University, Zaria, January, 1964.* London: International African Institute and Oxford University Press, 1966.

Liebow, Elliot. *Tally's Corner: A Study of Negro Streetcorner Men.* Boston: Little, Brown, 1967.

Lienhardt, Godfrey. *Divinity and Experience: The Religion of the Dinka.* Oxford: Clarendon Press, 1961.

Little, Kenneth. *West African Urbanization: A Study of Voluntary Associations in Social Change.* Cambridge: Cambridge University Press, 1965.

Lloyd, P. C. *Africa in Social Change.* Rev. ed. Baltimore: Penguin Books, Penguin African Library, 1969.

Long, Charles H. "Archaism and Hermeneutics," in *The History of Religions: Essays on the Problem of Understanding,* edited by Joseph M. Kitagawa with the collaboration of Mircea Eliade and Charles H. Long. Chicago: University of Chicago Press, 1967.

Lynd, Robert S. *Knowledge for What? The Place of Social Science in American Culture.* New York: Grove Press, 1964.

McAllester, David P. *Enemy Way Music: A Study of Social and Esthetic Values as Seen in Navaho Music.* Papers of the Peabody Museum of

American Archaeology and Ethnology, Harvard University, vol. 41, no. 3. Cambridge, Mass.: Peabody Museum of American Archaeology and Ethnology, 1954.

McCall, George J., and Simmons, J. L., eds. *Issues in Participant Observation: A Text and Reader*. Reading, Mass.: Addison-Wesley, 1969.

McCutchen, Leighton. "Psychology of the Dream: Dream without Myth," in *The Dialogue between Theology and Phycology*, edited by Peter Homans. Chicago: University of Chicago Press, 1968.

McHugh, Peter. *Defining the Situation: The Organization of Meaning in Social Interaction*. Indianapolis: Bobbs-Merrill, 1968.

Malraux, André. *The Voices of Silence*. Translated by Stuart Gilbert. Garden City, N.Y.: Doubleday, 1953.

————. *The Metamorphosis of the Gods*. Translated by Stuart Gilbert. Garden City, N.Y.: Doubleday, 1960.

Manis, Jerome G., and Meltzer, Bernard N., eds. *Symbolic Interaction: A Reader in Social Psychology*. 2d ed. Boston: Allyn and Bacon, 1972.

Mann, Thomas. *Doctor Faustus: The Life of the German Composer Adrian Leverkühn as Told by a Friend*. Translated by H. T. Lowe-Porter. New York: Random House, Vintage Books, 1971.

Mannheim, Karl. *Ideology and Utopia: An Introduction to the Sociology of Knowledge*. Translated by Louis Wirth and Edward Shils. New York: Harcourt, Brace, Harvest Books, 1936.

Manoukian, Madeline. *Tribes of the Northern Territories of the Gold Coast*. Ethnographic Survey of Africa: West Africa, part 5. Edited by Daryll Forde. London: International African Institute, 1952.

————. *The Ewe-Speaking People of Togoland and the Gold Coast*. Ethnographic Survey of Africa: West Africa, part 6. Edited by Daryll Forde. London: International African Institute, 1952.

Marcuse, Herbert. *One Dimensional Man: Studies in the Ideology of Advanced Industrial Society*. Boston: Beacon Press, 1964.

Mbiti, John S. *African Religions and Philosophy*. Garden City, N.Y.: Doubleday, Anchor Books, 1970.

Mead, George H. *Mind, Self, and Society from the Standpoint of a Social Behaviorist*. Edited by Charles W. Morris. Chicago: University of Chicago Press, 1962.

Mead, Margaret. *From the South Seas: Studies of Adolescence and Sex in Primitive Societies*. New York: William Morrow, 1939.

————. "The Implications of Culture Change for Personality Development," in *Readings in Anthropology*, vol. 2, *Readings in Cultural*

Anthropology, edited by Morton H. Fried. New York: Thomas Y. Crowell, 1959.

Merton, Robert K. *Social Theory and Social Structure*. Rev. and enl. ed. Glencoe, Ill.: Free Press, 1957.

Mills, C. Wright. *The Sociological Imagination*. New York: Oxford University Press, 1959.

Mphahlele, Ezekiel. "The Fabric of African Cultures," *Foreign Affairs* 42, no. 4 (1964): 614–27.

Myers, Charles S. "A Study of Rhythm in Primitive Music," *British Journal of Psychology* 1 (1905): 397–406.

Nadel, Siegfried Frederick. *Nupe Religion*. London: Routledge and Kegan Paul, 1954.

Nash, Denison, and Wintrob, Ronald. "The Emergence of Self-Consciousness in Anthropology," *Current Anthropology* 13, no. 5 (December 1972): 527–42.

Nietzsche, Friedrich. *The Case of Wagner* and *Nietzche contra Wagner*. Translated by Anthony M. Ludovici. Vol. 8 of *The Complete Works of Friedrich Nietzsche*, edited by Oscar Levy. London: George Allen & Unwin, 1911.

——. *The Birth of Tragedy out of the Spirit of Music*. Translated by Francis Golffing. Garden City, N.Y.: Doubleday, Anchor Books, 1956.

——. *The Use and Abuse of History*. Translated by Adrian Collins. New York: Liberal Arts Press, 1957.

Palmer, Richard E. *Hermeneutics: Interpretation Theory in Schleiermacher, Dilthey, Heidegger, and Gadamer*. Evanston, Ill.: Northwestern University Press, 1969.

Park, Robert Ezra. *Human Communities: The City and Human Ecology*. Vol. 2 of *The Collected Papers of Robert Ezra Park*, edited by Everett Cherrington Hughes et al. Glencoe, Ill.: Free Press, 1952.

Parrinder, Geoffrey. *African Traditional Religion*. London: Hutchinson's University Library, 1954.

——. *Religion in Africa*. Baltimore: Penguin Books, Penguin African Library, 1969.

——. "God in African Mythology," in *Myths and Symbols: Studies in Honor of Mircea Eliade*, edited by Joseph M. Kitagawa and Charles H. Long with the collaboration of Jerald C. Bauer and Marshall G. S. Hodgson. Chicago: University of Chicago Press, 1969.

Paul, Benjamin D. "Interview Techniques and Field Relationships," in *Anthropology Today: An Encyclopedic Inventory*, edited by A. L. Kroeber. Chicago: University of Chicago Press, 1953.

Petock, Stuart Jay. "Expression in Art: The Feelingful Side of Aesthetic Experience," *Journal of Aesthetics and Art Criticism* 30, no. 3 (spring 1972): 297–309.

Philipson, Morris, ed. *Aesthetics Today.* New York: World, Meridian Books, 1961.

Présence Africaine. *Colloque sur les religions: Abidjan, 5/12 Avril 1961.* Paris: Présence Africaine, 1962.

Radin, Paul. *Primitive Man as Philosopher.* New York and London: D. Appleton, 1927.

―――. *The World of Primitive Man.* New York: Henry Schuman, 1953.

Rapaport, David, ed. and trans. *Organization and Pathology of Thought: Selected Sources.* Austen Riggs Foundation Monograph, no. 1. New York: Columbia University Press, 1951.

Rattray, R. S. *The Tribes of the Ashanti Hinterland.* Vol. 2. Oxford: Clarendon Press, 1932.

Read, Kenneth E. *The High Valley.* New York: Charles Scribner's Sons, 1965.

Redfield, Robert. *Human Nature and the Study of Society.* Vol. 1 of *The Papers of Robert Redfield,* edited by Margaret Park Redfield. Chicago: University of Chicago Press, 1962.

―――. *The Little Community* and *Peasant Society and Culture.* Chicago: University of Chicago Press, Phoenix Books, 1967.

Ricoeur, Paul. "The Model of the Text: Meaningful Action Considered as a Text," *Social Research* 38, no. 3 (autumn 1971): 529–62.

Rieff, Philip. *Freud: The Mind of the Moralist.* Garden City, N.Y.: Doubleday, Anchor Books, 1961. 3d ed. Chicago: University of Chicago Press, 1978.

―――. *The Triumph of the Therapeutic: Uses of Faith after Freud.* New York: Harper & Row, Harper Torchbooks, 1968.

Riesman, David. *Individualism Reconsidered and Other Essays.* Glencoe, Ill.: Free Press, 1954.

―――. with Glazer, Nathan, and Denney, Reuel. *The Lonely Crowd: A Study of the Changing American Character.* Abr. ed. New Haven: Yale University Press, 1961.

Rilke, Rainer Maria. *Sonnets to Orpheus.* Translated by M. D. Herter Norton. New York: W. W. Norton, Norton Library, 1962.

Rougemont, Denis de. *Love in the Western World.* Translated by Montgomery Belgion. Rev. ed. Greenwich, Conn.: Fawcett Publications, Fawcett Premier Books, 1966.

Schapiro, Meyer. "Style," in *Aesthetics Today,* edited by Morris Philipson. New York: World, Meridian Books, 1961.

Scully, Vincent. *The Earth, The Temple, and The Gods: Greek Sacred Architecture.* Rev. ed. New York: Frederick A. Praeger, 1969.

Seznec, Jean. *The Survival of the Pagan Gods: The Mythological Tradition and Its Place in Renaissance Humanism and Art.* Translated by Barbara F. Sessions. New York: Harper & Row, Harper Torchbooks/The Bollingen Library, 1953.

Shapiro, David. *Neurotic Styles.* Austen Riggs Center Monograph Series, no. 5. New York: Basic Books, 1965.

Simpson, George Eaton. "The Shango Cult in Nigeria and in Trinidad," *American Anthropologist* 64 (1962): 1204–19.

Smith, Edwin W., ed. *African Ideas of God: A Symposium.* London: Edinburgh House Press, 1950.

Smith, Wilfred Cantwell. "Comparative Religion: Whither—and Why?" in *The History of Religions: Essays in Methodology,* edited by Mircea Eliade and Joseph M. Kitagawa. Chicago: University of Chicago Press, 1959.

Spradley, James P., and McCurdy, David W., eds. *Conformity and Conflict: Readings in Cultural Anthropology.* Boston: Little, Brown, 1971. Especially Edward T. Hall and William Foote Whyte, "Intercultural Communication," and Robert B. Edgerton, "A Friend Who Misunderstands."

Staniland, Martin. *The Lions of Dagbon: Political Change in Northern Ghana.* Cambridge: Cambridge University Press, 1975.

Stein, Maurice R. *The Eclipse of Community: An Interpretation of American Studies.* New York: Harper & Row, Harper Torchbooks, 1964.

————, and Vidich, Arthur, eds. *Sociology on Trial.* Englewood Cliffs, N.J.: Prentice-Hall, Spectrum Books, 1963. Especially Barrington Moore, Jr., "Strategy in Social Science"; Joseph Bensman and Arthur Vidich, "Social Theory and Field Research"; and Alvin Gouldner, "Anti-Minotaur: The Myth of Value-Free Sociology."

Stetson, R. H. "A Motor Theory of Rhythm and Discrete Association," 2 parts, *Psychological Review,* 12 (1905): 250–70, 293–350.

Stone, Gregory P., and Farberman, Harvey A., eds. *Social Psychology through Symbolic Interactionism.* Waltham, Mass.: Ginn-Blaisdell, 1970.

Strachey, Lytton, *Elizabeth and Essex: A Tragic History.* Harmondsworth, Middlesex, England: Penguin Books, 1971.

————. *Eminent Victorians.* New York: Harcourt, Brace & World, Harbrace Paperbound Library, n.d.

Strauss, Anselm L. *Mirrors and Masks: The Search for Identity.* n.p.: Sociology Press, 1969.

Sunday, William Ashley [Billy]. "Dancing, Drinking, Card-Playing," in *20 Centuries of Great Preaching: An Encyclopedia of Preaching,* edited by Clyde E. Fant, Jr. and William M. Pinson, Jr. Vol. 7, *Watson [Maclaren] to Rufus Jones.* Waco, Texas: Word Books, 1971.

Tait, D. Unpublished Mss. A & B. Library of The Institute of African Studies, University of Ghana, Legon, Ghana.

Tempels, Placide. *Bantu Philosophy.* Translated (from a French translation) by A. Rubbens. Paris: Présence Africaine, 1969.

Trimingham, John Spencer. *Islam in West Africa.* Oxford: Clarendon Press, 1959.

_____. *The Influence of Islam upon Africa.* New York: Frederick A. Praeger, 1968.

Turnbull, Colin M. *The Forest People: A Study of the Pygmies of the Congo.* Garden City, N.Y.: Natural History Library and Doubleday, Anchor Books, 1962.

_____. *The Lonely African.* Garden City, N.Y.: Doubleday, Anchor Books, 1963.

_____. *The Mountain People.* New York: Simon and Schuster, 1972.

Turner, Victor W. *Schism and Continuity in an African Society: A Study of Ndembu Village Life.* New York: Humanities Press, 1957.

_____. *The Drums of Affliction: A Study of Religious Processes among the Ndembu of Zambia.* Oxford: Clarendon Press and International African Institute, 1968.

_____. *The Ritual Process: Structure and Anti-Structure.* Chicago: Aldine, 1969.

Tutuola, Amos. *The Palm-Wine Drinkard and His Dead Palm-Wine Tapster in the Dead's Town.* New York: Grove Press, 1953.

Tyler, Stephen A., ed. *Cognitive Anthropology.* New York: Holt, Rinehart and Winston, 1969.

Underwood, Richard A. "Myth, Dream, and the Vocation of Contemporary Philosophy," in *Myths, Dreams, and Religion,* edited by Joseph Campbell. New York: E. P. Dutton, 1970.

Vansina, Jan. *Oral Tradition: A Study in Historical Methodology.* Translated by H. M. Wright. Chicago: Aldine, 1965.

Vidich, Arthur J. "Participant-Observation and the Collection and Interpretation of Data," *American Journal of Sociology* 60 (1955): 354–60.

_____. "Paul Radin and Contemporary Anthropology," *Social Research* 32, no. 4 (winter 1965); 375–407.

_____; Bensman, Joseph; and Stein, Maurice R., eds. *Reflections on Community Studies.* New York: Harper & Row, Harper Torchbooks, 1971.

Wallerstein, Immanuel. *Africa: The Politics of Independence.* New York: Vintage Books, 1961.

Watts, Alan W. "Western Mythology: Its Dissolution and Transformation," in *Myths, Dreams, and Religion,* edited by Joseph Campbell. New York: E. P. Dutton, 1970.

Weber, Max. *The Methodology of the Social Sciences.* Translated and edited by Edward A. Shils and Henry A. Finch. Glencoe, Ill.: Free Press, 1949.

Weiss, Paul. *The World of Art.* Carbondale: Southern Illinois University Press, 1961.

Whyte, William Foote. *Street Corner Society: The Social Structure of an Italian Slum.* Chicago: University of Chicago Press, 1955.

Wirth, Louis. *On Cities and Social Life: Selected Papers.* Edited by Albert J. Reiss, Jr. Chicago: University of Chicago Press, 1964.

Index

Abdulai, Naa, 204
Abiodun, Dele, 115
Abstraction, issues of, 20–21, 30–32, 37, 141, 153–54,
189, 200–201, 216–17, 218. *See also* Alienation; Ethnocentrism; Interpretation; Mediation; Participation
Accentuation, 53, 86, 96–100, 117–20, 123, 200–201, 209.
See also Cross-rhythms; Improvisation; Musicians, African, creative sensibility of; Off-beat
Adam Alhassan, Alhaji, 16–19, 65, 132
Adaptability, 156, 165
Ade, Sunny, 115
Adekunle, Prince, 115
Adowa (Akan dance beat), 128
Adzenyah, Abraham, 50
Adzogbo (Fon dance beat), 45–47, 57
Aesthetics: aesthetic command, 14–15, 113, 125–27, 140,
151, 167–68; aesthetic effect, 30, 32–36, 92–95, 141–43,
163; and dance, 143–44, 149–51, 220; and ethics, 25,
36–37, 137, 139–40, 143, 168–69; interpretation of, 30–
33, 184, 194–96, 214, 216–17, 218; and music, 96–98,
106–11, 122–27; and sculpture, 168–69, 171. *See also*
African music, aesthetic orientation to; Art; Coolness;
Criticism; Ethics; Expression; Improvisation; Style
Afiadenyigba, 11, 48
Aflao, 48
Africa '70 Band, 72–73. *See also* Kuti, Fela Anikulapo
African Brothers Band, 70, 116, 211
African culture-area, 192
African dance. *See* Dance
African music: aesthetic orientation to, 48–51, 87–88, 93,
125–27, 143, 155; compared to classicism, 1–2, 66, 112,
217; continuity of, in Americas, 29, 73–74, 195; and
dance, 50, 143–51; as focus for values, 35–37, 125–27,
140, 143, 149–51, 153–55, 166–67, 173–82; generalizations about, 28–30, 35–37, 40, 116–17, 153–55, 192,
194–96, 197–98, 208, 216–17; history of, 61–65, 202–3;
institutionalization of, 34–37, 48, 83–84, 93–95, 118,
129–30, 155–72; use of language in, 75–82; openness
of, 59–60, 113–14, 157; and politics, 35, 72–73, 82–84,